Communications in Computer and Information Science 948

Commenced Publication in 2007
Founding and Former Series Editors:
Phoebe Chen, Alfredo Cuzzocrea, Xiaoyong Du, Orhun Kara, Ting Liu,
Dominik Ślęzak, and Xiaokang Yang

More information about this series at http://www.springer.com/series/7899

Moises Torres · Jaime Klapp
Isidoro Gitler · Andrei Tchernykh (Eds.)

Supercomputing

9th International Conference, ISUM 2018
Mérida, Mexico, March 5–9, 2018
Revised Selected Papers

 Springer

Editors
Moises Torres ⓘ
University of Guadalajara
Guadalajara, Jalisco, Mexico

Jaime Klapp ⓘ
Instituto Nacional de Investigaciones
Nucleares
La Marquesa, Mexico

Isidoro Gitler ⓘ
CINVESTAV-IPN
Mexico City, Mexico

Andrei Tchernykh
CICESE
Ensenada, Mexico

ISSN 1865-0929 ISSN 1865-0937 (electronic)
Communications in Computer and Information Science
ISBN 978-3-030-10447-4 ISBN 978-3-030-10448-1 (eBook)
https://doi.org/10.1007/978-3-030-10448-1

Library of Congress Control Number: 2018963970

This Springer imprint is published by the registered company Springer Nature Switzerland AG
The registered company address is: Gewerbestrasse 11, 6330 Cham, Switzerland

Preface

High-performance computing (HPC) or supercomputing in research and development continues to be of significant importance to highly developed countries and those evolving. As researchers, we have come to depend on the power of these machines to compute high volumes of data to find timely results. The ability to perform complex calculations in high volumes of data would have taken hours, days, weeks and sometimes months to process 30 years ago, but today with the processing power that HPC machines manage, we are able to take decisions faster from the analysis of our results, hence saving time, money, and sometimes even lives. Thus, this 9th International Supercomputing Conference in México fostered the continuous growth of HPC in Mexico and Latin America to advance in research and applications.

We recognize that supercomputing is more than an essential tool and instrument for contemporary science and technology. It has turned out to be, together with the development of basic theory and experimentation, the third crucial pillar for the improvement of our understanding of nature, analysis of society, and technological advancement. Nowadays, current research in applied mathematics, physics, biology, engineering, medicine, and environmental sciences relies more and more on supercomputing. It is allowing us to expand basic research and experimentation in areas such as astrophysics, cosmology, fluid dynamics, elementary particle physics, medicine, and life sciences. Supercomputing has proven to be equally essential for developing and understanding a wide range of advanced science and technology topics that are directly related to our daily lives, including global warming forecasting and simulations of natural disasters that help minimize the damage from events such as earthquakes, tsunamis, torrential rains, and typhoons among others. Other areas benefiting from supercomputing are genome analysis for gene therapy and protein analysis for drug design, the development of new devices and materials, car crash simulations, jet engine design, and many more. HPC enables the design of models and running computer simulations of phenomena before passing through an experimental phase, with great economic savings, but more importantly allowing us to provide results within days or weeks when months or even years were required in the past.

It is worth noting that Mexico has significant experience in the uses of supercomputers, which began in 1991, when UNAM installed a Cray YMP. Afterwards, Mexico appeared in the Top 500 supercomputing list several times: for example, the case of the oil industry (Top 83, Top 84, and Top 85 in the list of November 2003). A few years later, UNAM and UAM placed computers in slots 126 (2006) and 225 (2008), respectively. Other outstanding projects in Mexico are the National Laboratory for High-Performance Computing in Mexico City (UNAM-UAM-CINVESTAV), the National Supercomputing Center of San Luis Potosi within the Instituto Potosino de Investigación Científica y Tecnológica (IPICYT), the Grids National Laboratory, the National Supercomputing Laboratory of the Southeast (LNS) from the Benemérita Universidad Autónoma de Puebla, and ABACUS CINVESTAV, which placed its supercomputer ABACUS-I in the 255 slot of the top 500 list of June 2015. In addition to these laboratories, there are new supercomputer centers in development by the University of Guadalajara and the University Autonomous of the State of México (UAEMEX). Although we have a platform and experience in supercomputing, these supercomputing resources are not enough to conduct research and development for a country like México. The continuous joint effort by national institutions, organizations, and government should impact positively, in the near future, the needs of computer power in academia, government, society, and industry to further advance research and development.

With an effort to continue to evolve in the uses of supercomputing and promote the use of these powerful machines in research and development in México and Latin América, the International Supercomputing Conference in México (ISUM) was founded by a group of researchers, supercomputing directors, IT directors, and technologists representing the largest research academic institutions along with the support of the largest technology vendors in México.

This conference was established to provide a space for researchers and technologists to present their research work related to HPC. Building on the experience of the previous eight editions, this ninth edition of ISUM was held in the historic and beautiful city of Mérida, Yucatán, México, where more than 400 attendees had the opportunity to hear five international keynote speakers, 15 thematic national and international speakers, and more than 60 research presentations. The conference covered topics in HPC architecture, networks, system software, algorithmic techniques, modeling and system tools, clouds, distributed computing, big data, data analytics, visualization and storage, applications for science and engineering, and emerging technologies. There were three workshops offered in artificial intelligence, cloud computing, and data analytics conducted by an international group of instructors. In addition, the conference had three round table discussions where important issues related to supercomputing were debated such as: strengthening graduate programs in supercomputing in Mexico, creating national and international project opportunities in supercomputing, and fostering the uses of supercomputing in industry for the development of México and Latin America. These open discussions gathered experts in the respective areas representing Mexico and Latin America including academia, industry, and government.

The central part of ISUM is the presentation of the latest research work conducted primarily but not limited to Mexico and Latin America. This book presents the selected works from more than 70 authors who have presented articles individually and collaboratively in ISUM. Each work was reviewed by three expert reviewers from an international group of experts in the respective area. These works are divided into three parts that include:

Part 1: Scheduling, Architecture, and Programming. In this section there are three works, one presents an algorithm designed to obtain results without the loss of information in several nodes of a mobile distributed environment; and the second presents a software that generates code that implements a microprocessor simulator based on features defined by the user. And the third article talks about container technology and its efficiency.

Part II: Parallel Computing. This part contains five works that strengthen the concept of parallel computing with various areas covered by these articles, which include a methodology for the design of parallel algorithms on language patterns, parallelized iterative closest point algorithm for 3D view fusion, evaluation of OrangeFS as a tool to achieve a high-performance storage and massively parallel processing in HPC cluster, a many-core parallel algorithm to correct the Gaussian noise of an image, and Amdahl's law extension for parallel program performance analysis on Intel Turbo-Boost multi-core processors.

Part III: Applications and HPC. We know that research today is becoming more dependent on the uses of HPC to examine problems in a wide array of research areas. This section shares 11 works covering a wide array of topics such as health, environment, and urban mobility. For example, in the area of health it presents the 3D image reconstruction system for cancerous tumor analysis based on diffuse optical tomography with Blender, data augmentation for deep learning of non-mydriatic screening retinal fundus images; it also has works that cover the environment including, fast random cactus graph generation, the use of HPC on volcanic tephra dispersion operational forecast systems, high-performance open source Lagrangian oil spill model, sea-surface temperature spatiotemporal analysis for the Gulf of California, 1998–2015, regime change simulation, computational study of aqueous solvation of vanadium (V) complexes, decision support system for urban flood management in the Cazones River Basin, use of high-performance computing to simulate cosmic-ray showers initiated by high-energy gamma rays, theoretical calculation of photoluminescence spectrum using DFT for double-wall carbon nanotubes. It also contains an article impacting urban mobility such as traffic signs entitled "The Traffic Sign Distance Estimation Based on Stereo Vision and GPUs." This work uses an algorithm to split the problem into parts and they are solved concurrently by the available massive processors into the stream processor units (SM). Their results show that the proposed algorithm accelerated the response time 141 times for an image resolution of 1,024x680 pixels, with an execution time 0.04 seconds for the accelerated estimation for traffic sign distance (AETSD) parallel version and 5.67 seconds for the sequential version. This book contains a number of articles that cover interesting topics that are worth diving into to obtain a new perspective on what the authors present. We invite you to take the time to browse through this book and examine the contribution of than 70 authors representing Mexico, Latin America, and Europe.

The book is aimed at senior undergraduate and graduate students, as well as scientists in the fields of HPC, computer sciences, physics, biology, mathematics, engineering, and chemistry who have interest in the solution of a large variety of problems involving supercomputers. The material included in this book is adequate for both teaching and research.

The editors are grateful to the institutions and people who made the 9th International Supercomputing Conference in México possible through their support: CONACYT, Julia Taqüeña Parga, Bemerita Universidad Autónoma de Puebla, Cesar Díaz Torrejón, Universidad Autónoma del Estado de México (UAEMEX), Luis Díaz Sánchez, Universidad de Guadalajara, Luis Gutiérrez Díaz de León, Universidad Autónoma de México (UNAM), Felipe Bracho Carpizo and Fabián Romo, Centro de Investigación Científica y de Educación Superior de Ensenada (CISESE), Raúl Rivera, Corporación de internet (CUDI), Carlos Casasús López Hermosa and Salma Leticia Jaliffe Villalón, Sociedad Mexicana de Supercómputo (SOMEXSU A.C.), Moisés Torres Martínez, and

Red Mexicana de Supercómputo (REDMEXSU) Consejo Técnico Académico (CTA). We give special recognition to our corporate sponsors that without their support this event would not have been possible. Special recognition to TEAM, Hewlett Packard Enterprise, Totalplay, CISCO, Fujitsu, IPICYT-CNS, IBM, NVIDIA, ITEXICO, and DDRMéxico.

The following individuals were instrumental in leading the evaluation of these works: Juan Manuel Ramírez Alcaraz, Alfredo Cristóbal Salas, Andrei Tchernykh, Cesar Díaz Torrejón, Erwin Martin, Isabel Pedraza, Isidoro Gitler, Jaime Klapp, Liliana Barbosa Santillán, Luis Díaz Sánchez, Luis Gutiérrez Díaz de León, Moisés Torres Martínez, Manuel Aguilar Cornejo, Raúl Hazas, Rene Luna, Salvador Castañeda, and Sergio Nemeschnow. We thank them for the time spent in coordinating the evaluation process of these research works.

We give special thanks to the ISUM national and local committees, and CIMAT-Merida for all their support in making this event possible. We give special thanks to Veronica Lizette Robles Dueñas, Karen Sanchez Jimenez, and Marlene Ilse Martinez Rodriguez and Angie Fernandez Olimón for all their support in organizing all the logistics of this successful edition of ISUM 2018.

In conclusion, we thank all the institutions who have supported this event throughout these nine editions, especially ISUM 2018: BUAP LNS-SURESTE, UdeG, UCol, UNISON, ININ, CUDI, IPN, UAM, UNAM, CICESE, CIMAT-Merida, UAEMEX, CNS-IPICYT, ABACUS-CINVESTAV, CONACYT, SOMEXSU A.C., and REDMEXSU.

October 2018   Moises Torres
                                                                Jaime Klapp
                                                             Isidoro Gitler
                                                          Andrei Tchernykh

Acknowledgments

The production of this book was sponsored by the Sociedad Mexicana de Super-computo (SOMEXSU A.C.), Red Mexicana de Supercomputo (REDMEXSU), Consejo Nacional de Ciencia y Tecnología (Conacyt), the Instituto Nacional de Investigaciones Nucleares (ININ), Universidad de Guadalajara, the Laboratorio de Matemática Aplicada y Computo de Alto Rendimiento of the Centro de Investigación y de Estudios Avanzados of the Instituto Politécnico Nacional through the "ABACUS" CONACyT grant EDOMEX-2011-C01-165873.

Contents

Applications and HPC

List of Contributors

A. Aldama-Díaz Facultad de Ciencias de la Computación, Benemérita Universidad Autónoma de Puebla, Puebla, México

Miguel Angel Aleman-Arce Centro de Nanociencias y Micro y Nanotecnologías del Instituto Politécnico Nacional, Mexico City, Mexico

Jesus A. Alvarez-Cedillo Instituto Politécnico Nacional, UPIICSA, Mexico City, Mexico

Teodoro Alvarez-Sanchez Instituto Politécnico Nacional, CITEDI, Tijuana, Mexico

Andrea Anguiano-García Centro de Ciencias de la Atmósfera, Universidad Nacional Autónoma de México, Mexico City, Mexico

M. Anzures-García Facultad de Ciencias de la Computación, Benemérita Universidad Autónoma de Puebla, Puebla, México

Eduard Ayguadé Barcelona Supercomputing Center, Barcelona, Spain; Universitat Politècnica de Catalunya, Barcelona Tech, Barcelona, Spain

Liliana Barbosa-Santillan University of Guadalajara, Zapopan, Jalisco, Mexico

Luis Barbosa-Santillan University of Guadalajara, Zapopan, Jalisco, Mexico

Carlos Bermejo-Sabbagh Tecnológico Nacional de México-I.T. Mérida, Mérida, Mexico

Norma A. Caballero Facultad de Ciencias Biológicas, Benemérita Universidad Autónoma de Puebla, Puebla, Mexico

J. Migliolo Carrera Facultad de Ciencias de la Computación, Benemérita Universidad Autónoma de Puebla, Puebla, México

S. Castañeda-Avila Center for Scientific Research and Higher Education of Ensenada, Ensenada, Baja California, Mexico

María Eugenia Castro Centro de Química, Instituto de Ciencias, B. Universidad Autónoma de Puebla, Puebla, Mexico

Ulises Cortés Barcelona Supercomputing Center, Barcelona, Spain; Universitat Politècnica de Catalunya, Barcelona Tech, Barcelona, Spain

A. Cristóbal Salas School of Engineering in Electronics and Communications, Universidad Veracruzana, Poza Rica, Mexico

Alfredo Cristóbal-Salas Laboratorio de Cómputo de Alto Rendimiento, Universidad Veracruzana, Veracruz, Mexico

Hugo Eduardo Camacho Cruz Universidad Autónoma de Tamaulipas - FMeISC de Matamoros, Tamaulipas, Mexico

J. M. Cuenca Lerma School of Engineering in Electronics and Communications, Universidad Veracruzana, Poza Rica, Mexico

Nora Leticia Cuevas-Cuevas Tecnológico Nacional de México-I.T. Mérida, Mérida, Mexico

Hugo Delgado-Granados Instituto de Geofísica, Universidad Nacional Autónoma de México, Mexico City, Mexico

Néstor David Espinosa-Torres Instituto de Energías Renovables (IER-UNAM), Temixco, Morelos, Mexico

Alejandro Flores-Lamas Centro de Investigación Científica y de Educación Superior de Ensenada, Baja California, México

D. Garcia-Gasulla Barcelona Supercomputing Center, Barcelona, Spain

Agustín García-Reynoso Centro de Ciencias de la Atmosfera, Universidad Nacional Autónoma de México, Mexico City, Mexico

Isidoro Gitler Mathematics Department, Cinvestav-IPN, Mexico City, Mexico

Sael González-Romero Centro de Investigación en Computación, Instituto Politécnico Nacional, Mexico City, Mexico

Raúl Gilberto Hazas-Izquierdo Departamento de Investigación en Física, Universidad de Sonora, Hermosillo, Sonora, Mexico

María del Carmen Heras-Sánchez Departamento de Matemáticas, Universidad de Sonora, Hermosillo, Sonora, Mexico

Cesar Alejandro Hernández-Calderón Centro de Investigación en Computación, Instituto Politécnico Nacional, Delegación Gustavo A. Madero, CDMX, Mexico

Dulce R. Herrera-Moro Centro de Ciencias de la Atmosfera, Universidad Nacional Autónoma de México, Mexico City, Mexico

Javier Martínez Juárez Centro de investigaciones en Dispositivos Semiconductores (CIDS) del ICUAP, Benemérita Universidad Autónoma de Puebla (BUAP), Puebla, Puebla, Mexico

Jesús Labarta Barcelona Supercomputing Center, Barcelona, Spain; Universitat Politèctnica de Catalunya, Barcelona Tech, Barcelona, Spain

Julio Antonio Lara-Hernández Centro de Ciencias de la Atmósfera, Universidad Nacional Autónoma de México, Mexico City, Mexico

M. Larios-Gómez Facultad de Ciencias en Sistemas Computacionales y Electrónicos, Universidad Autónoma de Tlaxcala, Tlaxcala, México; Facultad de Ciencias de la Computación, Benemérita Universidad Autónoma de Puebla, Puebla, México

Neiel Israel Layva-Santes Centro de Investigación en Computación, Instituto Politécnico Nacional, Delegación Gustavo A. Madero, CDMX, Mexico

Neiel Israel Leyva-Santes Centro de Investigación en Computación, Instituto Politécnico Nacional, Mexico City, Mexico

Cederik de León Laboratorio Nacional de Supercómputo del Sureste de México, Benemérita Universidad Autónoma de Puebla, Puebla, Mexico

Ma. de Lourdes Cantú Gallegos Universidad Autónoma de Tamaulipas - FMeISC de Matamoros, Tamaulipas, Mexico

J. E. Lozano-Rizk Center for Scientific Research and Higher Education of Ensenada, Ensenada, Baja California, Mexico

J. A. David Hernández de la Luz Centro de Investigaciones en Dispositivos Semiconductores (CIDS) del ICUAP, Benemérita Universidad Autónoma de Puebla (BUAP), Puebla, Puebla, Mexico

José Luis López-Martínez Universidad Autónoma de Yucatán, Tizimín, Yucatán, Mexico

Julio Cesar González Mariño Universidad Autónoma de Tamaulipas - FMeISC de Matamoros, Tamaulipas, Mexico

Eduardo San Martín-Martínez Centro de Investigación en Ciencia Aplicada y Tecnología Avanzada del Instituto Politécnico Nacional, Mexico City, Mexico

F. Medrano-Jaimes Center for Scientific Research and Higher Education of Ensenada, Ensenada, Baja California, Mexico

Francisco J. Melendez Lab. de Química Teórica, Centro de Investigación. Depto. de Fisicoquímica, Facultad de Ciencias Químicas, Benemérita Universidad Autónoma de Puebla, Puebla, Mexico

Amilcar Meneses-Viveros Computer Science Department, Cinvestav-IPN, Mexico City, Mexico

H. L. Monroy Carranza School of Architecture, Universidad Veracruzana, Poza Rica, Mexico

Guillermo B. Morales-Luna Computer Science Department, Cinvestav-IPN, Mexico City, Mexico

Jonathan Moreno Barcelona Supercomputing Center, Barcelona, Spain

E. Ulises Moya-Sánchez Barcelona Supercomputing Center, Barcelona, Spain; Posgrado en Ciencias Computacionales, Universidad Autónoma de Guadalajara, Guadalajara, Mexico

Lisset Noriega Lab. de Química Teórica, Centro de Investigación. Depto. de Fisicoquímica, Facultad de Ciencias Químicas, Benemérita Universidad Autónoma de Puebla, Puebla, Mexico

Mireya Paredes-López Mathematics Department, Cinvestav-IPN, Mexico City, Mexico

Ferran Parrés Barcelona Supercomputing Center, Barcelona, Spain

Jose Manuel Perez-Aguilar Lab. de Química Teórica, Centro de Investigación. Depto. de Fisicoquímica, Facultad de Ciencias Químicas, Benemérita Universidad Autónoma de Puebla, Puebla, Mexico

Jesús Humberto Foullon Peña Universidad Autónoma de Tamaulipas - FMeISC de Matamoros, Tamaulipas, Mexico

Marco Antonio Ramírez-Salinas Centro de Investigación en Computación, Instituto Politécnico Nacional, Delegación Gustavo A. Madero, CDMX, Mexico

R. Rivera-Rodriguez Center for Scientific Research and Higher Education of Ensenada, Ensenada, Baja California, Mexico

M. J. Robles-Águila Centro de Investigaciones en Dispositivos Semiconductores (CIDS) del ICUAP, Benemérita Universidad Autónoma de Puebla (BUAP), Puebla, Puebla, Mexico

A. P. Rodríguez Victoria Centro de Investigaciones en Dispositivos Semiconductores (CIDS) del ICUAP, Benemérita Universidad Autónoma de Puebla (BUAP), Puebla, Puebla, Mexico

Carlos Rojas-Morales Centro de Investigación en Computación, Instituto Politécnico Nacional, Delegación Gustavo A. Madero, CDMX, Mexico

Rosario Romero-Centeno Centro de Ciencias de la Atmósfera, Universidad Nacional Autónoma de México, Mexico City, Mexico

Humberto Salazar Laboratorio Nacional de Supercómputo del Sureste de México, Benemérita Universidad Autónoma de Puebla, Puebla, Mexico

Jacobo Sandoval-Gutierrez Universidad Autónoma Metropolitana, LERMA, Mexico City, Mexico

B. Santiago Vicente School of Engineering in Electronics and Communications, Universidad Veracruzana, Poza Rica, Mexico

Juan D. Santiago-Domínguez Laboratorio de Cómputo de Alto Rendimiento, Universidad Veracruzana, Veracruz, Mexico

Bardo Santiago-Vicente Laboratorio de Cómputo de Alto Rendimiento, Universidad Veracruzana, Veracruz, Mexico

A. Alejandra Serrano-Rubio Computer Science Department, Cinvestav-IPN, Mexico City, Mexico

Abraham Sánchez Posgrado en Ciencias Computacionales, Universidad Autónoma de Guadalajara, Guadalajara, Mexico

Homero Toral-Cruz Universidad de Quintana Roo, Chetumal, Quintana Roo, Mexico

Joel Antonio Trejo-Sánchez CONACyT-Centro de Investigación en Matemáticas, Sierra Papacal, Yucatán, Mexico

G. Trinidad-García Facultad de Ciencias de la Computación, Benemérita Universidad Autónoma de Puebla, Puebla, México

Felipe Trujillo-Romero Universidad de Guanajuato, DICIS, Salamanca, Guanajuato, Mexico

José Eduardo Valdez-Holguín Departamento de Investigaciones Científicas y Tecnológicas, Universidad de Sonora, Hermosillo, Sonora, Mexico

S. Ivvan Valdez Universidad de Guanajuato, DICIS, Salamanca, Guanajuato, Mexico

Andrés Vela-Navarro Tecnológico Nacional de México-I.T. Mérida, Mérida, Mexico

Enrique González Vergara Centro de Química, Instituto de Ciencias, B. Universidad Autónoma de Puebla, Puebla, Mexico

Luis Alfonso Villa-Vargas Centro de Investigación en Computación, Instituto Politécnico Nacional, Delegación Gustavo A. Madero, CDMX, Mexico

Luis Villaseñor Laboratorio Nacional de Supercómputo del Sureste de México, Benemérita Universidad Autónoma de Puebla, Puebla, Mexico

Edgar Villavicencio-Arcadia University of Guadalajara, Zapopan, Jalisco, Mexico

Miguel Zapata Ophthalmology, Hospital Vall d'Hebron, Barcelona, Barcelona, Spain

Jorge Zavala-Hidalgo Centro de Ciencias de la Atmósfera, Universidad Nacional Autónoma de México, Mexico City, Mexico

Olmo Zavala-Romero Centro de Ciencias de la Atmósfera, Universidad Nacional Autónoma de México, Mexico City, Mexico; Department of Radiation Oncology, University of Miami Miller School of Medicine, Miami, FL, USA

Scheduling, Architecture, and Programming

A Scheduling Algorithm for a Platform in Real Time

M. Larios-Gómez[1,2](✉), J. Migliolo Carrera[2](✉),
M. Anzures-García[2](✉), A. Aldama-Díaz[2](✉),
and G. Trinidad-García[2](✉)

[1] Facultad de Ciencias en Sistemas Computacionales y Electrónicos,
Universidad Autónoma de Tlaxcala, Tlaxcala, México
mlg_y@yahoo.com
[2] Facultad de Ciencias de la Computación,
Benemérita Universidad Autónoma de Puebla, Puebla, México
migliolo.jair@gmail.com, marioanzuresg@gmail.com,
aviel.aldama@gmail.com, tgarcia@cs.buap.mx

Abstract. We propose a scheduling algorithm that was designed and implemented to obtaining the results for assigning tasks based with miss deadline among several nodes of a mobile distributed environment, taking into account the delay quality, achieving in such a way that the data of a mobile device can be transferred and located in a network. This method was intended to give a real-time scheduler, which allowed the obtaining of good results without loss of information. Also, we proposed to develop a mechanism to maintain and construct a scheduler to from the beginning.

Keywords: Real-time systems · Distributed environments
Embedded software system · High-performance computing

1 Introduction

The scheduling tasks in the current computer systems are the basis of its optimal functioning. Scheduling is demanded in embedded software design, mainly by the communication between the host system and the base system. Also, it is the fundamental part of the mobile distributed systems (MDS), real time systems (RTS) and in the high performance computation (HPC).

Real-time systems are strongly included and used in the latest generation of aircraft, spacecraft, robot control, communication between wireless mobile devices (WMD), etc. In distributed mobile devices (DMD), real-time algorithms must have the ability to respond immediately by having time constraints and with respect to the use of their limited resources [1, 3].

In a MDS, we have a set of devices $m_i \in M$ i = 1, 2, 3... s. The metric used is based on the minimization of the sum of the weight in determined times, based on a cost of sending a packet between two nodes. This metric is important since in the DMD, the difference of values is imparted on the complemented system, this proposed metric is based on [4, 5], where different algorithms based on theorems of process scheduler on

M. Torres et al. (Eds.): ISUM 2018, CCIS 948, pp. 3–10, 2019.
https://doi.org/10.1007/978-3-030-10448-1_1

uniprocessors and multiprocessors measuring the computation time required for the determined scheduler that satisfies the partial order and resource constraints.

The study of the DMS, RTS and HPC was taken as a starting point, and reactive protocol algorithms [2], depending on the convenience of the application or applications [6]. For this reason, these applied to a platform capable of running in real time. This platform allows mobile devices to tasks scheduling in real time. The algorithm and methodologies was simulated under a high performance computing architecture, specifically in a node of the supercomputer in LNS-BUAP, with the adequate resources to perform the tests and obtain the desired results.

In implementation of a MDS, it was applied to a network connection based on p2p nodes. Once this network configuration was obtained, the scheduler algorithm was designed and implemented in order to observe the delay quality. At the p2p nodes, roles were assigned to each of the peers: sending node, receiving node, bridge node and router node. It can be seen as a local state, depending on the requirements and restrictions of resources to carry out the communication; in this MDS the nodes can communicate with neighboring nodes by means of a suitable entity configuration, in a range of transmission from an emitter to a receiver in a neighborhood L. The communication in this neighborhood, describes a dynamic topology, this makes difficult to establish and maintain a communication route between the nodes v_i and v_j, taking into account that $i \neq j$ and vi, vj $\in$ V, where V is the set of nodes in a mobile network, presumably remote due to the limited disposition for communication in a given time.

The routing algorithms in an SDM environment, are based on message flooding, as a search mechanism for routes in an L neighborhood, sending messages in neighborhoods of nodes, using Ad Hoc SLR networks [7].

The analysis, design and implementation of a scheduler algorithm based on consensus, guaranteed the execution of periodic, aperiodic and sporadic tasks with appropriation in the simulated dynamic environments, complying with strict time constraints (deadline) [4]. In this proposal, such characteristics were provided for consensus management on decision making [8, 9].

The analysis of the infrastructure, as well as the tools required to carry out the design and implementation of the proposed algorithms and methods, were coupled to a software tool capable of measuring the times of the process planners.

The scheduling algorithm was based on the assignment of tasks for MDS. For this, it was used in a multi-agent environment with uncertainty in execution times, based on the metrics previously proposed for the scheduling of tasks a priori [10].

2   State of the Art

In [4] the approach to the problem about consensus and agreement is described. The agreement between the processes in a distributed system is a fundamental requirement for a wide range of applications. Many forms of coordination require that the processes exchange information, which serves to negotiate processes with processes and reach a common understanding, before taking specific actions of the application.

In this paper, we propose the use of Ad Hoc networks, for validating their results in networks with intercommunication topologies and dynamic changes. Another work with novel proposals on consensus-based planning algorithms is [11], in this work the problem was redirected for distributed systems with non-linear multi-agent and a controller is applied to directed and non-directed gaps, plus this control allows you to work in fixed and changeable topologies. The application of consensus and agreements in multi-agent environments distributed and design of observers can be found in [12], this work is based on the rules of neighborhoods L for the coordination of multi-agent. In the search for an active leader, the dynamics of the agent to be followed with interactive control inputs are described.

In [13] being discussed the application of the results for the consensus problem based on multi-agent systems, the use of Ad Hoc networks is based on the Laplacian matrix of the network that achieves consensus in a finite time using Lyapunov functions, In this way a special distributed map is proposed for the class of non-directed graphs, these maps are used in [14], where an exhaustive analysis and the design of cooperative strategies for the grant are proposed, another contribution is the introduction to the necessary and sufficient conditions for two discontinuous distributed algorithms that achieve the minimum and maximum consensus in finite time and an asymptotically granted consensus.

An example of a SDM applications can be found in [16–18], these works focuses on the problem of determining an optimal route; through a route discovery algorithm. The AEC is applied to a distributed environment (DE) using an adjacency matrix, then the numerical distance is used to apply the consensus for the mobile topology study case expressed in Eq. (1).

$$y_i^k = \frac{\sum_{k=1}^m w\left(i, J_i^h\right) f_{\left(i, J_i^h\right)}^k (\rho)}{\sum_{k=1}^m w_{\left(i, J_i^h\right)}} \qquad (1)$$

where:

y_i^k It is the winner of the consensus with the interaction i.

$w\left(i, J_i^h\right)$ It is the level of agreement with respect to the input pairs.

$f_{\left(i, J_i^h\right)}^k (\rho)$ Availability function of the neighbors of L_i.

For example in [17], we can observe the application of fuzzy control based on the Takagi-Sugeno theory, in this experiment, they were based on commercial platforms, applying the Takagi-Sugeno methodology for the control with fuzzy logic. Both quadrocopters and helicopters were established three regulation points:

$$\theta = -45°, \ \theta = 0° \ y \ \theta = 45°$$

These conditions are important for obtaining the desired quantifications, although they are limited to only three sets of them. This non-linear model is independent of the positions of de ψ y θ. This research covers the area of drones, as in the works [14, 15] a modeling using Euler-Lagrange is presented for the drone-helicopter in 2DoF. Based on this model, an FF-LQR control is applied to control a miniature helicopter regulating the axis at an angle pitch (θ) with FF. The FF + LQR + I control uses an integrator in the feedback loop to reduce the error in steady state. Using the FF and proportional integral velocity (PIV) the angle θ is adjusted and only with the PIV is the yaw angle (ψ) controlled.

The LQR control effectively adjusts the set of frequencies without calculating the control law and the reconfiguration itself impacting on the transition. It is noteworthy that this last reconfiguration decreases the performance index caused by a use of the network outside its bandwidth or due to a low sampling of the transmission outside the planning region in the angles and velocities in θ and ψ.

Another research work, which highlights the analysis and design of control systems in NCS networks, is found in [17], here an LQR (Linear-Quadratic Regulator) control applied to delays in a real-time system is evaluated. It is located in an NCS. Another research work is presented in [18], where a proposal for helicopter control is presented. The objective is to maintain the desired angle of pitch and yaw, through two propellers with two motors as actuators, in addition to other use cases such as the simulation of a magnetic levitation system, with an electric magnet as an actuator, and two sensors that measure the position of a steel ball and the current of the electro magneto. To show the design application of an NCS, packet loss is presented in a remote communication between computers or mobile devices, based on the UDP protocol. The designed control is applied to both cases of study, using the model and the imperfections. Feedback matrices are designed for each discrete sub-model through an LQR design.

3   Design and Implementation of the Algorithm

Having the scheduler σ(t) whose processes are generated in an expansion tree, such processes as a set of P, set of resources R, and set of tasks J, as shown in Eqs. 2 and 3.

$$\sigma(t) : R^+ \rightarrow N \tag{2}$$

$$G{<}P, R, J, A> p_i \in P, r_i \in R, j_i \in J \tag{3}$$

where

G: acyclic graph connected
A: edges between processes, resources and tasks

The algorithm proposed in Fig. 1, highlights the management, creation and scaling of processes with a specific deadline. The processes have the task of sending messages in a determined time, creating a process by message, in this way the metric based on time is obtained. The time constraints are considered, and a tardiness or exceeding time E_i is generated as a function of the lateness L_i, as illustrated in Eq. 4.

$$E_i = \max(0, L_i) \tag{4}$$

The scheduler proposed in this work falls into the non-preemptive category, since it does not allow context switching.

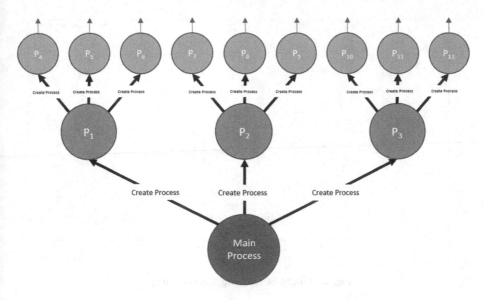

Fig. 1. Tree of processes

The tests were made in a node assigned by the laboratory LNS-BUAP, using instances of the operating system with a micro-kernel called Minix. This has basic resources of an operating system [19], being ideal for the execution of scheduling algorithms. These instances were made with a tool for the administration of the computing cloud it's called OpenStack allowed for the execution of a considerable number of Minix instances, testing of at 1000 instances and handling of 1000 processes.

In Fig. 1, the execution cycle of processes tree send messages through the UDP remote communication protocol is expressed. Executed by each of the peers instantiated in Minix hosted in the host.

4   Results

The results obtained are mainly focused on the proposal of a real-time scheduler algorithm, such as it support decision-making in groups of mobile agents in a community of WMD. Achieving results in mobile devices. Giving proposals to improve the operation of robots and mobile devices. The application of algorithms and methodologies that were used to perform the expected results were simple and with a good performance response.

Figure 2, shows how the processes reach their deadline executing simple tasks with arbitrary quantum times, measured in milliseconds, as well as the results obtained by the tests carried out in a node of the LNS laboratory. It should be noted that 92% of the processes achieved their dead-line established a priori. Starting with 980 processes, a constant with respect to time is observed. The interpretation of this statement tells us that the scheduler has a brief improvement with respect to the scope of the deadline. After a processing time, 92.99% of processes reaching their deadline. The remaining 7% achieved a considerable improvement in the range of 1.8 s to 2 s.

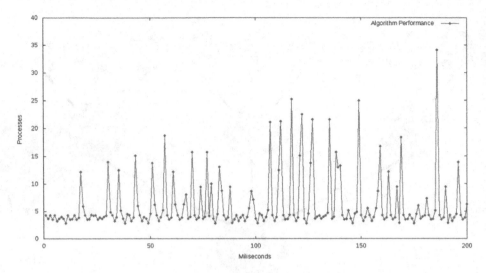

Fig. 2. Processes reaching their deadline.

In Table 1 we present the estimated average of the number of processes and their scope of the deadline.

In the obtained results did not pass the time of transitions between the times and the time that each step of the piece depends on the accomplishment of one task to another; In terms of CPU time, we can find processes that need time intervals along which there is a long or long process during the indefinite time that, consequently, are the processes that do not reach their established deadline. This being the premise of the timeshare processes since, as is known, it is difficult to always guarantee compliance with deadlines.

Table 1. Representation of estimated deadline.

Interval	Average deadline
0–99	11.1547
100–199	11.5528
200–299	10.0025
300–399	10.3498
400–499	8.9831
500–599	8.9050
600–699	8.6645
700–799	7.4945
800–899	6.8368
900–999	5.3706

Thanks to the fact that you can see the behavior of the processes and their tasks, it opens the way to the development of effective mechanisms for the baking of these, for example, a static planning. Already knowing periods and execution times, an execution plan can be established a priori, as is done in the nearest term planning (EDF), taking on the task whose deadline is closest to expire.

5 Conclusions

The executions were performed on a node assigned by the LNS-BUAP supercomputer lab, using instances of the reduced operating system with a microkernel-based systems called Minix. The micro-kernel has basic resources of an operating system, being ideal for the execution of the algorithms of planning. These instances were carried out with a tool for the administration of the cloud of computation. The tool called OpenStack allowed the execution of a considerable number of Minix instances, several tests were performed with at least 1,000 instances and a handling of 1,000 processes.

Acknowledgment. The authors acknowledge to the people from the National Laboratory of Supercomputing of Southeast of Mexico that belongs to the CONACYT national laboratories, for all the technical assistance and the computational resources.

References

1. Severance, C.: Andrew S. Tanenbaum: the impact of MINIX. J. Computer **47**(7), 7–8 (2014). https://doi.org/10.1109/MC.2014.175
2. Corson, M.S., Macker, J., Batsell, S.G.: Architectural considerations for mobile mesh networking. In: Proceedings of IEEE Military Communications Conference, MILCOM 1996 (1996)
3. Park, V.D., Corson, M.S.: A highly adaptive distributed routing algorithm for mobile wireless networks. In: Proceedings of IEEE Sixteenth Annual Joint Conference of the IEEE Computer and Communications Societies. Driving the Information Revolution, INFOCOM 1997 (1997)
4. Cheng, A.M.K.: Real-Time Systems: Scheduling, Analysis, and Verification. Wiley (2003)
5. Stankovic, J.A., Spuri, M., Di Natale, M., Buttazzo, G.C.: Implications of classical scheduling results for real-time systems. Computer **28**(6), 16–25 (1995)
6. Sengul, C., Kravets, R.: Bypass routing: an on-deman local recovery protocol for ad hoc networks. Ad Hoc Netw. **4**(3), 380–397 (2006)
7. Ramasubramanian, V., Haas, Z.J., Sirer, E.G.: SHARP: a hybrid adaptive routing protocol for mobile ad hoc networks. In: Proceedings of the 4th ACM International Symposium on Mobile Ad Hoc Networking & Computing, pp. 303–314. ACM (2003)
8. Gómez, J.A.H., Pérez, H.B.: Global scheduling of confined tasks based on consensus. IEEE Latin Am. Trans. **13**(3), 825–834 (2015)
9. Arellano-Vázquez, M., Benítez-Pérez, H., Ortega-Arjona, J.: A consensus routing algorithm for mobile distributed systems. Int. J. Distrib. Sens. Netw. **11**, 510707 (2015)
10. Kshemkalyani, A.D., Singhal, M.: Distributed Computing: Principles, Algorithms, and Systems. Cambridge University Press, Cambridge (2011). Capítulo 14

11. Cortés, J.: Finite-time convergent gradient flows with applications to network consensus. Automatica **42**(1), 1993–2000 (2006)
12. Cortés, J.: Distributed algorithms for reaching consensus on general functions. Automatica **44**(3), 726–737 (2008)
13. Hui, Q., Haddad, W.M.: Distributed nonlinear control algorithms for network consensus. Automatica **44**(9), 2375–2381 (2008)
14. Hong, Y., Chen, G., Bushnell, L.: Distributed observers design for leader-following control of multi-agent networks. Automatica **44**(3), 846–850 (2008)
15. Esquivel-Flores, O., Benítez-Pérez, H., Ortega-Arjona, J.: Issues on communication network control system based upon scheduling strategy using numerical simulations. INTECH, Open Access Publisher 2016 (2012)
16. Castillo, O., Benítez-Pérez, H.: A novel technique to enlarge the maximum allowable delay bound in sampled-data systems. In: Congreso Nacional de Control Automático 2017, 4–6 Octubre, Monterrey, Nuevo León, Mexico (2017)
17. Mendez-Monroy, P., Benitez-Perez, H.: Supervisory fuzzy control for networked Control systems. ICIC Express Lett. **3**(2), 233–238 (2009)
18. Mancina, A., Faggioli, D., Lipari, G., et al.: Real-Time Syst. **43**, 177 (2009). https://doi.org/10.1007/s11241-009-9086-5
19. Larios, M., et al.: Scheduling: a graphical interface for applying a process scheduling algorithm. In: Applications of Language & Knowledge Engineering. Research in Computing Science, vol. 145, pp. 119–126 (2017). ISSN 1870-4069

Automatic Code Generator for a Customized High Performance Microprocessor Simulator

Alfredo Cristóbal-Salas[1]([⊠]), Juan D. Santiago-Domínguez[1]([⊠]),
Bardo Santiago-Vicente[1]([⊠]), Marco Antonio Ramírez-Salinas[2]([⊠]),
Luis Alfonso Villa-Vargas[2]([⊠]), Neiel Israel Layva-Santes[2]([⊠]),
Cesar Alejandro Hernández-Calderón[2]([⊠]),
and Carlos Rojas-Morales[2]([⊠])

[1] Laboratorio de Cómputo de Alto Rendimiento,
Universidad Veracruzana, Blvd. Adolfo Ruiz Cortines No. 306,
Col. Obras Sociales, 93240 Veracruz, Mexico
acristobal@uv.mx, juansd97458@gmail.com,
bardosantiago.v@gmail.com
[2] Centro de Investigación en Computación, Instituto Politécnico Nacional,
Av. Juan de Dios Bátiz, Esq. Miguel Othón de Mendizábal Col. Nueva Industrial
Vallejo, Delegación Gustavo A. Madero 07738, CDMX, Mexico
{mars, lvilla}@cic.ipn.mx,
israel.leyva.santes@gmail.com, hdzces@gmail.com,
crojasmrls@gmail.com

Abstract. This paper presents a software that generates code that implements a microprocessor simulator based on features defined by user. Software receives a set of microprocessor architecture description that includes: number of cores, operations to be executed in the ALU, cache memory details, and number of registers, among others. After configuration, the software generates Java code that implements the microprocessor simulator described. Software can generates more than forty different codes depending on the configurations defined. Each simulator follows a standard four stages pipeline: fetch, decode, execute and store. Code generator has been used as a learning tool in an undergraduate course with interesting effects in the student's learning process. Preliminary results show that students understand better how a microprocessor works and they felt ready to propose new microprocessor architectures.

Keywords: Code generator · Microprocessor · Simulator · Architecture
ISA

1 Introduction

In Mexico, The quality of teaching in higher education is regulated by a civil organization called "Consejo para la Acreditación de la Educación Superior, A.C." (COPAES). Within this civil association is "Consejo de Acreditación de la Enseñanza de la Ingeniería A.C." (CACEI) which is responsible for quality of teaching engineering [1]. CACEI has defined three orientations for computer engineering academic Programs: System information, hardware and software [2] (see Table 1).

© Springer Nature Switzerland AG 2019
M. Torres et al. (Eds.): ISUM 2018, CCIS 948, pp. 11–23, 2019.
https://doi.org/10.1007/978-3-030-10448-1_2

Table 1. CACEI evaluation for engineering academic programs with topics in the area of microprocessors.

	Science of the engineering	Applied engineering and engineering design
Computer engineering: system information	Concurrency and parallelism, computer organization	Digital technology
Computer engineering: hardware	Concurrency and parallelism, computer organization, basic electricity and electronics, digital electronics	Computer architecture: memory, central processing unit, I/O units, peripherals and interfaces, design techniques for systems with microprocessors and microcontrollers
Computer engineering: software	Concurrency and parallelism, computer organization, basic electricity and electronics, digital electronics	Computer architecture: memory, central processing unit, I/O units

This civil association has a reference framework in use since 2018; in this new reference framework, all skills defined in an academic program must be developed and there should be an artifact that makes evident the skills fulfillment. In other words, if there is a specific skill defined as a part of a course, this skill must be demonstrated by documenting all projects made by students [3]. For example, let's consider the following skill: "Students design a microprocessor considering energy efficiency". This skill should be evaluated with an artifact where students participate in the design process of a microprocessor microarchitecture that explicitly considers energy studies.

2018 CACEI's new reference-framework for quality education brings new challenges for microprocessors design courses. Computer engineers graduating in this new framework should demonstrate mature knowledge in the design, implementation and testing of a microprocessor microarchitecture. In order to fulfill these new requirements, this paper presents a learning tool where students can design a custom microprocessor simulator based on customizable features by the user. This simulator would allow them to understand the flow of information within the datapath, how instructions are processed, and consequently, how the microprocessor's design influences the execution of a program.

The paper is organized as follows: Sect. 2 describes code generator design; in Sect. 3, the microprocessor simulator implementation is presented. Section 4 presents how to generate HPC microprocessors. Section 5 presents the microprocessor simulator as an educational tool, and finally some preliminary results and conclusions are discussed.

2 Code Generator Design

As presented in Fig. 1, code generator is a software-based tool that takes a Java-code template and modifies it according to the information provided by user, as the main input for the code generator. Code modifications include code replacement and code insertion. The resultant code runs a microprocessor simulator with the features required by the user, being possible to execute machine code. More information about these input information is presented next.

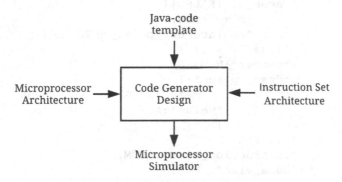

Fig. 1. Code generator block diagram.

2.1 Instruction Set Architecture – ISA

In general, the ISA describes each instruction available in the ALU for execution. Also, it describes how to decode the instruction identifying the operation code and the addresses for input data. All this information is introduced in the code generator as a JSON string according to the following syntax notation:

```
ISA={(NUM  :  {"name"  :  STRING,
               "OPCODE": STRING,
               "type": STRING,
               "encoding": { (STRING:NUM-NUM)⁺},
               "code"  : STRING
               }(,|λ))⁺
      }
```

2.2 Microprocessor Microarchitecture MAC

The MAC describes the microprocessor components and their configuration. Information contained in the MAC usually defines electronic description of a microprocessor elements, for instance: number of cores, cache memories, registers, bus bandwidth, flags among others. Code generator software receives the MAC information also as a JSON string that describes microprocessor features. This input information follows the syntax notation presented below:

```
ARCH={
    "Cores": NUM,
    "Cache_L1":FALSE|{
            "size":NUM,
            "replacement_policy":STRING},
    "Cache_L2":FALSE|{
            "size":NUM,
            "replacement_policy":STRING},
    "Cache_L3":FALSE|{
            "size":NUM,
            "replacement_policy":STRING},
    "flags"    : ({
     "number":NUM,
     "description":{
                "name":STRING,
                "value":NUM
                }
    (,|λ)})⁺,
    "instruction_size": NUM,
    "data_size": NUM,
    "memory_size": NUM,
    "registers":{
        (
        "number":NUM,
        "description":{
                "name":STRING,
                "value":NUM
        }
        (,|λ))⁺
        }
    }
```

3 Microprocessor Simulator Implementation

In this section, more information about the Java-code that implements the microprocessor simulator is presented. A part of the validation process for this simulator it is
important to compare the resultant Java-code with other simulators available in the
market. In Table 2, several microprocessor simulators are compared; these simulators
were originally described in [4–9].

Microprocessors are compared considering the following features: microprocessor's features customization, execution of multiple architectures, visual programming
from the interface, present microprocessor architecture to user, benchmarking programs
execution, loading of a custom ISA, showing the microprocessor's state, allowing input
code in assembler language, simulator has a graphical user interface.

Table 2. Microprocessor simulators and their characteristics.

	CALVIS32	Saksham	Emu8086	Simula3MS	Spim	DrMIPS
Features customization	–	O	–	–	–	–
Multiple microarchitectures	–	O	–	–	–	–
Visual programming in the interface	O	–	–	–	–	O
Show microprocessor architecture on screen	–	O	–	O	–	O
Execute benchmarking programs	O	O	O	O	O	O
Custom instruction set	O	O	O	O	–	O
Show microprocessor current state	–	O	O	O	O	O
Code in assembler	O	O	O	O	O	O
Graphical user interface	O	–	–	O	–	O

According to the information previously presented, the requirements needed to design a new microprocessors simulator are:

- Memory and registers visualization. Microprocessor class should have methods to show the current values of classes' attributes, such as: main memory, registers, flags, and cache memory (if defined).
- Code availability. Java-code should be always available to user.
- Simulator documentation. Java-code should have documentation using Javadoc.
- Project download. Microprocessor code should be available for download as a compressed file.

In Fig. 2, the class diagram for the microprocessor simulator is presented. Simulator contains eight classes: Processor, Control Unit, Arithmetic-Logic Unit, Core, Register, Main memory, L1 Cache, L2 Cache. Detail information about each class is presented next.

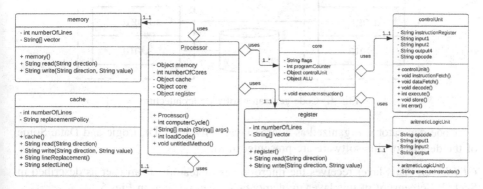

Fig. 2. Example of a class diagram for a customized microprocessor simulator.

3.1   Code Generator Implementation

The code generator is a software implemented in PHP language with user interface written in HTML5, CSS, and Javascript. This software captures the ISA and microprocessor microarchitecture and generates object oriented code written in Java according to the description in Sects. 2.1 and 2.2. The generator's use-cases are presented in Fig. 3 and its software architecture is presented in Fig. 4.

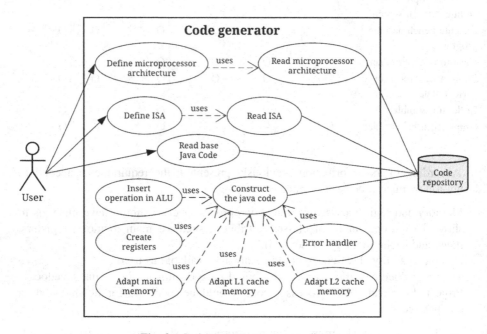

Fig. 3. Code generator use-cases diagram.

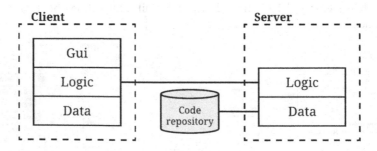

Fig. 4. Code generator software architecture.

Code generator is organized as a three layer software: GUI, Logic and Data. Some of the details for this software are presented next.

GUI Layer. This layer receives the microprocessor features from user as described in Sect. 2. Screenshot of this layer implementation can be seen in Fig. 5.

Logic Layer. This layer reads template Java-code that implements a microprocessor and modifies its methods and attributes to adapt it to user requirements. The modifications can be one of the following strategies:

Code replacement. This strategy replaces code-tags with information defined by user. For instance, in the code,

```
String[] CacheMemory = new String[<MAXSIZE>];
```

The tag <MAXSIZE> would be replaced by the number 64 when user defines a cache memory array consisting of 64 registers.

Code insertion. This strategy is applied when user defines a microprocessor that includes a L1 cache memory or several cores as microprocessor elements are specified. For example, let's consider the next code

```
public static void main(String[] args) {
MEMORY=new memory();
CU= new controlUnit();
ALU= new aritmeticLogicUnit();
<CACHE_CODE>
int output;

CU.programCounter="100110";
do{
output=Microprocessor.executeInstruction();
}while(salida==0);
}
```

The tag <CACHE_CODE> should be replaced with the code

```
L1 = new cacheMemory();
```

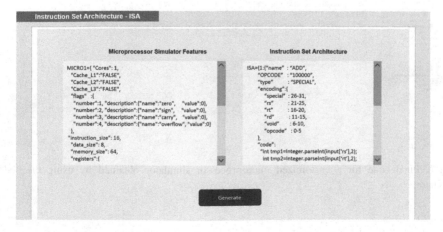

Fig. 5. Defining a microprocessor using the code generator.

This tags are replaced with information provided by user. Data layer. This layer retrieves the Java-code for microprocessor simulator from code repository. Once Java-code is modified, the generator compresses code and makes it available for download (see Fig. 6). Figure 7 shows the interface running microprocessor simulator project.

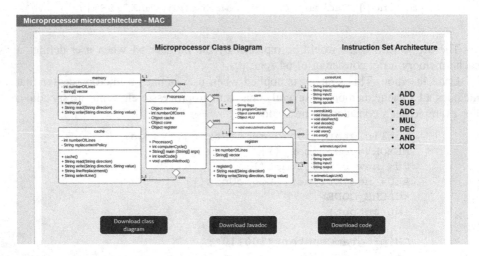

Fig. 6. Access to the microprocessor simulator generated.

Fig. 7. Final code for a customized microprocessor simulator obtained by using the code generator.

4 Generating HPC Microprocessors

Microprocessor performance is in terms of some of its features, such as: instructions per cycle, number of processing elements, energy consumption, or the inclusion of additional hardware such as: cache memory, co-processors, hardware accelerators, etc. All these terms are considered when defining performance variables such as: energy efficiency, number of operations per second, instruction-level parallelism, among others.

The code generator, presented in this paper, can produce customized Java code that implements microprocessor simulators with different features that can be considered as high performance. In Table 3 a list of Java-code templates is presented; from this table, it is possible to see that user can choose between several predefined microprocessor architectures; once selected, user can continue defining the rest of the microarchitecture. This Java-code templates include code-tags which are substituted by final values defined by user according to the explanation in Sect. 3.

Table 3. Microprocessor microarchitectures produced by the code generator.

Architecture	Cores	Cache	Registers	Word size	ISA
One-core	1	None, L1	User defined	User defined	User defined
Dual-core	2	L1, L2	User defined	User defined	User defined
Quad-core (2 Dual-core)	4	L1, L2	User defined	User defined	User defined
Six-core (3 Dual-core)	6	L1, L2, L3	User defined	User defined	User defined
Octa-core (2 Quad-core)	8	L1, L2, L3	User defined	User defined	User defined
Many-core (full parallel)	User defined	L1	User defined	User defined	User defined

5 Simulator as an Educational Tool

This section discusses the use of the code generator described in this paper as a learning tool in a computer architecture undergraduate course. The main idea behind this learning tool is to allow students to understand microprocessor design by using UML notation to describe its components, and its behavior. Microprocessor implementation is viewed as a software development problem where all techniques and standards applied for this area have to be used to design a microprocessor. As all software development, a microprocessor should consider the following elements: a software requirement system, software design, implementation and a test bench environment to ensure the correct implementation.

This fundamental idea behind this research is to see microprocessor design as the implementation of a computational model instead of a series of electronic circuits. In other words, students with software orientation should see a microprocessor as a function that transforms input data into output data. This idea happens to be the fundamental definition for a Turing Machine or a Finite State Automata. Thus, the hypothesis to demonstrate is: "undergraduate students, from the area of computer engineering, understand better how to design a microprocessor when they see the process as a object oriented software development compared to the use of assembly code programming learning technique". To prove this hypothesis students from the Computational Technologies Engineering undergraduate academic program at Universidad Veracruzana were selected as target population. As sample population, 20 students from fifth semester (out of seven semesters) were selected.

5.1   Experimentation

As part of the experimentation, students took a 40 h. course about microprocessors design. In this course, students solved five laboratory practices considering the topics: memory addressing modes, arithmetic operations, logic operations, conditionals, and cycles. These practices contained more than 50 instructions to be executed for an x86 architecture. Students solved these operations using an x86 microprocessor architecture emulator called EMU8086.

In a second stage, students were required to use the Java project that implements an x86 microprocessor architecture obtained by the code generator. Students run the java project using the Oracle Netbeans IDE to run exactly the same instructions as the previous laboratories practices. All instructions were executed using the DEBUG option available in Netbeans were students could check step-by-step how instructions were executed.

After experimentation, students were directed to answer a survey to measure their confidence about the knowledge acquired during the course. As can be seen in Fig. 8, most of the students, 100% of them, reported that having the Java code that implements a microprocessor simulator helps them to understand how microprocessor elements work together to execute instructions. This result is quite remarkable compared to the initial 11% of the students who claimed to understand how a microprocessor works using only a microprocessor emulator.

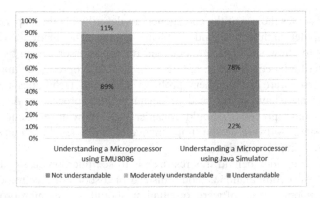

Fig. 8. Improvement in the understanding on how a microprocessor work when using a microprocessor emulator and when using the Java-code microprocessor simulator.

Figure 9 shows more details about how the simulator help students to understand a microprocessor microarchitecture. In this figure, students talk about how the simulator helps them to identify the microprocessor elements, how these elements interact, how to design an ISA and how to execute programs using the ISA designed. In all of these variables, more than 60% of the students report to understand better the microprocessor. In this figure, it is possible to observe that students still have problems to understand how to design and implement an ISA. More research on this topic is required.

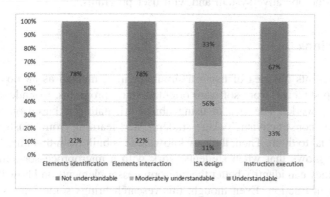

Fig. 9. Students' opinion on how understandable are the concepts microprocessor microarchitecture and instruction set architecture.

Fig. 10. Photographic evidence of students participating in the course and answering the final survey.

In Fig. 10, some photographic evidence is presented when students attended the course and when students answered the survey after using the microprocessor simulator. Students also comment that Java simulator requires to be more user-friendly because all instructions are written in machine code and they expected assembly code. Also, they prefer more time to explore the simulator and more practices that include more details about how to implement a microprocessor in hardware. Finally, students were interested in understanding how to implement a compiler and a run-time system. This new interest confirm the idea that students really understand how a microprocessor interacts with the operative system and with user programs.

6   Conclusions

This paper presents the idea of using a simulator implemented as an object oriented project to help students, from software oriented study programs, to understand how a microprocessor works. The idea of using object orientation is based on the learning strategy called "constructivism" where students start learning from constructs that are known and usual to them. Then, the new knowledge is built from this initial constructs. This research shows that when students work with a microprocessor simulator with open source, they can identify better the microprocessor elements and how they interact to execute an instruction. Even though, this research brings some interesting results, there are still more research to be done because it is necessary that students know how to implement a microprocessor in hardware. Thus, this research is just a step forward in this direction.

Finally, microprocessor simulator contributes to fulfill the new requirements proposed by the 2018 CACEI's framework for accreditation of engineering undergraduate study programs where students have to demonstrate full developed skills by presenting products as evidence of their learning process.

Acknowledgements. Authors would like to thank to students from Facultad de Ingeniería en Electrónica y Comunicaciones, Universidad Veracruzana and students from Centro de Investigación en Cómputo, Instituto Politécnico Nacional who participated during the research activities. Likewise, authors would like to thank to both institutions authorities who make possible this research collaboration.

References

1. CACEI A. C. http://www.cacei.org.mx/nvfs/nvfs01/nvfs0101.php. Accessed 12 Feb 2018
2. CACEI A. C.: Marco de Referencia 2018 del CACEI en el Contexto Internacional, pp. 143–145 (2017)
3. CACEI A. C.: Marco de Referencia 2018 del CACEI en el Contexto Internacional, p. 67 (2017)
4. Grace-Alcalde, J., Chua, G., Marlowe-Demabildo, I., Ahsley-Ong, M., Luis-Uy, R.: CALVIS32: customizable assembly language visualizer and simulator for Intel x86-32 architecture. In: IEEE Region 10 Conference (TENCON 2016), pp. 214–217 (2016)

5. Vasudeba, A., Kumar-Sharma, A., Kumar, A.: Saksham: customizable x86 based multi-core microprocessor simulator. In: IEEE First International Conference on Computational Intelligence, Communication Systems and Networks, pp. 220–225 (2009)
6. Alegrechi, D., Almirón, E.: Introducción al entorno emu8086 Archive https://www.dsi.fceia.unr.edu.ar/images/downloads/digital_II/Introduccion_emu8086_v1.4.pdf. Accessed 12 Feb 2018
7. Cocheiro, R., Loureiro, M., Amor, M., Gonzáles, P.: Simula3MS: simulador pedagógico de un procesador. In: Actas de las XI Jornadas de Enseñanza universitaria de la Informática, pp. 490–495 (2005)
8. Larus, J.: SPIM A MIPS32 Simulator. http://pages.cs.wisc.edu/~larus/spim.html. Accessed 12 Feb 2018
9. Nova, B., Ferreira, J.C., Araújo, A.: Tool to support computer architecture teaching and learning. In: 1st International Conference of the Portuguese Society for Engineering Education, pp. 1–8 (2013)

Use of Containers for High-Performance Computing

F. Medrano-Jaimes$^{(\boxtimes)}$, J. E. Lozano-Rizk, S. Castañeda-Avila,
and R. Rivera-Rodriguez

Center for Scientific Research and Higher Education of Ensenada,
Ensenada, Baja California, Mexico
{hmedrano,jlozano,salvador,rrivera}@cicese.mx

Abstract. The past decade, virtual machines emerged to solve many infrastructure problems and practical use of computing resources. The limitations of this type of technology, are in the sense of resource overload because each virtual machine has a complete copy of an operating system plus different libraries needed to run an application. Containers technology reduces this load by eliminating the hypervisor and the virtual machine for its operation, where each application is executed with the most elementary of a server, plus a shared instance of the operating system that hosts it. Container technology is already an essential part of the IT industry, as it is a simpler and more efficient way to virtualize Micro-Services with workflow's creations support in development and operations (DevOps). Unlike the use of virtual machines, this solution generates much less overhead in the kernel host and the application, improving performance. In the high-performance computing (HPC) there is a willingness to implement this solution for scientific computing purposes. The most important and standard technology in the industry is Docker, however is not a trivial and direct adoption of this standard for the requirements of scientific computing in a HPC environment. In the present study, a review of research works focused on the use of containers for the HPC will be carried out with the objective of familiarizing the user and system administrator of HPC in the use of this technology, and how scientific research projects can get benefit from this type of technology in terms of mobility of compute and reproducibility of workflows.

Keywords: Containers · Virtual machines · High-performance computing

1 Introduction

In "full virtualization" or "hardware level virtualization", a system has a operating system that runs a process called the hypervisor, this one is capable of communicating directly with the host kernel, which can be very useful in some cases. Above the hypervisor sits the virtual hardware layer, that sometimes has a bypass to the physical layer, and then above that is the kernel for the operating system installed on the virtual machine.

Container-based virtualization was developed to improve the sharing of computing resources, allowing multiple isolated namespaces and facilitating the creation and maintenance of customized environments according to specific user and applications requirements. These containers, create abstractions of the guest processes directly

© Springer Nature Switzerland AG 2019
M. Torres et al. (Eds.): ISUM 2018, CCIS 948, pp. 24–32, 2019.
https://doi.org/10.1007/978-3-030-10448-1_3

without the need of an OS guest reducing the overhead of creating a new virtual machine with an operating system guest for each application [1]. Figure 1 represents a general architecture for hypervisor-based and container-based virtualization.

One of the most important and standard container technology is Docker. Docker uses the Linux kernel namespaces to provide resources isolation and is considered an extension of LCX (Linux Containers), in which their containers share the kernel with the Operative System, so the File System and the processes that are executed are also visible and manage from the host OS [2]. Docker also extends LXC with more kernel and application-based features to manage data, processes and advanced isolation within the host OS and gives services and applications with their full dependencies via Docker Hub with an open source platform where everyone can create and upload new containers [3].

In this document we present a technology review about container's platform designed to work in HPC environments and its usages or scientific computing. The reminder of the paper is organized as follows: Sect. 2 presents a background about how HPC applications use containers. Section 3 gives a description about containers technology focused on the HPC for scientific computing. Section 4 describes how HPC applications use containers and finally in Sect. 5 concludes this work.

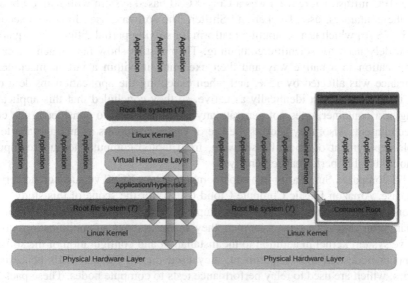

Fig. 1. General architecture for hypervisor-based and container-based virtualization [5].

2 Background

In this section, we identify some recently efforts that has been done for container's technology used for scientific computing in HPC.

There are works that involve the use of Docker for HPC applications. In [4] their study was based on the Docker integration with the message passing interface (MPI) framework. Such integration is considered as a difficulty for the adoption of

Docker containers for HPC. However, they emphasize a series of solutions to be able to execute MPI applications through Docker containers. They developed a program wrapper for MPICH that the user will call instead of the mpiexec command. The idea in this wrapper is send to mpiexec the necessary parameters for its execution in addition to the variables required to run the Docker container, in a certain way, it creates the docker network, communicates with the MPI files and the parameters necessary to be able for job scheduling, create a container from the image specified by the user, and some administrative tasks job's execution. An important aspect to consider is the security since the Docker daemon has restricted access, and although the wrapper allows sending additional information to be able to create the container, it is necessary to be specified by the HPC administrator which options are considered safe for Docker container execution. In their results they focused only on the integration of Docker and MPI, and how the use of the containers allows the execution of applications with special configurations and requirements without the need to make adjustments for each application in the HPC native system.

In [5] conducted a study where their primary objective was to carry out a comparative running a scientific application to evaluate its performance, in this case, from native, virtual machine and using a container. The tests were running in a workstation and the HPC infrastructure used was a Cray XC30-based system with native libraries, and in the containers, used Docker and Shifter. The software used for tests execution was FEniCS [6] which is a computing platform for solving partial differential equations and is widely used for scientific computing. Their results show that, when executing this application in a native way and then executing it within a virtual machine, its performance was affected by 15%, and when executing the application inside a container, it behaves almost identically as native, so they concluded that this application running in a container, does not generate any additional load to consider in the computer equipment. Also, they address the use of Linux containers as an approach to the portable deployment of scientific software, from laptop computer to supercomputer, with no noticeable performance penalty.

In [7] compared Singularity in a supercomputer Cray XC30 versus a cloud service, in this case, Amazon Elastic Compute Cloud (EC2), for the scope of this study, we'll focus only in tests running in Cray supercomputer. In order to achieve the execution of Singularity on the Cray supercomputer, they made a series of modifications to the operative system kernel in addition to the installation and configuration of the software in compute nodes. In their experiment, they used the HPCG and IMB benchmarks packages, which are used to relay performance tests to compute nodes. These packages were executed natively on both the supercomputer and then did the same using containers deployment for each package. Test results presented show that, in the case of the IMB package (used for connectivity evaluation), using a Singularity container with the Cray native MPI library, they achieved a 99.4% efficiency in the bandwidth between two adjacent nodes, however, when using a container with the Intel MPI library, performance was significantly affected, reaching a 39.5% efficiency. Regarding HPCG Package (used to measure applications performance), performance tests were run inside a Singularity container using the native Cray MPI libraries and the Intel MPI libraries. The results showed that, with Intel MPI libraries, there was an overload of 18.1% compared when using native Cray libraries in the Singularity container. After analyzing the results, they concluded that the Singularity container does not add any consideration load using the vendor's native libraries (in this case Cray), and they consider as a good proposal the use of singularity containers to carry out scientific applications and maximize the use of supercomputer's computing resources.

As we mentioned above, the Docker philosophy has in mind mobility as maneuverable as possible, that is to say in an easy way, it bases its architecture that focuses on microservices, it can be cataloged as an SOA architecture. Due to the nature of the microservices in Docker, you can easily package in a container, and satisfy the required transportation through the Docker management. In business applications are based on a set of components that are agglutinated to be a solution and these can easily be done independently through a microservice, this tells us that each microservice itself discovers its requirements and solves them. These same characters make the Docker a system without security and unable to scale in a desirable way as other application require data and processing capacity such as HPC applications, so all of these aspects can be considered as a limitation to use Docker for HPC applications.

3 Bringing Containers to HPC

It's already known, that the IT world is benefiting from the development and use of containers, in the HPC world the experts deal with some non-trivial issues for deploying containers in a HPC environment, as we reviewed in the previous section. The system admins use Linux modules, package managers and even python virtual environments as an effort to provide the users with environments to run their tasks in a cluster without interfering with another user process. However, this solution doesn't fix the problem of portability. In the case that the user needs to run his task in a different cluster, all the dependencies available by Linux module or package managers would need to be installed first in the new cluster in order to reproduce his work.

Containers look like a proven path to deal with the dependency problem, and when we think in containers we must talk about Docker. The main goal of Docker is to enable users and system administrators to separate application from infrastructure so they can ship and run applications quickly. These applications are mostly for the microservice architecture.

The use of containers in science is somehow different, the focus in not necessarily in development and operations (devops), rather in the ability to provide mobility, and reproducibility of workflows using a environment of choice in different HPC clusters. And also leveraging the shared resources of the cluster to scale their workflow.

There are a few factors that prevents Docker being used in a HPC environment. The first and most important is security, since when the user runs a docker container, the container process is being spawned by a root owned Docker daemon, and when this happens the user theoretically could escalate their privileges in the HPC environment. In a real production cluster is very weird and irresponsible if a sysadmin let their users use root privileges. Another big problem is the integration of docker with HPC resources managers and schedulers, which are necessary for shared resources. In this sense, efforts have been done to integrate it, but they tend to result in a "hack" of the Docker functionality or a cluster being built on top of a cluster [4, 7].

4 Containers Technology for HPC: Review

In this section, we describe some HPC containers solutions used for scientific computing applications running in an HPC computing environment. These solutions are Charliecloud, Shifter, and Singularity. They are currently being used in production systems (most of them in academic and research centers) and their developments communities continue with software maintenance and improvements. These solutions allow users to create their software stack (often called User Defined Software Stack UDSS) using a container format (commonly a docker image), allowing application portability to bring their environment to the HPC center for running instances of their container image. Also, they allow the possibility to use the shared cluster resources from a container image and can use OpenMPI, MPICH, Intel MPI, Infiniband, distributed storage systems (LUSTRE) and GPU's.

Charliecloud is an open-source, lightweight implementation on containers for HPC developed by Los Alamos National Security LLC in 2017 [8]. The Charliecloud design goal is simplicity. In this sense, the solution achieves isolation by using user namespaces only for accessing a few important system calls, and keeps all the processes on center-owned resources, unprivileged. The container preparation workflow consists in allowing the user create their own UDSS in a privileged environment (user computer) with docker, when this image is tested and ready for deployment, the image is flattened for distribution in a tar file using Charliecloud commands. The tar file needs to be copied to the cluster and unpacked typically in a local storage or distributed filesystem (this step can be done during the job allocation time). At the end, the container execution is done by the Charliecloud commands (ch-run) that mounts the container image to the host, set up the namespaces and changes the container root directory to the user image. Charliecloud uses the shared resources of the cluster to run the programs in the container images, for example using host MPI infrastructure to run. Regarding the use of Charliecloud with GPUs, there is no work that proves this. Not too many features, options, or security boundaries are implemented in charliecloud; they keep it simple in the guidance that is unnecessary complicate the issue of running contained workflows in the HPC.

Shifter is an open-source framework developed by NERSC. It was one of the first projects that use the containerization to an advanced supercomputing architecture, specifically on Cray systems. After several attempts of implementations alternatives to work with containers (CHOS, MyDock, CRAY_ROOTFS) [9], Shifter surged a solution based on scalability and performance for running and configuring the containers, access to the shared cluster resources and compatibility with its job manager. This solution was originally based on chroot to achieve isolation. Shifter contrary to Charliecloud is more robust, with user-driven functionality and also requires more commitment for the system administrator to set up all details needed. In production environments shifter needs one node in the cluster to act as an "Image Gateway", this node is a Docker installation with daemon "dockerd" running. The Image gateway receives the user request from the "docker pull" command in the login nodes, establishing communication to the root owned docker daemon, and get the images from docker-hub or a private registry of images that the shifter installation provides to hold private workflows. The container image is converted to an ext4 format (optional) and shared to the compute nodes or copy to a distributed file system. After the Image Gateway does this step, the user can submit the job using one of the available images already deployed. For this purpose, Shifter integrates itself with the workload managers (according to the Shifter developing team it can be done with Torque/Moab, ALPS, and Slurm) by adding directives to the batch scripts where the user can define the running images and binding paths. Shifter offers the possibility for the user to run MPI applications, no matter the MPI version needed, in the case that the user needs specific versions of MPI that are not backward supported by the host MPI infrastructure, this will not perform as well as the native MPI. Cluster shares resources like GPU, MPI infrastructure, and high-performance interconnection can be used, and in most cases, the documentation offers examples for the Cray specific services available, like MPICH, and Cray Aries network.

Singularity is also an open-source implementation, originally developed by Lawrence Berkeley National Laboratory, now Syslabs. Singularity is an implementation that provides custom docker images, and standardized container image formats to run in HPC infrastructure. As primarily use case, Singularity brings mobility of computing to both users and HPC centers. Its goal is to support existing and traditional HPC resources as quickly as installing a single package into the host OS [7]. The isolation in Singularity containers images uses a reduced list of namespaces, and the security model is the same as POSIX Linux paradigm. Singularity achieves computing mobility by utilizing a single distributable image format that encapsulates the UDSS, all standard UNIX file permissions apply. This feature facilitates the mobility and also reproducibility which gives the user the certainty that container's code has not changed. Singularity offers an approach for container's content validation integrating a hashing algorithm SHA256. Another Singularity design goal is to support the usage of shared HPC resources, implementing code to natively support technologies such as Infini-Band, MPI, and Lustre. This aspect is considered as a big difference between the others HPC containers solutions, even if support is available in Shifter and Charliecloud, the native support gives the user a "Linux natural feeling" when using Singularity. For example, the user can pipe standard output, error output, IPC (Internal process communication) to the internal container process. The workflow for standard usage is as follows: the user locally in an owned resource creates his UDSS, that can be bootstrapped from the docker repository and then modified to adapt it to his requirements, the resulting image can be a tar file, a standard Linux directory, or an image file with ext3 or squashfs file systems; These options provide a different type of functionality. Then the user distributes the container image to the cluster, this can be done by transferring the image, or it can be "pulled" from a docker-hub like cloud site that the Singularity team deployed, called "Singularity Container Registry" (singularity-hub. org) where the registered users can upload and share the container images exclusively for the singularity container image format. After that in the HPC cluster, the user calls a shell session in the container, or executes a specific binary or script inside the container without the need root privileges. The shared resources can be accessed natively, this means that in the case for the MPI infrastructure, the local commands are used to call the binary inside the container, with no difference with the regular interaction with MPI jobs in a native manner.

4.1   HPC Containers Technology Analysis

After review above, we can mention that Charliecloud is the easier to use and it implies not much effort for users and sysadmin, because the software provides simple straight forward commands. This simplicity tends to be interpreted as a lack of robustness in the solution however for some problems simplicity is the best option. On the other side, Shifter can be considered as a proven solution for working with Docker containers, which requires more commitment in the installation and maintenance for the sysadmins. Shifter has a lot of functionalities and tools for the end users. Even if Shifter is an open-source solution, the documentation is focused on the Cray architecture, although it can be installed in a different HPC architecture. Singularity is considered as a solution for HPC applications, its software is like a Linux service that allows a sysadmin to define and configure according to the cluster policies. Singularity is supported and developed by a team which is focused on the scientific use of containers in HPC. Also provides a cloud service for storing and sharing singularity containers thriving on the singularity goal which is the mobility of compute. The development team is working to add new features like data containers, which are mainly encapsulating the generated data with the deltas in a different persistent overlay, and keeping it valid thru hash algorithms.

Another important aspect is in R/W jobs. Shifter and Singularity discovered that when running jobs that are not optimized for distributed filesystems, (the type of jobs that need to write and read many small files) they improve the performance by running the jobs inside the container, in this manner, the distributed filesystem metadata calls are reduced just to one, the one used in the container image. A general comparison is presented in Table 1.

Table 1. HPC containers technology general comparison

	Charliecloud	Shifter	Singularity
Security model	User Namespaces	SUID/chroot	SUID/user namespaces
Root daemons	No	Yes, for image gateway	No
Network configuration	No	Yes, for image gateway	No
MPI support	OpenMPI	MPICH	OpenMPI, MPICH, Intel MPI *
GPU support	In development	Yes	Yes
High-speed network support	Yes	Yes	Yes
Job scheduler support	Agnostic	Slurm	Agnostic. Plugin for slurm available
Sysadmin limits configuration	No	Yes	Yes
Image format	Docker image, tarball	Docker image, tarball	Singularity format, Docker image, tarball, squashFS
cgroup resource restriction	No, let the workload manager handle the resources	Yes	No, let the workload manager handle the resources
Licence	Open-source apache license	Open-source	Open-source

5   Conclusions

The use of containers for applications that run in HPC environments, has created solutions such as those described in the previous section, in which their results, in general, have been satisfactory and also identify some limitations in order to exploit the computing resources of the HPC infrastructure. In this way, there still a lot of work to be done, but certainly the use of containers for HPC is growing day by day due to the advantages they offer, as the one called "reproducibility of science" [11]. With the contribution to its scientific activity and the publication of the results subject to the scrutiny of the scientific community, in most cases and based on the scientific method, it is desired or presumed that the results of science were more reproducible facial, here, in this case, we did not always ask only the "Reproducibility" of Science, so that whoever could repeat without much problem the results of other experiments, but of the same nature. With this fact of not being able to reproduce the actions easily, the learning time for another scientist to reproduce the experiments can take equal or more time than the original scientist, and some cases are impossible to reproduce them. In this particular case, containers could provide a strong solution to reproducibility of science, allowing scientists to create an image with the application and data needed to run the experiment either on any computing platform.

HPC Containers technology is in growth, and we considered this is an excellent moment to contribute to the development and instrumentation of the tendencies towards the containers, either Singularity, CharlieCloud, Shifter, among others. Our future work involves the applications or numerical model's portability used in research areas such as bioinformatics, earth, ocean as well as atmospheric sciences to get the benefit of HPC containers technology.

References

1. Adufu, T., Choi, J., Kim, Y.: Is container-based technology a winner for high performance scientific applications? In: 17th Asia-Pacific Network Operations and Management Symposium (APNOMS), pp. 507–510. IEEE (2015)
2. Beserra, D., Moreno, E., Takako, P., et al.: Performance analysis of LXC for HPC environments. In: 9th International Conference on Complex, Intelligent and Software Intensive Systems, pp. 358–363 (2015)
3. Kovács, Á.: Comparison of different Linux containers. In: 40th International Conference on Telecommunications and Signal Processing (TSP), pp. 47–51. IEEE (2017)
4. Bayser, M., Cerqueira, R.: Integrating MPI with docker for HPC. In: IEEE International Conference on Cloud Engineering, pp. 259–265. IEEE Computer Society (2017)
5. Hale, I.J., Li, L., Richardson, C., Wells, G.: Containers for portable, productive, and performant scientific computing. Comput. Sci. Eng. **19**, 40–50 (2017)
6. FEniCS. http://fenicsproject.org. Accessed 21 Feb 2018
7. Younge, A., Pedretti, K., Grant, R., Brightwell, R.: A tale of two systems: using containers to deploy HPC applications on supercomputers and clouds. In: 9th International Conference on Cloud Computing Technology and Science, pp. 74–81. IEEE Computer Society (2017)

8. Priedhorsky, R., Randles, T.: Charliecloud: unprivileged containers for user-defined software stacks in HPC. In: Proceedings of the International Conference for High Performance Computing, Networking, Storage and Analysis, Article no. 36 (2017)
9. Gerhardt, L., Bhimji, W., et al.: Shifter: containers for HPC. In: Journal of Physics: Conference Series (2017)
10. Kurtzer, G., Sochat, S., Bauer, M.: Singularity: scientific containers for mobility of compute. PLoS ONE 12(5), e0177459 (2017). https://doi.org/10.1371/journal.pone.0177459
11. Pattinson, D.: Plos One launches reproducibility iniciative. http://blogs.plos.org/everyone/2012/08/14/plos-one-launches-reproducibility-initiative/. Accessed 18 Feb 2018

Parallel Computing

Generic Methodology for the Design of Parallel Algorithms Based on Pattern Languages

A. Alejandra Serrano-Rubio[1]([✉]), Amilcar Meneses-Viveros[1],
Guillermo B. Morales-Luna[1], and Mireya Paredes-López[2]

[1] Computer Science Department, Cinvestav-IPN, Mexico City, Mexico
aserrano@computacion.cs.cinvestav.mx
[2] Mathematics Department, Cinvestav-IPN, Mexico City, Mexico

Abstract. A parallel system to solve complex computational problems involve multiple instruction, simultaneous flows, communication structures, synchronisation and competition conditions between processes, as well as mapping and balance of workload in each processing unit. The algorithm design and the facilities of processing units will affect the cost-performance ratio of any algorithm. We propose a generic methodology to capture the main characteristics of parallel algorithm design methodologies, and to add the experience of expert programmers through pattern languages. Robust design considering the relations between architectures and programs is a crucial item to implement high-quality parallel algorithms. We aim for a methodology to exploit algorithmic concurrencies and to establish optimal process allocation into processing units, exploring the lowest implementation details. Some basic examples are described, such as the *k-means* algorithm, to illustrate and to show the effectiveness of our methodology. Our proposal identifies essential design patterns to find models of Data Mining algorithms with string self-adaptive mechanisms for homogeneous and heterogeneous parallel architectures.

Keywords: Pattern language · Methodology · Parallel algorithm design
Data Mining algorithms

1 Introduction

Parallel computing is based on partition of a computational problem into sub-problems to be executed simultaneously by several processing units and is characterized by the potential to improve the performance, the cost-performance, and the productivity [1]. The constant demand for more significant computing power has evolved this area, from architecture to systems and specialised libraries. Parallel Computing is firmly established in intensive numerical processing [2]. Several parallel systems have been proposed to solve numerical problems, e.g. in [3] a parallel solution of Cholesky factorization is proposed to invert symmetric positive definite linear systems; in [4] a parallel diffuse genetic mining algorithm is proposed based on a master-slave architecture responsible for extracting association rules. However, a parallel system not only has multiple streams of instructions running simultaneously but also involves other

© Springer Nature Switzerland AG 2019
M. Torres et al. (Eds.): ISUM 2018, CCIS 948, pp. 35–48, 2019.
https://doi.org/10.1007/978-3-030-10448-1_4

challenges, as communication structures, synchronisation and competition between processes, coupled with the mapping process and workload balance.

The cost-performance ratio of an algorithm is affected by its design, and by the characteristics of the processing units. Methodologies such as *Partition, Communication, Agglomeration and Mapping* (PCAM) [4], *Partition, Granularity, Agglomeration and Mapping* (PGAM) [5], and *Decomposition, Agglomeration, Orchestation and Mapping* (DAOM) [6], expose the analysis and design of parallel algorithms as decomposition and assignment tasks of different processing elements. We propose a generic methodology that captures the main characteristics of the current methodologies and adds the experience of expert programmers through a pattern language [7]. Our proposal provides a high-level methodology for fast prototyping of parallel algorithms implementations reducing the execution time and with minimum programming effort.

Section 2 describes the background, Sect. 3 the generic methodology for parallel algorithm design, and Sect. 4 the strategies to parallel *k-means*. Last section summarises the main conclusions and sketches future work.

2 Parallel Methodologies

A sequential algorithm consists of a single flow of instructions, each executed exclusively at a given time by a single processing unit. In parallel computing more than just one processing units execute instructions simultaneously; aiming to achieve higher performance [4]. Our methodology addresses the parallelism based on partition a computational problem N into a set $T = \{t_1, t_2, \ldots, t_n\}$ of n tasks, treated concurrently by a set $P = \{p_1, p_2, \ldots, p_k\}$ of k processing units. Each task is composed by a series of instruction or data sets processed simultaneously. The decomposition of the problem N is performed by three different mechanisms: *Domain decomposition*, where the corresponding storage set D is partitioned according to the processing units; *Functional decomposition*, where the instruction set I is divided in n clusters to be processed; and a combination of the above as *activity parallelism* [3, 9]. A parallel computer consists of a set P of processing units, connected through communication channels in order to work cooperatively [3, 7]. Any communication channel is determined by processing and communications. For instance, in shared memory environments, communication is quick and uniform in access time, due to the closeness between processing units. In distributed memory systems, the communication times variate depending on the characteristics of the network, communication protocols, bandwidth and other factors causing non-uniform access to memory. Furthermore, the granularity of the processes should be analysed as the relationship between the amount of computation and the communication structure formed by the processing units. Finally, factors such as mapping and load balance directly affect the performance of the algorithm. The uniform load distribution between the processing units allows to perform a similar amount of work and to remain busy for most of the time. Mapping strategies provide a load balance that is not always ideal, however, they avoid occurrences of idle processors.

2.1 PCAM Methodology

PCAM was proposed by Ian Foster [4]. It starts with a computational problem N; from which a set T is to be executed simultaneously by the processing array P. A *synchronization* is established within the given architecture by communication channels $c_{ij} = (t_i, t_j)$ between tasks, forming m processes $Q = \{Q_1, Q_2, \ldots, Q_m\}$ where $Q_i = \{t_{i1}, t_{i2}, \ldots, t_{ir}\}$ consists of r tasks sharing similar characteristics. This process is known as *agglomeration*, whose goal is to define an efficient *mapping*, namely the allocation $Q \to P$ of parallel processes into processing units.

2.2 DCOM Methodology

In [5], it is described the methodology *Decomposition, Communication, Orchestration* and *Mapping*. Initially, N is broken down into a set T of tasks. The purpose of this phase is to get enough tasks to keep processors busy. Immediately and through an assignment, the elements of the set T are grouped to form a set of processes Q. The *orchestration* creates a specific structure determining access to data, communications, and synchronisation, aiming to reduce the costs and general expenses of parallelism administration through the organization of data structures and the programming of temporary tasks. Finally, the processes are mapped onto the set P. *Mapping* decides which processes run in each processing unit.

2.3 PGAM Methodology

Partition, Granularity, Agglomeration and *Mapping* are considered in [6] to improve the parallel algorithms performance within own execution architectures. The input problem N is partitioned into a task set T, where each t_i is performed in parallel. The granularity $G : t_i \mapsto G(t_i)$ is adjusted to get the map $T \to P$ [6].

3 A Generic Methodology Based on a Pattern Language

We consider the main aspects of the three methods described above. We consider five steps: *Partition, Agglomeration, Granularity, Communication* and *Mapping*. The methodology starts with a computational problem N to be partitioned into a task set T which in turn is treated concurrently by a processor set P. Then a set Q is identified, each element q_i represents the *agglomeration* of r tasks with similar characteristics, $r \leq n$. A *granularity analysis* $G : t_i \mapsto G(t_i)$ is involved to reduce communication costs between task groups. Finally, a *mapping* is a common stage among methodologies whose goal is to reduce the total execution time in a destination architecture. The steps of the generic methodology are:

- **Partition analysis:** It partitions N into a set T, and it does not require that $|T| = |P|$, as in [3, 7]. It is recommended that the granularity specification of the algorithm is maximal and $|T| \geq |P|$. Therefore $|T|$ may vary dynamically at runtime or be defined statically at the computation beginning, besides the maximum number of tasks executed at any time is limited by the maximum number of processing units [7], hence the goal is to maximize scalability and minimize latency produced in process communication. Scalability refers to how the performance of a given partition changes when processing units are added, while latency is the time a message takes in the communication channel. However, the partitioning scale may indicate the minimum number of processing units used to solve the problem.

- **Agglomeration analysis:** In this phase a process set Q is identified. The minimum number of processors used to solve the problemis determined, as well as the load balance in each processing unit, including the processing time, data management time and the communication time.
- **Granularity analysis:** Granularity is the metric representing the relation between processing times with communication times [6, 7]. For each t_i

$$G(q_i) = \frac{t_{process}}{t_{com}} \tag{1}$$

where $t_{process}$ is the time that a processing unit requires to solve the process q_i, while t_{com} is the required communication time among processing units. Typically, the computation of a process is separated by communication periods given by synchronization events, and the relation between processing and communication derives in three granularity types: fine, average and coarse grain. $G(q_i)$ depends on the algorithm and the target architecture. Although it is possible to increase the granularity of q_i, in some cases, it is better to increase the granularity of the agglomeration of t_j in q_i, than to reduce the partition sizes.

- **Communication analysis:** This step optimizes performance of communication operations between executions of recurring processes, therefore, the communication structure C must satisfy the communication requirements between $c_l = (q_i, q_j)$. The objective of this phase is to coordinate the process execution, avoiding the addition of channels and unnecessary communication operations.
- **Multiprocessor scheduling or mapping** aims to minimize the total execution time of parallel systems, since process allocation into processing units improves the overall system performance. An allocation capable of multiplexing among the available processing units must be considered. Otherwise, some processing units may be inactive. *Mapping* is an NP-Complete problem [4], so locality is a relevant aspect when reducing communication times among pairs of processes whose information exchange is of fine granularity. Different methodologies have been proposed to address mapping, showing good performance in general cases [9]. However, the *agglomeration* step assists when the number of processes is close to the number of processing units [1, 10].

3.1   The Pattern Language

The key to implement high-quality parallel algorithms is the development of robust design subject to the relations between the architecture and the program expression. In this section, we describe a pattern language, which is defined as a set of four design spaces containing a set of design patterns, each describing solutions to exploit parallelism in recurrent problems, reflecting the experience of expert programmers in Parallel Computing.

The first design space in the pattern language is *"Finding concurrency"*. This design space is related to the structure of the computational problem and aims to exploit any parallelism opportunity within the algorithm at a high level. The patterns included in this space conform three groups:

- *Decomposition patterns*, which are used to decompose N in a set T, where each t_i can be executed simultaneously. Any t_i represents a subset of instructions or data to be processed in a relatively independent way.
- *Dependency analysis patterns* used to group the elements of T and possible dependencies among them. The *task-grouping* pattern groups each component of T in a set Q to simplify the dependency analysis. The pattern of task ordering establishes a logical order to satisfy the different restrictions on each element of q_i. Finally, it is analysed how the components of the storage data are shared between each element of the set T through a data exchange pattern.
- *Design evaluation pattern*, which is responsible to qualify the decomposition of the problem and the analysis of dependencies. If the design is right, it can be passed to the next design space "Algorithm structure".

The *"Algorithm structure"* is the next design space and its objective is to analyze the structure of the algorithm in order to propose mechanisms to exploit previously defined parallelism. The design patterns grouped at this level describe general strategies for exploiting parallelism and are classified into three groups:

- *Patterns based on the execution* of parallel tasks. The design pattern to be used is chosen based on how the task listing; therefore if the tasks are grouped linearly, then the partitioning mechanism to be used is based on patterns of *task parallelism*. Otherwise, the patterns are based on *divide and conquer strategies* which divide the problem into independent subproblems and recombine the sub-solutions into a general solution. The *task parallelism* patterns analyse the dependencies between the q_i. If there are no dependencies (i.e., task queues), the *embarrassingly parallel* pattern is used. In another case, it is necessary to analyse whether the dependencies are separable, namely, they involve single-write update operations or associative accumulation in shared data structures; or they are protected, which include the reading and writing of a variable during the simultaneous execution
- *Patterns based on data decomposition*. Two patterns are identified: based on *geometric decomposition*, which decomposes T into discrete subspaces that share data between each one of them; and the pattern based on the *decomposition of recursive structures data*
- *Patterns based on the organization of the data flow*. They use the *Pipeline* pattern, which is a global solution resulting from the union of partial solutions obtained by a processor in different clock cycles. On the other hand, the *event-based coordination* pattern assumes that the problem can be divided into semi-independent task groups that interact irregularly. The interaction is determined by the flow of data between them

The *"Support structure"* is the third design space and represents an intermediate stage between the *"Algorithm structure"* and *"Implementation mechanisms"* design spaces. We analyse the source code of a parallel algorithm emphasising the construction of parallel solution. The design patterns here form two groups:

- Patterns for program structure, which, in addition to analyze the interactions between the different processing units, allow the organisation of a program with the objective of dynamically balancing the work.
- Patterns for the data structure responsible for the explicit analysis of the secure exchange of data between a set of parallel processes. The main of this phase is to obtain an efficient and easy to understand program.

Here, the SIMD and MIMD architectures are auxiliary support structures.

Finally, the *"Implementation mechanisms"* give the fourth design space. This space contains mechanisms for efficient allocation of previous design spaces to a programming environment. These mechanisms manage the interaction of the data with the processes and processing units. Three groups are described:

- *Management of processing units* to establish mechanisms allowing simultaneous execution
- *Synchronization*, whose objective is to impose restrictions on the events order for execution in the processing units. The elements are barriers, traffic lights and mutual exclusion mechanisms
- *Communication* based on the memory mechanisms of the destination architecture. The main types of communication are message passage and the collective communication between shared memory mechanisms

Since most of these patterns are related to low-level coordination events, their consequences tend to be located in a small part of the problem, and their implementation depends directly on the used environment. Mostly, the implementation mechanisms are primitives of parallel programming environments.

3.2   Pattern Language Applied to the Generic Methodology

We have described a generic methodology that captures the main characteristics of the methodologies already proposed. The generic methodology is defined by five stages: *Partition, Agglomeration, Granularity, Communication* and *Mapping* (PAGCM). A pattern language consisting of four design spaces to allow efficient descriptions of parallel algorithms has been described. The objective of our proposal is to obtain a generic parallel methodology allowng the design of efficient algorithms and reflects the experience of expert programmers (see Fig. 1). Each phase of the methodology is mapped to a specific design space of the pattern language. Our methodology is divided into two phases: (1) Parallel analysis and (2) the analysis of the relation between the algorithm and the architecture. The phases are defined at high and low levels respectively. In phase (1), the problem is *partitioned* by identifying the potentially parallelizable sections using patterns in the *"Finding concurrency"* design space. Also, the *agglomeration* analysis is performed for each of the sections defined above. During this analysis, the algorithm structure is analyzed in order to efficiently exploit the previously defined sections and to determine the problem granularity. This phase is carried out using the patterns of the *"Algorithm structure"* design space. In step (2), the patterns to analyze the *communication* between the processing units and their assignments are described by the patterns in the *"Support structure"* design space. Finally, the *"Implementation mechanisms"* map into a parallel destination architecture.

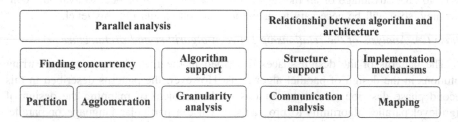

Fig. 1. Implementation of a pattern language to a generic design methodology for parallel algorithms.

Each of these phases is described in more detail in the next sections.

Phase (1): concurrency analysis

It is necessary to define a data structure or critical tasks derived from the decomposition of N and the dependency analysis of the elements that make up the set T, and thereafter the set Q to coordinate the parallel execution of the entities. Firstly, the code sections more computationally intensive are selected. Next, we should identify their tasks and data structures. Decomposition pattern must be selected to exploit the concurrency of the algorithm. A decomposition of tasks is chosen if the overhead associated with the dependency administration is small in comparison with the total execution time of the program. On the other hand, the decomposition of data establishes that the data must be classified according to their locality to choose the appropriate association for each task. Upon the entities identification to decompose N, dependency analysis is made on the set T. Since the efficiency of a parallel algorithm is proportional to the fraction of time spent in calculating a problem, dependencies between tasks should require little time to manage data communication and management of time constraints.

Therefore, it must be recognized how tasks should be grouped to ensure that a task set with the same characteristics is executed in the same q_i process. An order must be introduced for Q to share data between each $t_i \in q_l$ and each $q_l \in Q$. Finally, the design of the algorithm is evaluated by analysing how regular each element of T is, its interactions and the dependencies between the data.

The next stage of the methodology focuses on the analysis of the granularity $G(q_i)$ of a process and the refinement of the parallel algorithm design, for which three main aspects must be considered:

- Target architecture, where $|P|$ is defined by the type of architecture we used, the bandwidth, the cost of an elementary operation t_c, the time of communication t_s and the time of sending a basic data represent by t_w.

- Fundamental organisation principle, which can be by tasks or by data.
- Identification of patterns through a decision tree (see Fig. 2), which begins at the top by analysing the basic principle of organisation and the type of concurrency. Then select one of the branches.

In most cases, a single pattern of the design space: *algorithm structure* will not allow to take advantage of all the opportunities arising with respect to available concurrency, so it will be necessary to use more than one pattern at this level.

Phase (2): Analysis of the relationship between algorithm and architecture

The patterns of the design spaces described in the first phase capture recurring solutions in the design of parallel algorithms. However, the patterns described in this second phase describe recurrent solutions to the problem of mapping the design of high-level parallel algorithms to programs that use a particular language or parallel library. In addition, we describe methodologies to structure the source code and share different data structures between the processes already defined. In this phase, an intermediate mechanism has been proposed for the high-level design and the implementation mechanisms that describe a mapping to a particular programming environment.

This mechanism is composed of five modules (see Fig. 3): Input data forming unit, control unit, unit for computational software modules, a unit for database operations and output data forming unit. The following describes each of them:

- The input data-forming unit, which represents the system parameters, SP described by the target architecture in the first phase and the algorithm parameters AP that will be considered. In this phase, we collect the data that will feed the objective function $T(AP, SP)$, whose purpose is the optimisation of the execution time of a parallel algorithm.
- In control unit, the patterns of the design space structure support are implemented, for which the parameters entered by the previous module must be validated, and the necessary heuristics will be applied for $\min T(AP, SP)$. Also, a communication structure $C = \{c_1, c_2, \ldots, c_l\}$ should be proposed where $c_l = (q_i, q_j)$ represents the communication requirements between processes. Finally, we propose the implementation of a library of elementary operations that considers both semantics and elementary arithmetic operations classified according to their computational complexity.
- Unit for computational software modules implements the last level of a pattern language: *implementation mechanisms*. The patterns in this level describe entities that strictly belong to particular programming environments, and have homogeneous and heterogeneous architectures. Here, access to information stored in different repositories (Unit for database operations) is allowed.
- Output data forming unit shows the results, in files that contain parameters with which the T function has been optimised, the total execution time and additional information.

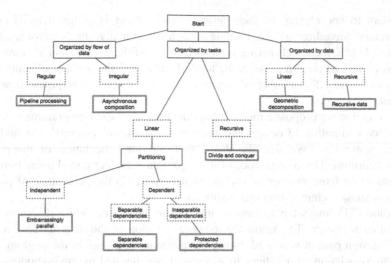

Fig. 2. Starting at the top of the tree, the concurrency and the major organising principle, select one of the three branches of the tree. Then follow the discussion below for the appropriate sub-tree [8].

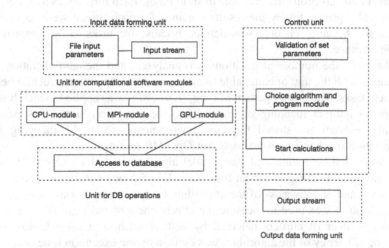

Fig. 3. Logical scheme of the design space "*Structure support*" and "*Implementation mechanisms*".

4 Design and Implementation of the Parallel *K-means* Algorithm with a Generic Methodology

K-means clustering algorithm [16] is quite relevant in data mining. Given *n* patterns, the main goal is to group each pattern in *k* clusters [17]. *K-means* algorithm assigns each object to the nearest cluster. Cluster centers are called centroids. The algorithm starts with an initial set of cluster centers, chosen at random. Then it iteratively assigns each pattern to one cluster. In each iteration, each object is assigned to its nearest cluster center according to the Euclidean distance. Finally, the centroids are re-calculated [18]. K-means clustering is known to be NP-hard [14], and its time complexity is $O(nki)$ where n represents the total of patterns, k the number of centroids in each iteration and i the number of iterations that the algorithm requires to achieve convergence.

In this section we propose a methodology helping non-expert programmers in high-performance computing to design and implement parallel algorithms with high performance at runtime. We describe the design and implementation of the parallel *k-means* algorithm. The convergence of the algorithm was determined using two main conditions: (1) a fixed number of maximum iterations; (2) the percentage of patterns that do not show a change between iterations.

Condition (1) limits the execution time of the algorithm, while (2) ensures the quality of each cluster. To exploit the temporal location of the data, a *"Task decomposition"* design pattern was used during the partitioning phase. In the agglomeration phase, the association of a pattern to a centroid was defined as the computationally intensive code section, and the overhead in the handling of possible dependencies is compensated. Fine-grain parallelism compensates the overload of management of tasks and threads. Also, a *"Divide and conquer"* design pattern was used, so that the problem was divided into sub-problems, solvable in short times. Each thread was assigned to the calculation of a group, finally the results obtained for each thread were reduced to a single thread. A static schedule was defined because the tasks to be performed are known in advance.

In phase (2), the number of iterations was analyzed, and the administration of the dependencies with the aim of being able to propose a communication structure between the different tasks. The design pattern of type *"Fork/Join"* was applied, which has as an advantage an indirect mapping of the tasks to the execution units. This pattern is particularly relevant for shared memory environments, so in the mapping phase, implementation mechanisms were based on OpenMP routines.

The sequential algorithm and the parallel algorithm based on OpenMP routines were developed in language C, in an Intel Xeon E3 v5 processor. In order to mea-sure the efficiency and effectiveness of the algorithm, two data repositories were generated *in silico*: *Group A* was used to measure the effectiveness of the algorithms, defined as the correct number of clusters detected by both algorithms; *Group B* was used to measure the efficiency of the algorithm, was defined by the execution time necessary to obtain a solution of data sets with different numbers of patterns and characteristics.

Group A. Characterized by 12 sets of patterns constructed *in silico*, to which a certain number of clusters have been implanted according to the number of patterns. Each data set was classified according to four criteria: (1) the patterns belonging to a cluster are contiguous; (2) the patterns belonging to a cluster are not contiguous; (3) the patterns belonging to a cluster are contiguous and additionally a random variable has been added that simulates the presence of noise; (4) the patterns belonging to a cluster are not contiguous and additionally a random variable has been added that simulates the presence of noise. Table 1 describes the characteristics of each of these matrices and the effectiveness represented by the comparison between the characteristics of the implanted clusters against the characteristics of the obtained clusters. The effectiveness of the algorithm sequential (s) and parallel (p) have been represented by the convention α_0–α_1(%) where α_0 and α_1 represent the number of clusters implanted and detected correctly, while (%) representing the percentage of effectiveness for each case of study. The comparison between the implanted and obtained clusters was made by analyzing patterns that were included in each cluster, such that the elements included in an implanted cluster were the same elements of a cluster reported by the algorithm.

Table 1. Effectiveness of the sequential and parallel *k-means* algorithm using a generic methodology. Effectiveness (s) represents the degree of effectiveness for the sequential algorithm, while Effectiveness (p) represents the degree of effectiveness for the parallel algorithm

Matrix	Size matrix	Classification	Effectiveness (s)	Effectiveness (p)
1	100×8	1	10-10(100%)	10-10(100%)
2	500×40	1	50-50(100%)	50-50(100%)
3	2500×200	1	250-250(100%)	250-250(100%)
4	100×8	2	10-10(100%)	10-10(100%)
5	500×40	2	50-50(100%)	50-50(100%)
6	2500×200	2	250-250(100%)	250-250(100%)
7	100×8	3	10-2(20%)	10-1(10%)
8	500×40	3	50-1(2%)	50-0(0%)
9	2500×200	3	250-2 (0.8%)	250-0(0%)
10	100×8	4	10-0(0%)	10-1(10%)
11	500×40	4	50-2(4%)	50-0(0%)
12	2500×200	4	250-2(0.4%)	250-0(0%)

In order to determine if a cluster had been correctly identified, it was taken into consideration that at least 95% of the patterns contained in a cluster were the same as those that had been implanted in the beginning. Since the algorithm is totally dependent on the initial configuration, in all experiments 1000 maximum iterations and a threshold of 0.0001 were defined. The number of implanted clusters is represented by 10% of the number of patterns. However, the results show that if the data set is exposed to noise situations, the number of iterations will increase, which puts the algorithm at a disadvantage in application problems. During this analysis the presence of outliers was not analyzed and since it is sensitive to the choice of initial centroids, the same centroids appear in all cases.

Group B. Characterized by 6 sets of patterns constructed *in silico*. The objective of this group is to measure the efficiency of both the sequential and the parallel implementations of *k-means* algorithm. The configuration parameters for the parallel algorithm are: Number of iterations represents 30% of the number of patterns in the set; the threshold was determined as 0.0001 in all cases; the number of clusters is determined as 10% number of patterns that make up the whole. The acceleration rate $S(n)$ with $n = 4$ threads is the quotient of the sequential time and the time required by the parallel algorithm. In the same way, the number of iterations necessary to obtain a solution to the problem is reported.

Table 2 shows that the acceleration rate is increases w.r.t. the number of patterns. The maximum acceleration rate approaches 1.91, verifying Amdahl's law. In addition, in most cases the algorithm never reaches the maximum number of iterations allowed, that is, it always converges taking into account the number of patterns that do not change from one iteration to another.

Table 2. Efficiency of the sequential and parallel *k-means* algorithm using a generic methodology.

Matrix	Size matrix	Number of clusters	Acceleration rate	Maximum iterations
1	100×8	10	0.5593	30-25
2	500×40	50	0.9133	150-106
3	1000×80	100	1.5643	300-62
4	5000×400	500	1.8623	1500-100
5	10000×800	1000	1.9113	3000-39
6	50000×4000	5000	1.9184	15000-45

On the other hand, Table 3 describes the percentage of time needed to obtain a solution.

Table 3. Comparison in percentage of execution time between sequential and parallel algorithm, (I/O is reading and writing time of, P is ratio of processing time and the total time).

Matrix	Sequential algorithm (%)	
	I/O	P
1	79.23	20.77
2	72.43	27.57
3	45.87	54.13
4	36.54	63.46
5	34.65	65.35
6	34.54	65.46

The analysis has been divided into two parts: percentage of time required to read and write data; and the percentage of processing time to group each data set. The results show that the algorithm is highly parallelizable because most of the computational time is used to process the data. Hybrid programming techniques exploiting the potential of GPUs may improve the performance of the algorithm.

Based on the results of Table 3, we compared the maximum performance described in Table 2 with the maximum performance that the parallel k-means algorithm can provide. Be the sequential program of the k-means algorithm and 65% of its code is highly parallelizable, yield and efficiency are calculated on 4 processing units. Assuming that it has a runtime of 1 unit of time. The system performance improvement factor is $S(n) = \frac{T(1)}{T(n)}$, while efficiency of the system with n processors is $E(n) = \frac{S(n)}{n}$, where $T(n)$ represents the execution time with n processing units. Consequently, the maximum performance of the *k-means* algorithm is, when $n \rightarrow 4$,

$$S_1(4) = \lim_{n \to 4} \frac{T(1)}{(1-p) + \frac{p}{n}} = \frac{1}{(1-0.65) + \frac{0.65}{4}} = 1.95, \tag{2}$$

where p is defined as 65% of the potentially parallelizable code. For acceleration rate $S_2(4) = 1.91$, as obtained in the experiments in Table 2, and $S_1(4) = 1.95$ as the maximum rate of acceleration, we conclude that our generic methodology allows the design and implementation of parallel algorithms showing a competitive performance, $S_1 \approx S_2$. Every parallel program has a sequential part that limits the acceleration in any given architecture. The Euclidean distance was used in the implementation of both algorithms, namely a good measure of adjustment degree (cohesion and separation) of the found centroids, however the final solution may not be optimal. It is necessary to choose a priori the number of centroids since the algorithm is not able to determine the optimal number of groupings to be formed.

5 Conclusions

The key to approach programming of parallel algorithms is to propose algorithm design methodologies that reflect the characteristics of the algorithm promptly regardless of the architecture where it is going to be implemented. A generic methodology was defined for the design of parallel algorithms based on a pattern language. This is a non-trivial project since the methodology exploits the concurrency and establishes optimal allocation of a process set to a set of processing units taking subject to lowest implementation details. While this statement may represent a contribution to the state of the art, an even higher objective was the methodology to identify essential design patterns within Data Mining algorithms enabling self-adaptation to homogeneous and heterogeneous architectures.

Experimentally, we have tested our methodology with algorithms related to Computational Linear Algebra, Classification and Data Mining and it has succeeded in finding patterns aiming to improvements in processing times, with string self-adaptive mechanisms for homogeneous and heterogeneous parallel architectures. As future work, we propose the to automate of this methodology for Data Mining algorithms, with the aim of refining the design and measuring the effectiveness of the methodology proposed in this work.

Acknowledgment. The authors thank the financial support by the Mexican CONACyT, as well as ABACUS: Laboratory of Applied Mathematics and High-Performance Computing of the Mathematics Department of CINVESTAV-IPN. Our institution provided the facilities to accomplish this work.

References

1. Fox, G.C., Williams, R.D., Messina, G.C.: Parallel computing works!. Elsevier, Amsterdam (2014)
2. Bientinesi, P., Herrero, J.R., Quintana-Ortí, E.S., Strzodka, R.: Parallel computing on graphics processing units and heterogeneous platforms. Concurr. Comput.: Pract. Exp. **27**(6), 1525–1527 (2015)
3. Aliaga, J.I., Sáez, R.C., Ortí, E.S.Q.: Parallel solution of hierarchical symmetric positive definite linear systems. Appl. Math. Nonlinear Sci. **2**(1), 201–212 (2017)
4. Hong, T.P., Lee, Y.C., Wu, M.T.: An effective parallel approach for genetic-fuzzy data mining. Expert Syst. Appl. **41**(2), 655–662 (2014)
5. Foster, I.: Designing and Building Parallel Programs, vol. 78. Addison Wesley Publishing Company, Boston (1995)
6. Chandy, K.M., Taylor, S.: An Introduction to Parallel Programming. Jones and Bartlett Publishers, Inc., Burlington (1992)
7. Culler, D.E., Singh, J.P., Gupta, A.: Parallel Computer Architecture: A Hardware/Software Approach. Gulf Professional Publishing, Houston (1999). ISO 690
8. Mattson, T.G., Sanders, B., Massingill, B.: Patterns for Parallel Programming. Pearson Education, London (2004)
9. Jamali, S., Alizadeh, F., Sadeqi, S.: Task scheduling in cloud computing using particle swarm optimization. In: The Book of Extended Abstracts, p. 192 (2016)
10. Kirk, D.B., Wen-Mei, W.H.: Programming Massively Parallel Processors: A Hands-on Approach. Morgan kaufmann, Burlington (2016)
11. Barney, B.: Introduction to parallel computing. Lawrence Livermore National Laboratory, vol. 6, no. 13, p. 10 (2010)
12. Almasi, G.S., Gottlieb, A.: Highly Parallel Computing. The Benjamin/Cummings Publishing, San Francisco (1988)
13. Brown, J., Bowling, A., Flynn, T.: Models of quality of life: a taxonomy, overview and systematic review of the literature. In: European Forum on Population Ageing Research (2004)
14. Aloise, D., Deshpande, A., Hansen, P., Popat, P.: NP-hardness of Euclidean sum-of-squares clustering. Mach. Learn. **75**, 245–249 (2009)
15. Benson, A.R., Ballard, G.: A framework for practical parallel fast matrix multiplication. ACM SIGPLAN Not. **50**(8), 42–53 (2015)
16. Cui, H., Ruan, G., Xue, J., Xie, R., Wang, L., Feng, X.: A collaborative divide-and-conquer K-means clustering algorithm for processing large data. In: Proceedings of the 11th ACM Conference on Computing Frontiers, p. 20. ACM, May 2014
17. Rajeswari, K., Acharya, O., Sharma, M., Kopnar, M., Karandikar, K.: Improvement in K-means clustering algorithm using data clustering. In: 2015 International Conference on Computing Communication Control and Automation (ICCUBEA), pp. 367–369. IEEE (2015)
18. Törn, A., Žilinskas, A.: Clustering methods. In: Törn, A., Žilinskas, A. (eds.) Global Optimization. LNCS, vol. 350, pp. 95–116. Springer, Heidelberg (1989). https://doi.org/10.1007/3-540-50871-6_5

A Parallelized Iterative Closest Point Algorithm for 3D View Fusion

S. Ivvan Valdez[✉] and Felipe Trujillo-Romero

Universidad de Guanajuato, DICIS,
Carr. Palo Blanco-Valle de Santiago km 3.5 + 1.8,
36700 Salamanca, Guanajuato, Mexico
si.valdez@ugto.mx

Abstract. The Iterative Closest Point Algorithm (ICP) is a widely used method in computer science and robotics, used for minimizing a distance metric between two set of points. Common applications of the ICP are object localization and position estimation. In this work, we introduce a parallel version of the ICP which significantly reduces the computational time, by performing fewer operations while maintaining a simple and highly parallelizable algorithm. Our proposal is based on the naive computation of closest pairs of points in two different sets, instead of comparing all possible pairs we approximate the closest pairs of points by means of searching in a plausible subset. The experiments are performed on a sample from the Stanford 3D Scanning Repository, used for the 3D cloud of points registration. For these case studies, the error, as well as the solution, are exactly the same than using the exact algorithm.

Keywords: Iterative Closest Point · Shared memory · Approximated ICP
3D cloud registration

1 Introduction

From its first apparition in 91–92 [1, 2] the Iterative Closest Point has been one of the most used algorithms for two clouds of points registration. This one can be seen by the great number of papers mentioning it in specialized literature. One example of those works is the one developed by Sun et al. [5] who used ICP in the final step of their method to automatic 3D point cloud registration. In [6] ICP is used in order to find the match between two faces, probing a face match to each of the gallery faces. Also, there are a lot of papers that talk about the implementation of ICP's variations. In this group we can mention the work done by Donoso et al. [7], they implemented three new ICP variants that improve scan matching for surface mining terrain. Bouaziz et al. in [8] present a new formulation of the ICP algorithm that avoids these difficulties by formulating the registration optimization using sparsity-inducing norms. Meanwhile, Du et al. [9] have proposed an isotropic scaling ICP algorithm with corner point constraints for avoiding local dissimilar affectations. On another hand, Mavridis et al. [10] proposed a hybrid optimization system using a combination of Simulated Annealing search with the standard Sparse ICP, in order to solve the underlying optimization problem.

© Springer Nature Switzerland AG 2019
M. Torres et al. (Eds.): ISUM 2018, CCIS 948, pp. 49–56, 2019.
https://doi.org/10.1007/978-3-030-10448-1_5

More close to the work presented here, we can mention to Langis et al. [11] who have implemented an ICP version which was tested on a 22-node Beowulf-class cluster obtaining remarkable results. In [12], it is presented a GPU implementation of an ICP that exploits the concept of shared memory parallelism on a general purpose graphics processing unit (GPGPU). Manojkumar and Reddy [13] have developed a parallel ICP in OpenMP with a speedup factor of 3.7 using 8 cores.

Our proposal considers an approximated version of the ICP. For the sake of be more precise, consider that the ICP largest computational cost is due to the search of the nearest neighbor of each point in the data set P in the model set X, hence we used a simple technique in order to define a subset in X, for the purpose of avoiding comparisons with all points in the model set.

The paper is organized as follows, in Sect. 2, we review the ICP standard implementation, in Sect. 3 we propose a simple modification, in Sect. 4 we provide of results and time analysis, and in Sect. 5 the general conclusions are presented.

2   The Iterative Closest Point Algorithm

The iterative closest point algorithm was first proposed by [1]. An iteration of such proposal is shown in Algorithm 1. It requires two data sets, the first is a given model set X, while the second is the set to be registered P, which is simply called as data set. Considering that the data set P is updated every iteration, it is labeled with the iteration number k, then the set P_k is the input in the k iteration and P_{k+1} is the output.

Algorithm 1. Iterative Closest Point Algorithm Iteration

Data: Model set: X with n_X points and dimension d_X.
Data set: P_k with n_P points and dimension d_P.
Result: Transformed data set P_{k+1}
1 Compute the closest points $Y_k = C(P_k, X)$;
2 Compute centers of mass $\mu_P = col.means(P), \mu_X = col.means(Y_k)$;
3 Compute the cross-covariance matrix Σ_{PX};
4 Compute rotation $R = VU^T$, where $UWV^T = SVD(\Sigma_{PX})$;
5 Compute translation $q_T = \mu_X - R\mu_P$;
   // Applying transformation
6 **for** $i = 1..n_P$ **do**
7 $\quad \lfloor \; P_{k+1,i} = RP_{k,i} + q_T$;

In Line 1, the closest points in X to each point in P_k is stored in Y_k. In line 2, the centers of mass, that is to say, the mean vectors, μ_X and μ_P, are computed for Y_k and P_k, μ_X is labeled with X because every point in Y_k belongs to X. In addition, notice that if P_k changes every iteration, then Y_k changes. In line 3, the cross-covariance matrix, that is to say, Σ_{PX} = cross-covariance (P_k, Y_k), is computed, then, we compute the singular value decomposition $UWV^T = SVD(\Sigma_{PX})$, in order to compute the optimal rotation matrix $R = VU^T$. Once the optimal rotation has been computed, the optimal translation q_T is computed too. Finally, in lines 6 and 7, the rotation and translation are applied on each point belonging to P_k, for the sake of computing P_{k+1}.

2.1 Analysis of the ICP

Most of the operations in the ICP are of linear order with respect to the number of points in X or P_k, with the notorious exception of computing the set Y_k. Computing the closest point of a set P_k to another set X is in the naive algorithm $O(n_X n_P)$, considering a comparison of each point in P_k to each point in X. There are other algorithms, which are considered $O(n_P \log n_X)$, nevertheless, this proposal is focused on the impact of simple parallelization schemes for shared memory more than in proposing a general cheaper algorithm, hence the algorithmic proposal must be highly parallelizable.

To proceed in the analysis, from a practical point of view, consider Table 1, which shows typical execution times of a C program for the ICP on the bunny dataset from Stanford repository [4]. The columns are times from the different tasks needed for a single iteration as follows:

- $Y_k = C(P_k, X)$ computes the indexes of Y_k set of the nearest points in X to each point in the set P_k.
- Copy X to Y copies the points on X to Y_k according to the indexes previously computed.
- Means computes the centers of mass of sets P_k and Y_k.
- Cross-cov computes the cross-covariance matrix between P_k and Y_k.

Table 1. Times collected from a typical execution of ICP on X = bun000.ply and P = bun045.ply from Stanford repository

Routine	$Y_k = C(P_k, X)$	Copy X to Y	Means	Cross-cov	SVD	Trans & Rot
Ite 1	5.385045	0.000313	0.000261	0.000376	0.000006	0.000483
Ite 2	5.288539	0.000332	0.000264	0.000374	0.000003	0.000527
Ite 3	5.265721	0.00014	0.000257	0.000373	0.000003	0.000483
Ite 4	5.273979	0.00014	0.000258	0.000374	0.000003	0.000482
Ite 5	5.265923	0.00014	0.000257	0.000373	0.000003	0.000483
Ite 6	5.283538	0.000141	0.000256	0.000373	0.000003	0.000496
Ite 7	5.277435	0.00015	0.000256	0.000373	0.000003	0.000497
Ite 8	5.268357	0.000141	0.000276	0.000405	0.000003	0.000483
Ite 9	5.30061	0.000143	0.000256	0.000373	0.000003	0.000497
Ite 10	5.270814	0.000143	0.000263	0.000388	0.000003	0.000496
Total	52.879961	0.001783	0.002604	0.003782	0.000033	0.004927
Perc.	99.975178%	0.003371%	0.004923%	0.00715%	0.000062%	0.009315%

- SVD computes the SVD decomposition of the cross-covariance matrix.
- The function Trans & Rot applies the rotation and translation to each point in P_k.

As can be seen, 99.98 of time is spent on computing the set Y_k. Hence, we focus on this routine.

3 Parallel ICP

In this section, we compare different parallelization schemes on shared memory (OpenMP), for the $Y_k = C(P_k, X)$ computation.

3.1 Straight-Forward Parallelization of the Closest Point Search

The straightforward parallelization is simply to compute distances among sets with a parallel for as shown in Algorithm 2. As can notice the algorithm is $O(n_P\, n_X/n_t)$, where n_t is the number of threads. The proposal preserves the general idea but intending to reduce the number of total operations.

Algorithm 2. Parallel computation of the closest point in X to each point in P

Data: Model set: X with n_X points.
Data set: P_k with n_P points.
Result: List of indexes π of the closest point in X to each point in P.
1 Open parallel **For**;
2 **for** *Each index* $i \in I_t, I_t \subseteq \{1...n_P\}$ *assigned to thread t* **do**
3    $d_i =$ distance(P_i, X_1);
4   **for** $j = 2..n_X$ **do**
5   **if** $distance(P_i, X_j) < d_i$ **then**
6        $d_i =$ distance(P_i, X_j);
7        $\pi_i = j$

3.2 Modified Parallelization of the Closest Point Search

The proposal considers sorting X and P sets by its first coordinate, such as other proposals based on plane partition. Then, we compute a starting searching point in X given the position of a point in P, by assuming that, even if the number of points is different, the relative position with respect to the first coordinate indicates that such points are similar. For the sake of clarification, Algorithm 3 shows our proposal.

Algorithm 3. Parallel *approximation* of the closest point in X to each point in P

Data: Model set: X with n_X points sorted by the first coordinate.
Data set: P_k with n_P points sorted by the first coordinate.
Result: List of indexes π of the closest point in X to each point in P.

1   Open parallel **For**;
2   **for** *Each index* $i \in I_t, I_t \subseteq \{1...n_P\}$ *assigned to thread* t **do**
3      $m_X = integer((i/n_P)(n_X))$;
4      $d_i = \infty$;
5   **for** $j = m_x..1$ **do**
6   **if** $d_i > |P_{i,0} - X_{j,0}|$ **then**
7   **if** $distance(P_i, X_j) < d_i$ **then**
8               $d_i =$ distance(P_i, X_j);
9               $\pi_i = j$
10   **else**
11   **break**;
12   **for** $j = m_x + 1..n_X$ **do**
13   **if** $d_i > |P_{i,0} - X_{j,0}|$ **then**
14   **if** $distance(P_i, X_j) < d_i$ **then**
15               $d_i =$ distance(P_i, X_j);
16               $\pi_i = j$
17   **else**
18   **break**;

Notice that the **for** loop in Line 2 is parted into two loops, which go above and below m_X and perform at many n_X operations, so the Algorithm 3, is the same order than Algorithm 2. According to our experiments, the actual number of operations are closer to $m_X/3$. The assumption that the index returned for each point in P be the actual closest point in X, depends on how close $X[m_X]$ is to P_i.

The routine in Algorithm 3 is integrated into the ICP algorithm, with the purpose of reducing the computational time, nevertheless, notice that we can not guarantee that the closest pairs be actually found. In order to ensure that the results are comparable with the original implementation and that the registration is verified from time to time, we apply Algorithm 2 every 5 iterations, and the modified Algorithm 3 the remaining.

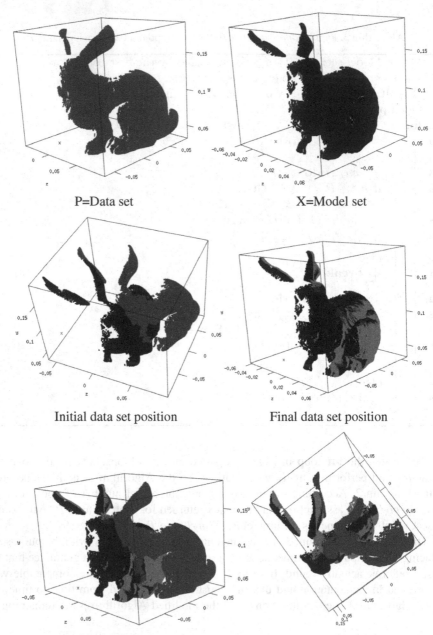

P=Data set

X=Model set

Initial data set position

Final data set position

Model, initial and final data sets from different views

Fig. 1. Points in model set X (black), data set P (blue), and registered data set P* (red) (Color figure online)

4   Results

In this section, we provide of graphical as well as numerical results to compare the naive Algorithm 2 with our approximation heuristic in Algorithm 3.

4.1   Graphical Results

Figure 1 shows the graphical results for the Bunny data set, using the 0 and 45° captures. Notice that the results are satisfactory, even though we are not looking for a better registration but for a reduced computational time.

4.2   Time Analysis

In Table 2 we present the times delivered by typical executions using 21 iterations with different threads or cores (each thread is on a physical core) and the final error. Notice that all errors are equal, thus, in this case, the computation is exact for all cases. Notice that even the sequential execution (1 thread) is improved with our modification. The SpeedUp with respect to the implementation of Algorithm 2 shows that the proposal significantly improves the execution time. The error is computed as the mean of the squared distances from each point in the data set P to its closest neighbor in the model set X. The SpeedUp 1 is computed with respect to Algorithm 2 using 1 thread, while SpeedUp 2 is computed using the serial Algorithm 3 versus the parallel. Notice that SpeedUp 1 compares the original with the proposal, while SpeedUp 2 compares the proposal scalability.

Table 2. Time and error of typical executions of Algorithms 2 and 3. Algorithm 2 performs the exact search while Algorithm 3 could only approximate the closest point.

Threads	Algorithm 2	Error A 2	Algorithm 3	Error A 3	SpeedUp 1	SpeedUp 2
1	117.268113	4.131643e-06	46.976999	4.131643e-06	2.496288	1
2	81.516636	4.131643e-06	28.932972	4.131643e-06	4.053096	1.623649
3	61.792432	4.131643e-06	23.438970	4.131643e-06	5.003126	2.004226
4	53.065775	4.131643e-06	19.823790	4.131643e-06	5.915524	2.369728

5   Conclusions and Future Work

This article presents a simple modification of the Iterative Closest Point algorithm (ICP) for improving the computation time. Even though the idea is not derived from the most efficient algorithm, the aim is to keep simple and highly parallelizable the algorithm, avoiding the use of recursive functions, which require memory in the application stack. The additional memory requirements of our proposal are minimal as well as the coding effort. Future work contemplates the extension to more efficient algorithms, a multi-scale approach as well as modifications to the ICP for the sake of escaping from local minima.

References

1. Besl, P.J., McKay, N.D.: A method for registration of 3-D shapes. IEEE Trans. Pattern Anal. Mach. Intell. **14**(2), 239–256 (1992)
2. Chen, Y., Medioni, G.: Object modelling by registration of multiple range images. Image Vis. Comput. **10**(3), 145–155 (1992). Range Image Understanding
3. Pomerleau, F., Colas, F., Siegwart, R., Magnenat, S.: Comparing ICP variants on real-world data sets. Auton. Robots **34**(3), 133–148 (2013)
4. Stanford-Computer-Graphics-Laboratory: Stanford 3D model repository (1994). http://graphics.stanford.edu/data/3Dscanrep/. Accessed 30 Nov 2017
5. Sun, J., Zhang, J., Zhang, G.: An automatic 3D point cloud registration method based on regional curvature maps. Image Vis. Comput. **56**, 49–58 (2016)
6. Mohammad Zade, H., Hatzinakos, D.: Iterative closest normal point for 3D face recognition. IEEE Trans. Pattern Anal. Mach. Intell. **35**(2), 381–397 (2013)
7. Donoso, F., Austin, K., McAree, P.: Three new iterative closest point variant methods that improve scan matching for surface mining terrain. Robot. Auton. Syst. **95**, 117–128 (2017)
8. Bouaziz, S., Tagliasacchi, A., Pauly, M.: Sparse iterative closest point. Comput. Graph. Forum **32**(5), 113–123 (2013)
9. Du, S., Cui, W., Zhang, X., Wu, L., Xiong, L.: Precise isotropic scaling iterative closest point algorithm based on corner points for shape registration. In: 2017 IEEE International Conference on Systems, Man, and Cybernetics (SMC), pp. 1811–1815, October 2017
10. Mavridis, P., Andreadis, A., Papaioannou, G.: Efficient sparse ICP. Computer Aided Geometric Design 35–36 (2015) 16–26 Geometric Modeling and Processing 2015
11. Langis, C., Greenspan, M., Godin, G.: The parallel iterative closest point algorithm. In: Proceedings Third International Conference on 3-D Digital Imaging and Modeling, pp. 195–202 (2001)
12. Qiu, D., May, S., Nüchter, A.: GPU-accelerated nearest neighbor search for 3D registration. In: Fritz, M., Schiele, B., Piater, J.H. (eds.) ICVS 2009. LNCS, vol. 5815, pp. 194–203. Springer, Heidelberg (2009). https://doi.org/10.1007/978-3-642-04667-4_20
13. Manojkumar, P., Reddy, G.R.M.: Parallel implementation of 3D modelling of indoor environment using microsoft kinect sensor. In: 2013 Fourth International Conference on Computing, Communications and Networking Technologies (ICC-CNT), pp. 1–6, July 2013

Evaluation of OrangeFS as a Tool to Achieve a High-Performance Storage and Massively Parallel Processing in HPC Cluster

Hugo Eduardo Camacho Cruz$^{(\boxtimes)}$ (ID), Jesús Humberto Foullon Peña,
Julio Cesar González Mariño (ID), and Ma. de Lourdes Cantú Gallegos

Universidad Autónoma de Tamaulipas - FMeISC dc Matamoros,
Sendero Nacional Km. 3. H. Matamoros, Tamaulipas, Mexico
hcamachoc@docentes.uat.edu.mx

Abstract. Nowadays, the requirements of modern software demand a greater computing power; numerous scientific and engineering applications request an increase in data storage capacity, be able to exchange of information at high speeds, as well as a faster data processing and better memory management. The implementation of personal computers interconnected to form a cluster and the use of distributed/parallel file systems are presented as a highly suitable alternative in the solution of complex problems that require these resources as their needs grow. The present work shows the evaluation of OrangeFS as a tool to achieve high performance storage and massive parallel processing. It takes advantage of the capacity of the hard drives included in each node of the cluster through the virtual file system and the network bandwidth, instead of having to add a more expensive type of storage. The tests carried out in a cluster with CentOS show that stripping a large file into small objects and distributed in parallel to the I/O servers provides that upcoming read/write operations runs faster; In addition, the use of the message passing interface in the development and execution of applications allows to increase the parallelism of the data in terms of processing due to the intervention of the multicore processor in each of the clients.

Keywords: OrangeFS · MPI · HPC cluster · Parallel file system

1 Introduction

Research on file systems are booming because file systems have a decisive influence on the performance of storage access in a computer system. The demands of the applications are increasingly greater which can cause bottlenecks due to the need to share data at high speeds, since they require a large capacity for processing, memory and even storage. This has led to the search for solutions that provide better benefits. In such circumstances some computer users implement high-performance dedicated equipment [13] to meet the demand for information and the time in which such information is processed; but the cost of such equipment, its maintenance and development is usually high, being not feasible for institutions or for users with limited resources. To solve this problem, some proposals arise, such as the parallelization of

© Springer Nature Switzerland AG 2019
M. Torres et al. (Eds.): ISUM 2018, CCIS 948, pp. 57–69, 2019.
https://doi.org/10.1007/978-3-030-10448-1_6

applications such as, for example, through MPI-IO [8, 10]; being able to decompose a problem into small parts and execute them in multiple processes simultaneously in the different processor cores increases the performance of the applications. Better yet, the performance of the applications can be increased if the tasks are executed on an HPC (High performance Computing) Cluster, since the parallelism by the implementation of multiple nodes and parallel file systems allows the distribution of data between the different I/O servers. By implementing a larger number of servers, the access time to data regarding the implementation of a single server is reduced, this is due to the distribution of data across multiple servers, since accessing parts of the file in parallel.

Currently we can find different distributed and parallel file systems [6, 7, 11]. However, a file system that we found interesting to evaluate was OrangeFS [14], and this is due to its facility to be installed and configured on HPC environments; since it is now part of the kernel version of Linux 4.6, which makes it easier for different Linux applications to increase the location of the data through this file system. It should be noted that OrangeFS avoids the acquisition of additional hardware or manipulate the partitions of existing storage devices. An important combination of this file system is that it can work with a great variety of interfaces depending on the client that is being managed (Linux, Windows, MacOSX, among others). With the Linux kernel interface, it is easy to use, since it is very similar to most systems that use the POSIX standard, however the performance through this interface is lower since it is not optimized for parallel I/O environments. To obtain the maximum performance, it is recommended to use the own interface of OrangeFS, since it offers direct access to the I/O servers through MPI-IO.

In this work, we evaluate OrangeFS, an open source file system developed by a group of experts in parallel computing, and whose objective is to achieve a high-performance storage, as well as a strong integration with MPI to obtain a massively parallel processing on HPC cluster environments. The rest of the article is organized as follows: Sect. 2 deals with related works, Sect. 3 shows the relevant aspects of OrangeFS, Sect. 4 presents some results and Sect. 5 presents the conclusions.

2   Related Work

A modern term for the concept of parallelization is defined as the division of a complex problem, into small problems, which can be sent through a high-speed network to the different nodes of a cluster so that they can be solved simultaneously and thereby get the results in less time. For this work we consider two main characteristics: High-performance storage and Massively parallel processing, this is achieved through the analysis of tools and methods used in the design, development and execution of applications that help solve complex problems in order to improve the performance of the systems. Mainly we focus on parallelizing applications by using message passing libraries via MPI-IO [15, 16] and the cluster deployment and use of the file system; the latter to increase in a greater proportion the parallelism in the I/O data.

2.1 High-Performance Storage

In similarity with distributed systems, a parallel file system is mounted on a client/server model whose objective is to work together to optimize the access time to the data. The difference with respect to the distributed file systems is that, in the parallels, the data is distributed across all the I/O servers; in this way it allows access in parallel to different data or the same data of a file. In the architecture of a parallel file system you can see that there is a large number of input/output servers, so there is an increase in bandwidth, thus reducing the time of access to data. Parallel file systems are used in most HPC clusters to provide high-performance storage. HDFS [5, 6] and Lustre [7, 17], are currently some of the most used systems in high-performance equipment [1, 9].

However, there are some systems such as HDFS, which implement data replication leading to having multiple copies of them on different I/O servers. While this can be a great advantage in terms of availability, requires additional hardware or greater capacity to store information; also causes an increase in the use of network bandwidth since it must be sending multiple TCP/IP messages since the client communicates with the NameNode to know which DataNode can be used for replication.

2.2 Massively Parallel Processing

Another benefit to be achieved using parallel file systems is to provide high-performance in I/O data operations. While parallel access to data allows to increase benefits; the performance is considerably improved by making use of the parallelization technique known as MPI-IO (Message Passing Interface-Input/Output). Some of these benefits can be seen in [3] and [4]. One of the main purposes of writing a parallel program is usually to get a computational model that allows studying a phenomenon more quickly. Works as the one presented in [12], evaluate the performance of a matrix multiplication application through sequential and parallel programming. The results for small operations clearly show how operations benefit from the caching of the local file system, however, by increasing the size of the operations and adding more nodes, the use of applications developed through the MPI-IO libraries shows an advantage with respect to sequential programming, since the execution times are reduced.

The following section gives a vision of the design and how the I/O accesses of the OrangeFS file system work.

3 OrangeFS Overview

OrangeFS [14], is a virtual file system based on PVFS2 [11]. It provides high-performance for scientific and engineering applications. Currently used in data-intensive applications, it decomposes a large file into small objects that are distributed over the multiple nodes of the cluster in a parallel manner, which allows subsequent I/O operations to run faster. This makes it a great tool to store, process and analyze large data. The main features of OrangeFS are: (1) It runs at the user level and works with different operating systems (Windows, Mac, and Linux), (2) Allows parallel access to data and metadata, (3) Reduces bottlenecks, (4) It provides different interfaces for the clients (Direct Interface, WebDAV, S3, FUSE, Hadoop and ROMIO), (5) It uses distributed directories, and (6) It implements security based on encryption.

1. *Metadata Server.* The metadata server is responsible for maintaining the attributes of files and directories, such as permissions, owners and location of data. Some of the operations that can be performed in a metadata server are: create, delete, open or close a file. This is achieved by communicating the client with the metadata server through the libpvfs library.
2. *I/O Servers.* They are responsible for storing and managing access to data located in the OrangeFS directories.
3. *Clients.* Users access the data stored in the OrangeFS directories through the clients. To do so, they have a library called libpvfs.

In OrangeFS each file and directory is composed of two or more objects: one contains metadata and the other the data of the file; objects can contain both data and metadata, as needed. This division and distribution of data is imperceptible for the users, since it only has a traditional view of the files, in other words, it is as if the user worked directly on the local file system. The file system servers operate on objects, each of which has its own unique identifier called handle, a bytestream, and key/value. The handle is used to locate objects. Bytestreams are sequences of bytes generally used to store file data. Key/value allows data to be stored and retrieved using a key. They are also used to store attributes and other metadata of the file. Some of the operations that can be performed in the metadata server are: create, delete, open or close a file. This is achieved by communicating the client with the metadata server through the libpvfs library. Other operations that can be performed are: write and read data. These operations are carried out directly on the I/O servers through libpvfs. In this case there is no communication with the metadata server. Figure 1 shows the composition of OrangeFS.

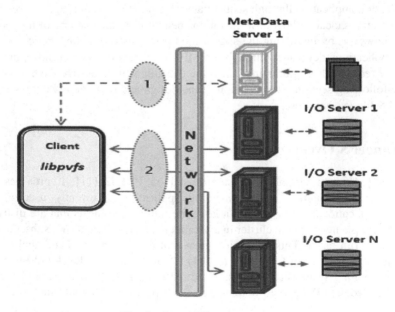

Fig. 1. OrangeFS components.

In OrangeFS the client communicates with the system interface through the application layer using different types of user-level interfaces. The system interface layer is an API made available to clients, which uses a series of state machines to execute the operations requested by the upper layer. These state machines launch new operations, executed and controlled by the JOB layer, each of which has an associated number to be identified. The operations executed by the JOB layer are sent to the servers through the FLOW layer, which is responsible for moving both operations and data from the clients to the servers. The FLOW layer, in turn, uses the BMI (Buffered Message Interface) layer, to have access to the network. BMI makes available to the FLOW layer, different modules that support different types of network. These modules make the client transparent to the type that is being used. The software layers in the server are practically the same as in the clients, except that the servers have a layer called TROVE, which is in charge of storing the data in the storage devices. This layer acts on both the metadata servers and the data servers.

3.1   Input/Output Operations

To better understand the operation of OrangeFS, it is necessary to describe how the input/output operations work. The documentation that addresses the particularities of the implementation of OrangeFS is scarce in its official website. The operations in OrangeFS are implemented as state machines, both in the clients and the servers. For the client's state machine to be launched to the I/O servers, the PVFS_isys_io function is required, because this function manages the read/write operations that the client requests and executes the state machine. A read/write request by the client to the I/O servers is done through the PVFS_sys_io function, which in turn calls the PVFS_isys_io function. This function contains a series of parameters that are initialized with the necessary data to be able to execute a read/write operation on the servers. Some of these parameters are: initial offset (file_req_offset), pointer to the client's local buffer (* buffer, the client's local buffer, it is a memory space reserved for reading/writing data from the client or writing data from the I/O servers), type of operation (io_type, read or write), size of the request required (aggregate_size). These values are sent to the client's state machine, which is responsible for executing the operations necessary to send/receive the data. The procedure followed in the OrangeFS reads and writings will be described below.

3.2   Read on OrangeFS

When a read operation is requested on OrangeFS, the PVFS_isys_io function is executed with the required parameters, indicating in the field io_type that the type of operation is read; that is, the value of this parameter is set to 1. Once the function is executed, a series of necessary checks to read a file is initialized. Some of these checks are: validate the file identifier (handle) and the file system identifier (fs_id), verify that the type of operation (read/write) has been correctly specified. So, when these checks are completed, a structure of type PINT_client_sm (structure for the state machine of the sm_p client) is filled with the requested parameters, and subsequently the client's state machine is sent to the I/O servers, which are responsible for returning the data from the file to the local buffer of the client (buffer). Figure 2 illustrates a read operation within the OrangeFS clients.

3.3   Write on OrangeFS

The data writes contained in the client's local buffer, like the readings, are executed through the PVFS_isys_io function, only this time the corresponding value of io_type is 2. After executing the function and validating the file identifier (handle), the file system identifier (fs_id), the type of operation (write) and performing some other operation, a structure of type PINT_client_sm (structure for the client state machine sm_p) is filled with the necessary parameters to launch the client state machine that contains a pointer to the client's local buffer with the written data that is to be sent to the I/O servers. The data to be written is distributed in blocks between the storage devices on the I/O servers. Each file will have several datafiles in each of the I/O servers. Figure 3 illustrates how a file is sent and distributed among the I/O servers.

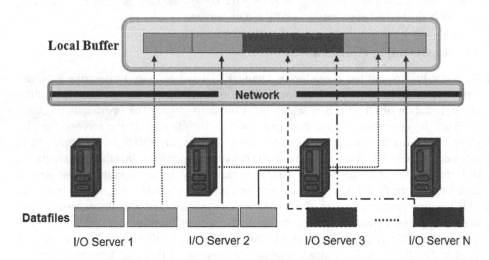

Fig. 2. Read-OrangeFS

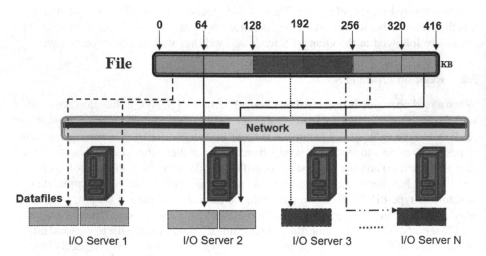

Fig. 3. Write-OrangeFS

4 Experimental Result

In this section we show the results obtained in OrangeFS and its integration with MPI. To obtain the results, a small cluster with the following characteristics was used: 8 nodes with Intel core i7 processors at 3.6 GHz, 12 GB DDR4 memory, SATA III hard disk at 2 TB 7200 RPM and Average Data Rate Read/Write 156 MB/s, a Gigabit Ethernet network card and a 24-port Gigabit Ethernet switch. As a measurement tool, a micro benchmark was used to execute an application that performs readings and writings operations on a file. The operations are executed from the client(s) to the storage space of the OrangeFS file system. To avoid the disk cache of the nodes (64 MB), a tool was developed that could replace the cached data before executing a new operation.

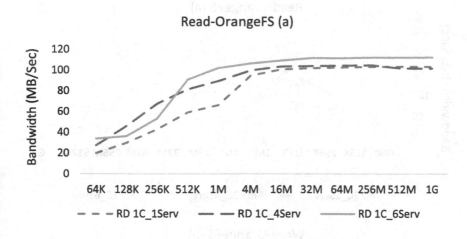

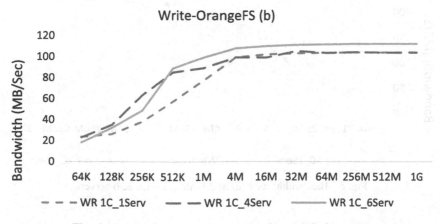

Fig. 4. Bandwidth: read (a) and write (b) - 1,4 & 6 servers

The first results were obtained using 1 metadata server, multiple I/O servers (1,4 & 6), 1 client, and the striping unit that OrangeFS uses by default (64 KB). As you can see in Fig. 4, in the operations of reading (a) and writing (b) we consider accesses of 64 KB, 128 KB, 256 KB, 512 KB, 1 MB, 4 MB, 16 MB, 32 MB, 64 MB, 256 MB, 512 MB and 1 GB. The bandwidth presents a penalty when the client accesses a single server against the access of 4 or more servers (6). In the tests, the servers only respond to the client's requests, no other application is running. In the case of 6 servers, it is observed how the bandwidth improves (+100 MB/s) when using files of more than 512 KB, which allows to deduce that decomposing a file and making use of all the servers (128,128, 64.64,64,64 KB) will increase the benefits for the distribution of data (high-performance storage) compared to having a server (512 KB) that writes in a single storage space.

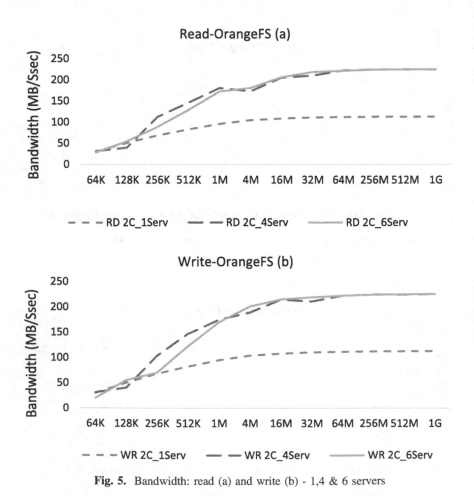

Fig. 5. Bandwidth: read (a) and write (b) - 1,4 & 6 servers

To achieve greater benefits, we implemented a second configuration to which 2 clients were added. Although these results (Fig. 5) show that for small accesses (<256 KB) the improvement is not significant, it is when the file size is greater; having an extra client doubles the bandwidth (220 MB/s) achieved by a single client. The results exceed the disk bandwidth (156 MB/s), since there are two clients accessing parts of the same file in parallel. Keep in mind that with OrangeFS you can improve the benefits of accessing a file if you use multiple clients and multiple input and output servers.

Table 1. Read OrangeFS vs lustre

File	Bandwidth OrangeFS 4C_4S	Latency OrangeFS 4C_4S	Bandwidth Lustre 4C_4S	Latency Lustre 4C_4S
128K	40.250	0.003105	38.100	0.003280
256K	79.690	0.003137	66.950	0.003734
512K	115.83	0.004717	132.29	0.003779
1M	262.29	0.003813	189.74	0.005454
4M	254.02	0.015747	315.80	0.012666
32M	329.24	0.097191	360.26	0.088825
64M	391.36	0.163529	391.57	0.639153
256M	412.22	0.621014	450.16	0.568675
1G	422.65	2.422776	474.76	2.156876

Table 2. Write OrangeFS vs lustre

File	Bandwidth OrangeFS 4C_4S	Latency OrangeFS 4C_4S	Bandwidth lustre 4C_4S	Latency lustre 4C_4S
128K	29.860	0.004186	32.370	0.003861
256K	76.750	0.003257	69.340	0.003605
512K	116.87	0.004278	104.02	0.004807
1M	254.49	0.003929	133.18	0.007509
4M	292.54	0.013673	301.80	0.132540
32M	384.94	0.083129	281.46	0.113692
64M	374.80	0.170757	288.03	0.222198
256M	400.87	0.638607	405.14	0.157968
1G	413.66	2.475435	461.92	1.108397

We made some final measurements and added a small comparison with Lustre (Tables 1 and 2). Each of the figures (Figs. 6 and 7) shows the lines belonging to OrangeFS and Lustre using MPI with 4 processes per client and I/O operations from 128 KB to 1 GB. Prior to these results, we implemented multiple stripping units in both file systems (from 64 KB to 1 MB), however not observing significant changes. Therefore, in the results shown, we wanted to use their default values. These graphs clearly reflect that executing OrangeFS with several clients, the operations of both reading and writing on the multiple servers, achieve greater data transfer (>400 MB/s) and disk access times (latency) are reduced. Although the results show a difference with Lustre we could see that OrangeFS, is a robust file system with great capacity for distribution and data processing.

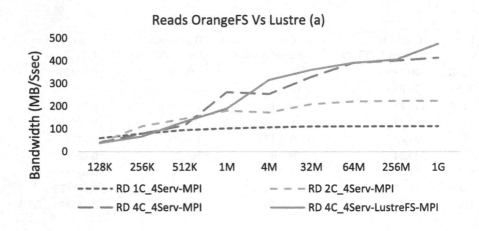

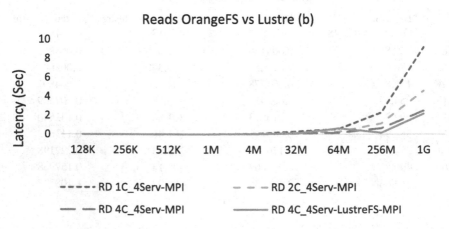

Fig. 6. Bandwidth (a) & latency (b): read OrangeFS vs lustre

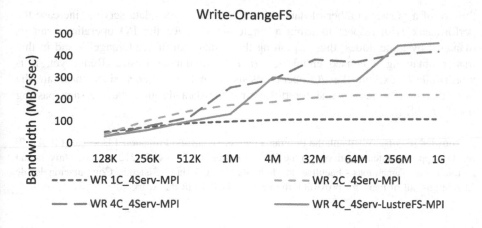

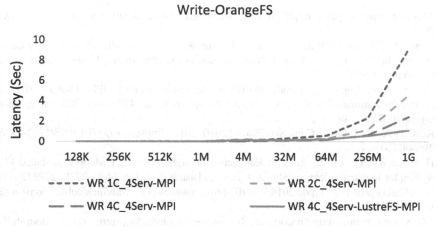

Fig. 7. Bandwidth (a) & latency (b): write OrangeFS vs lustre

5   Conclusions

The experimental tests performed on OrangeFS where the data are in constant modification have allowed us to see the advantages that can be expected about high-performance storage and massively parallel processing. The results show that in the input/output operations on small files, the obtained performance is lower if put in comparison with large files. That is, because data striping is 64 KB by default; performing operations below this value does not show significant improvement with respect to using the local file system. Although accessing again the data that was previously read/written could benefit from the local caching, this type of access is rare for applications that demand an intensive load of data. However, when you access files of a larger size (>64 KB), the results improve significantly. This is thanks to the fact that the operations are distributed in the different I/O nodes; It is worth mentioning that the use of a greater number of data servers, as well as metadata servers, increase the performance with respect to using a single server since the I/O operations can be managed by more nodes, thus exploiting the parallelism of the OrangeFS and in that matter obtaining a consequential performance similar to Lustre. Better yet, it is worthwhile to execute the I/O operations using multiple clients, since these are the ones that will be responsible for processing the data through the message passing interface (MPI).

Acknowledgments. We thank the Programa para el Desarrollo Profesional Docente (PRODEP) for the support granted mentioned in the Official Letter No. 511-6/17/8212, and the Universidad Autónoma de Tamaulipas - Facultad de Medicina e Ingeniería en Sistemas Computacionales de Matamoros, all of them for providing the means to carry out this work.

References

1. Abacus-I Supercomputer. http://www.abacus.cinvestav.mx/caracteristicas. Accessed 03 Dec 2017
2. Carns, P.H., Ligon III, W.B., Ross, R.B., Thakur, R.: PVFS: a parallel file system for Linux clusters. In: Proceedings of the Extreme Linux Track: 4th Annual Linux Showcase and Conference (2000)
3. Dickens, P.M., Logan, J.: A high performance implementation of MPI-IO for a Lustre file system environment. Concurrency Comput.: Pract. Exper. **22**, 1433–1449 (2010). https://doi.org/10.1002/cpe.1491
4. Riahi, H., et al.: J. Phys.: Conf. Ser. **396**, 042050 (2012). https://doi.org/10.1088/1742-6596/396/4/042050
5. Hua, X., Wu, H., Li, Z., Ren, S.: Enhancing throughput of the Hadoop Distributed File System for interaction-intensive tasks. J. Parallel Distrib. Comput. **74**(8), 2770–2779 (2014). https://doi.org/10.1016/j.jpdc.2014.03.010. http://www.elsevier.com/inca/publications/store/6/2/2/8/9/5/index.htt
6. HDFS Architecture. http://hadoop.apache.org/docs/stable/hadoop-project-dist/hadoop-hdfs/HdfsDesign.html#Introduction. Accessed 12 Oct 2017
7. Lustre. wiki.lustre.org/images/6/64/LustreArchitecture-v4.pdf. Accessed 1 Sept 2017
8. Message Passing Interface Forum. MPI: A Message-Passing Interface Standard, Version 2.2. University of Tennessee (2009)
9. Miztli Architecture. http://www.super.unam.mx/index.php/home/acerca-de?start=2. Accessed 02 Jan 2018
10. MPICH is a high performance and widely portable implementation of the Message Passing Interface (MPI) standard, mpich.org. http://www.mpich.org/documentation/guides/. Accessed 20 Dec 2017
11. PVFS2 Team: "Parallel Virtual File System, Version 2", September 2003. http://www.pvfs.org/pvfs2-guide.html
12. Sampath, S., Sagar, B.B., Subbaraya, C.K., Nanjesh, B.R.: Performance evaluation of parallel applications using MPI in cluster based parallel computing architecture. In: Proceeding of International Conference on "Emerging Research in Computing, Information, Communication and Applications" (2013). ISBN 9789351071020
13. Top500 Homepage. https://www.top500.org/. Accessed 02 Jan 2018

14. The OrangeFS Project, OrangeFS 2.9 Documentation, Orangefs.org. http://docs.orangefs.com/v_2_9/index.htm. Accessed 09 Feb 2018
15. William Gropp, Ewing Lusk and Anthony Skjellum: Using MPI, 3rd Edition (2014)
16. William Gropp, Torsten Hoefler, Rajeev Thakur and Ewing Lusk: Using Advance MPI, 1st Edition (2014)
17. Wu, Y., et al.: J. Phys.: Conf. Ser. **219**, 062068 (2010). https://doi.org/10.1088/1742-6596/219/6/062068

Many-Core Parallel Algorithm to Correct the Gaussian Noise of an Image

Teodoro Alvarez-Sanchez[1], Jesus A. Alvarez-Cedillo[2(✉)], and Jacobo Sandoval-Gutierrez[3]

[1] Instituto Politécnico Nacional, CITEDI, Tijuana, Mexico
talvarez@citedi.mx
[2] Instituto Politécnico Nacional, UPIICSA, Mexico City, Mexico
jaalvarez@ipn.mx
[3] Universidad Autónoma Metropolitana, LERMA, Mexico City, Mexico
j.sandoval@correo.ler.uam.mx

Abstract. The digitization of information is abundant in different areas related to digital image processing; its primary objective is to improve the quality of the image for a correct human interpretation or to facilitate the search of information patterns in a shorter time, with fewer computing resources, size and low energy consumption. This research is focused on validating a possible implementation using a limited embedded system, so the specified processing speed and algorithms that redistribute the computational cost are required. The strategy has been based on parallel processing for the distribution of tasks and data to the Epiphany III. It was combined to reduce the factors that introduce noise to the image and improve quality. The most common types of noise are Gaussian noise, impulsive noise, uniform noise and speckle noise. In this paper, the effects of Gaussian noise that occurs at the moment of the acquisition of the image that produces as a consequence blur in some pixels of the image is analyzed, and that generates the effect of haze (blur). The implementation was developed using the Many-core technology in 2×2 and 4×4 arrays with (4, 8, 16) cores, also the performance of the Epiphany system was characterized to FFT2D, FFT setup, BITREV, FFT1D, Corner turn and LPF and the response times in machine cycles of each algorithm are shown. The power of parallel processing with this technology is displayed, and the low power consumption is related to the number of cores used. The contribution of this research in a qualitative way is demonstrated with a slight variation for the human eye in each other images tested, and finally, the method is a useful tool for applications with resources limited.

Keywords: Frequency domain · Many-core · Parallel algorithms
Parallel processing · Gaussian noise

1 Introduction

In recent years, applications in the processing of images have increased, in which the objective is to improve their quality (of the image and a correct human interpretation or to facilitate the search for information in the processed image. Motivation to use, the use of new technologies to solve computational problems with high-performance

© Springer Nature Switzerland AG 2019
M. Torres et al. (Eds.): ISUM 2018, CCIS 948, pp. 70–86, 2019.
https://doi.org/10.1007/978-3-030-10448-1_7

computing systems that have become indispensable, when it is required to have a response in a shorter time of the result.

At present, there are several systems among them, computer clusters and hybrid CPU-GPU systems that each have different characteristics and capabilities that can be applied to multiple problems. Image processing is an area that requires solving applications in a shorter time (real time), which is applicable in various areas of scientific research. The high-performance systems take advantage of all the computational processing resources using tools that measure the time of uses of the core, in which the cores are specially designed to perform matrix operations that run in parallel, this is by the number of nuclei that have the computer system. Also, you can choose the distribution of code and execution in this system many-core: the one, how, and where, the program will be executed in the many-core.

The rest of the article is organized as follows. Section 2 provides a general description of the Epiphany III system. Section 3 describes characteristics of the pixel of f at any point (x, y), and as well as the function of the frequency domain in the Fourier Transform in two dimensions. Section 4 shows the decomposition of the data and tasks that Epiphany III will perform the multiplication of matrices, mathematical approach. Section 5 contains the procedure flow, response times, execution of the algorithm in parallel on the Epiphany III system and filtered image. Section 6 presents the results. Section 7 presents conclusions obtained as well as results and future work.

2   Many-Core System

Epiphany III is a system that incorporates a memory, and distributed cores called the many-core system, as shown in Fig. 1, which are characterized by low power consumption and computing power. This combination of different levels of software and hardware, which allows operations in the cores in a way, concurrent or parallel in each of the cores, in this system, is used a scheme of the cores have access to the same shared main memory.

The many-core system has a shared distributed memory space, which also addresses a low memory consisting of 232 bytes. The addresses are treated as unsigned numbers, from 0 to (232 - 1). This space is considered as a set of 230 words (Word) of 32 bits in which any nucleus access, which is connected through a topology of type "2D mesh", this system also can access the memory of concurrent form. It this avoids overload or blockages in the topology and shared distributed memory, that are factors affecting the high-performance system [12].

The Epiphany III system is a many-core system with 16 cores, among its virtues, the system has a scaling of nuclei, this allows to increase the computing power of the parallel system. This system has an energy consumption of 1 W per 50 Gigaflops in simple precision calculations; these cores with 65 nm (nanometer) were manufactured. This technology that can be running at a speed of 1 GHz with RISC technology, the 16 cores have the same architecture [4–9], and each core has 32 KB (16 KB code and 16 KB data) as local memory.

With this memory capacity in the Epiphany III system, you will have an image of (128 × 128 pixels) that is equivalent to 16 KB which is the memory space for data.

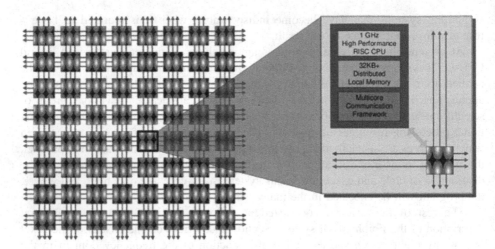

Fig. 1. Main components of the Epiphany III architecture [18].

3 Image Processing

A digital image can be projected in two dimensions on a numerical matrix in which it is composed of a finite number of elements, each of which has a value, which represents a bi dimensional light intensity function f (x, y), where x and y, indicate the coordinates of the value of f at any point (x, y), which is proportional to the luminosity (or level of gray) of the image at that point called pixels.

A pixel p with coordinates (x, y) has four neighbors, horizontal and vertical, whose coordinates are given by: $(x + 1, y)$, $(x - 1, y)$, $(x, y + 1)$, $(x, y - 1)$. This set of pixels is called the four neighbors of p and as N4 (p) is denoted. The four diagonal neighbors of p have coordinates $(x + 1, y + 1)$, $(x + 1, y - 1)$, $(x - 1, y + 1)$, $(x - 1, y - 1)$ and are denoted by ND (p). We also have another arrangement, which will be called the 8-neighbors of p, denoted by N8 (p). In Fig. 2, the neighboring pixels concerning the central pixel (x, y) see Fig. 2.

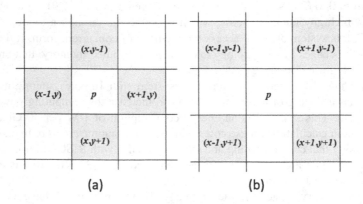

Fig. 2. (a) Horizontal and vertical pixel neighborhood (x, y), (b) Diagonal pixel neighborhood $(x + 1, y + 1)$.

An image is contaminated when some of its pixels have been altered or transformed, losing the original B/W or color information. This can be due to several factors, among which are the environmental conditions during the acquisition, or by the own quality of the transducer devices of the CCD camera, as well as the light levels, the temperature sensors, the movement sensors of the camera or blur, device noise, these factors that affect the quality of the image obtained [1]. A peculiar factor is the noises of the camera these are the following: Gaussian noise, uniform noise, speckle noise, impulsive noise [2, 19].

An image containing noise is eliminated by applying filters to eliminate noise. If you initially have an image with noise (IR), which is restored by eliminating noise to finally obtain a filtered image (IF). Noise filtering is a process to discriminate between the original information of the image and the noisy data, which prevent the correct interpretation of the information. The filtering stage of the image is probably the most common task in digital image processing, edge detection, pattern recognition, etc., is a fundamental step in computer vision systems in which images are used to perform an automatic analysis or human inspection [20].

There are several filters and detection methods to reduce or eliminate the noise presented by a digital image. Filters can be based on the spatial domain or the frequency domain. Based filters perform operations on the frequency domain in the Fourier transform of the image. On the other hand, the methods based on the spatial domain are shown on the pixels of the image.

Filters in the frequency domain consist of modifying the Fourier transform to achieve a specific objective and then calculating the inverse transform to obtain the processed result. The Fourier transform is seen as a transformation from the spatial domain to the frequency domain without losing information about the image. We can mention the low pass and high pass filters that are used to attenuate the low and high frequencies respectively. The filters in the spatial domain consist of an operation on the pixels of the neighborhood. The filtering creates a new pixel with coordinates equal to the coordinates of the center of the neighborhood and whose value is the result of the filtering operation. If the operation is performed on the pixels of the image, the filtering is spatial linear. Otherwise, it is non-linear.

In this research work, we have used the fast Fourier transform, based on the frequency domain, to improve the quality of the image and eliminate Gaussian noise in the test image.

Frequency Domain

A sinusoidal function in two dimensions is characterized by its phase, its frequency of oscillation and its direction of oscillation. Also, a sinusoidal function can be expressed in the space of two dimensions as shown in Eq. 1:

$$f(m, n) = \sin\{2\pi(Um + Vn)\}. \tag{1}$$

Where are the spatial coordinates (in pixels), are the two frequencies (cycles/pixel). The argument of the sine is the radians. The frequency and direction of maximum oscillation are:

$$\Omega = \sqrt{U^2 + V^2}, \quad \theta = arctan\left\{\frac{V}{U}\right\}. \tag{2}$$

It is usual to work with the frequencies normalized to the size of the image M × N.

$$(u, v) = (MU, NV). \tag{3}$$

Where now the dimensions are cycle/image. The expression of the sinusoidal is now:

$$f(m, n) = sin\left\{2\pi\left(\frac{u}{M}m + \frac{v}{N}n\right)\right\}. \tag{4}$$

The frequencies U, V have a period of 1. It this means that the same image is obtained for U = 0.2 and U = 1.2.

$$sin(\alpha + \beta) = sin(a) \cos(\beta) + \cos(a) \sin(\beta). \tag{5}$$

A signal can be decomposed into a sum of sine functions (harmonics) with different frequencies; the Fourier transform gives us the proportion in which each of them contributes. For example, in Fig. 3, we have a sinusoidal signal y (x) and the magnitude of the Fourier transform of the said signal.

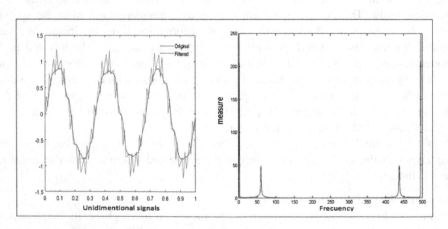

Fig. 3. (a) Signal y (x); (b) Magnitude of the Fourier transform.

Fourier Transforms in Two Dimensions

$$F(U, V) = \sum_{m=0}^{M-1}\sum_{n=0}^{N-1} f(m, n)e^{-j2\pi(Um + Vn)}.$$

The Fourier transform F (U, V) is a continuous function that must be discretized. Its inverse transform:

$$f(m,n) = \int_0^1 \int_0^1 F(U,V)e^{j2\pi(Um+Vn)}\,dU dV. \tag{6}$$

Making a change of variable: $U = \dfrac{u}{M}, V = \dfrac{V}{n}$.

$$F(u,v) = \frac{1}{MN}\sum_{m=0}^{M-1}\sum_{n=0}^{N-1} f(m,n)e^{-j2\pi\left(\frac{u}{M}m+\frac{v}{N}n\right)}.$$

$$f(m,n) = \frac{1}{MN}\sum_{u=0}^{M-1}\sum_{v=0}^{N-1} F(u,v)e^{-j2\pi\left(\frac{u}{M}m+\frac{v}{N}n\right)}.$$

Where now the indexes range from $0 < u < M - 1$, and $0 < v < N - 1$.

$$F(u,v) = |F(U,V)|. \tag{7}$$

It is known that U can have these values of $0 < U < 1$, then also the values M, that is to say, that u = UM, that will be obtained the value of u = 1, ..., M.

Therefore, we have that the Fourier Transform can make a transformation of one domain (in space) to another domain (in frequency) without losing information of the image. The representation of image information in the frequency domain which has advantages, when applying some algorithms that determine specific properties of the image. Each harmonic will pick up a level of detail, of what the variation of gray levels is like especially.

$$F(U,V) = R(U,V) + JI(U,V). \tag{8}$$

Where,

$$R(U,V) = \sum_{m=0}^{M-1}\sum_{n=0}^{N-1} f(m,n)\cos 2\pi(Um+Vn) \tag{9}$$

$$I(U,V) = \sum_{m=0}^{M-1}\sum_{n=0}^{N-1} f(m,n)\sin 2\pi(Um+Vn) \tag{10}$$

The algorithms are applied to the spectrum of magnitude,

$$|F(U,V)| = \sqrt{R^2(U,V) + I^2(U,V)}. \tag{11}$$

The phase is calculated with the following expression:

$$ang(F(U, V)) = \arctan \frac{I(U, V)}{R(U, V)} \qquad (12)$$

Usually, the information of the phase is not used in the analysis of the image, because it usually has several random ones, although its information is crucial to reconstruct the original image. Since the Fourier transform is a periodic function, then a period of M × N is sufficient to represent. Remember that M and N represent the size of the image.

An image is constructed whose level of gray is proportional to the magnitude of the Fourier transform; it can also be represented graphically to the Fourier transform. The characteristics that can be obtained from an image represented by its frequency spectrum are grouped by zones; these characteristics are described below:

- The homogeneous zones in the image will cause the spectrum energy to be concentrated in the low frequencies.
- Zones with many edges are the frequent transitions of gray levels that will lead to a spectrum of high-frequency components.
- If there is any regularity in the image, that is, repeating patterns, it will give rise to peaks of equal intensity separated at a normal distance.

Next, we have the expression that will improve the visualization of the image. In Fig. 4, the color tone intensities are shown.

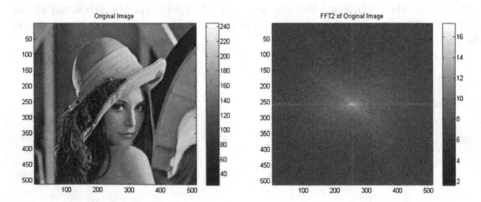

Fig. 4. Visualization of the discrete Fourier transform.

4   Distribution of Tasks and Data to the Epiphany System III

The Epiphany III system is used for the development of this research, it has the ability to implement the neutral programming model with the compatibility with the other methods of parallel programming, including SIMD - Single Instruction Multiple Data, SPMD - Single Program Multiple Data, master-slave programming, Multiple

Instruction Multiple Data - MIMD, static and dynamic data flow, systolic array, shared memory multi-threads, message passing and Sequential Communication Processes (CSP).

Next, in Fig. 5, the distribution of tasks (instructions) and the sequence of execution of tasks with a single core are shown. To accelerate the mathematical calculation, it is possible to use several cores simultaneously. First, the tasks are distributed in matrices A, B. Due to the structural nature of a matrix, the distribution of tasks in small blocks is adequate.

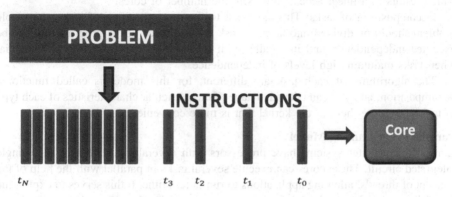

Fig. 5. Sequential execution.

For this distribution, the programming model SPMD (Single Program Multiple Data) is used, which is responsible for distributing the execution for each of the cores, as shown in Fig. 6.

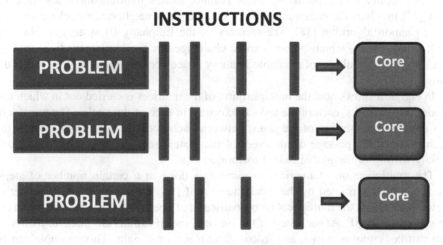

Fig. 6. Execution SPMD

Decomposition of Data and Tasks

Depending on the nature of the problem, you can choose between two approaches to decompositions: data decomposition or task decomposition.

Data decomposition (instructions): This approach refers, to the decomposition of data, that must be processed, and distributed. In this way, the instructions can be executed in parallel in different cores. This approach is appropriate when the data parts can be processed independently. With n cores, this speeds up the problem n times faster if you had run a single kernel. Except for the minimum delay involved in the initial distribution of the workload or data, and the final collection of the results of the data, which results in a linear acceleration with the number of cores.

Decomposition of tasks: This approach to the decomposition of tasks, the whole problem should be divided into tasks. A task is a sequence of the program that can be executed independently and in parallel with other tasks. This approach is beneficial when tasks maintain high levels of independence.

The algorithms of each task are different, for this model is called functional decomposition, and you can take advantage of the particular characteristics of each type of task to execute them in the kernel that is more convenient for that purpose.

Parallel Programming Model

Currently, computer systems have processors with several cores, that is, in a single integrated circuit. These cores can execute several tasks in parallel with the help of the concept of threads, allowing applications to run in less time. It this serves to exploit the parallelism available at the hardware and concurrent level at the software level; the application must be decomposed and distributed in different cores. In this way each available kernel executes tasks in parallel along with the other kernels. The executions have to be synchronized in some stages of the application.

Parallel Programming

The multiplication of matrices is a fundamental mechanism that is used in many scientific applications. The algorithm of parallel matrix multiplication described by Sapir [17] involves the communication of data between neighboring nuclei according to the Cannon algorithm [18]. The memory of the Epiphany III system is relatively small in each core, which presents some challenges in the implementation, making necessary the careful use of available memory space for communication between the cores.

In Fig. 7, it shows how the multiplication of the matrices is carried out in which it is divided into 16 tasks, each of the tasks is executed in each of the nuclei. The transfer of data during the execution of the tasks, between each node, is carried out through the mechanism, of the passage of messages of the system many-core of Epiphany III. or directly writing in the global shared memory.

The multiplication of matrices in parallel is done in a certain number of steps, which can be determined by the quadratic root of P $(\sqrt{P})$, where P is the number of nuclei, each task is the multiplication of matrices that operates on the set of data that are the size of $\sqrt{P}X\sqrt{P}$. At each step of the process, modifications are made to matrix C, then matrix A moves down, and matrix B moves to the right. This example can be programmed using the standard "C" ANSI programming language. The Epiphany III system provides specific functions to simplify the programming of many-core, but its use is not mandatory, this system allows programmers to innovate at all levels. The algorithm implemented in the Epiphany III system with 16-cores, operating at 1 GHz, which solves the multiplication of matrices of 128 × 128 in 2 ms. As the performance of the Epiphany III system grows linearly, with the core number, when adequate programming and data distribution models are used, a cost/performance optimized system will be available [10, 11, 13, 16, 23].

To exploit the parallelism in the platform in hardware, it is suggested that the application should be the decomposition of different tasks (code portions). In this way, each of the cores could execute a part of the program in parallel concerning other cores.

The decomposition of the tasks must be followed by a synchronization of the different parties involved to ensure consistency.

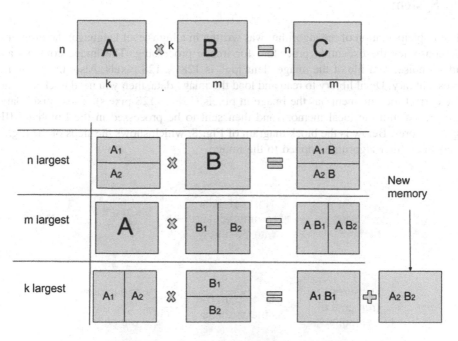

Fig. 7. Data flow in matrix multiplication [18].

In the previous figure, we have schematically a matrix that can be presented mathematically. For simplicity, opt for the multiplication of matrices. This multiplication can be represented by the following expression:

$$C_{ij} = \sum_{k=0}^{N-1} \left(A_{ij} B_{kj} \right) \qquad (13)$$

Where A and B are the input matrices, C is the result matrix of Ai and Bj, in which the coordinate (i, j) that is (row, column), are elements of the matrix. The procedure for programming the multiplication of matrices in a single core is shown below:

$$\text{for } (i = 0; \ i < M; \ i + +)$$
$$\text{for } (i = 0; \ j < M; \ j + +)$$
$$\text{for } (i = 0; \ k < K; \ k + +)$$
$$C[i][j] + \ = A[i][k] * B[k][j]$$

The previous pseudo code was written in standard C/C++ language, which is compiled and executed in a single core.

Now if the matrices A, B, are executed in each core of the system and that the results of the matrix C are placed in the local memory of the core.

5   Execution of the Parallel Algorithm in the Epiphany III System

The implementation of the algorithm was written in a high-level language; the program demonstrates the execution procedure for image processing. The image contains an added noise, said file of the image "lena.jpg" is 128 × 128 pixels. Also, the program uses a library, Devil library to read and load the image data, then you need to check that the correct measurement has the image in pixels (128 × 128 pixels). These pixel data are loaded into the local memory and then sent to be processed in the Epiphany III system cores. Below is the block diagram of Fig. 8, which shows the steps of the high-frequency filter algorithm applied to the image.

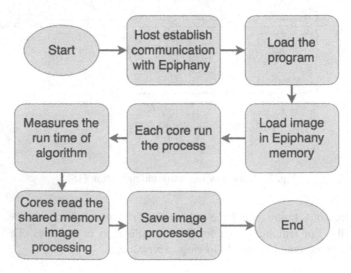

Fig. 8. Parallel execution.

The program ends up creating an image without noise, called "lena.lpf.jpg" of 128 × 128 pixels.

Recalling that the algorithm used the programming model SPMD (Single Program Multiple Data) that is responsible for distributing the execution for each of the cores [21, 22].

Figure 9 shows the execution times of the algorithms implemented on the Epiphany III system. In this application all the cores are synchronized to access the shared memory, allowing a smooth sending of data between cores.

```
Loading original image from file "../../lenna.jpg".

Width: 128  Height: 128  Depth: 1  Bpp: 24

Writing image to Epiphany
...................
GO!
Done!                                                        I

Finished calculation in 593200 cycles (0.989 msec @ 600 MHz)

FFT2D        -   284435 cycles (0.474 msec)
   FFT Setup -      189 cycles (0.000 msec)
   BITREV    -     8996 cycles (0.015 msec)
   FFT1D     -   127230 cycles (0.212 msec x2)
   Corner Turn -   4491 cycles (0.007 msec)
LPF          -    22225 cycles (0.037 msec)

Reading processed image back to host
.................

Saving processed image to file "../../lenna.lpf.jpg".
```

Fig. 9. Algorithm execution times.

Figure 10 shows two images: (a) you have the image of firewood with noise, and the image (b) shows the image of firewood without the noise.

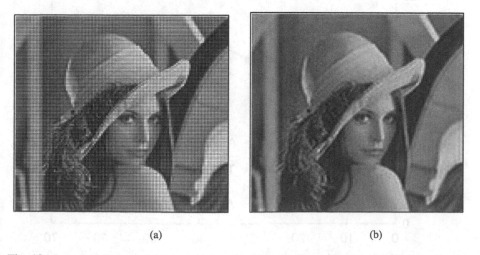

(a)   (b)

Fig. 10. Image of "Lena": (a) image with noise [23], (b) image filtered with fft_2d using the epiphany system III.

6 Results

The parallel algorithm was implemented in the high-level program in which it was executed, using arrays of 2×2 and 4×4 of the cores. The comparison based on the execution times of the algorithm. See Fig. 11.

The comparison of Bandwidth is shown in Fig. 12.

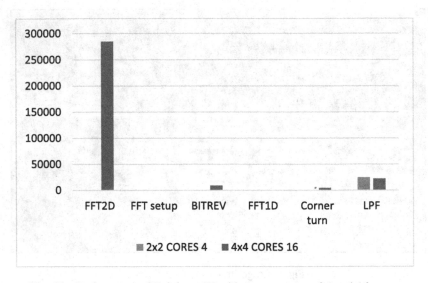

Fig. 11. Performance of Epiphany III with arrangements of 4 and 16 cores.

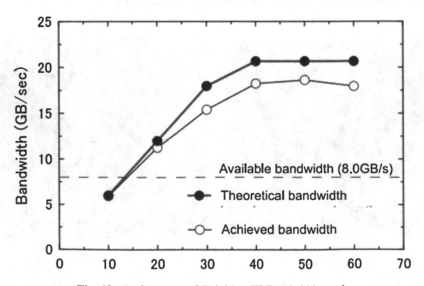

Fig. 12. Performance of Epiphany III Bandwidth used.

The following table shows the execution times of the 2 × 2 and 4 × 4 core clusters (Table 1).

Table 1. Execution times.

Cores	2 × 2 Cores 4	4 × 4 Cores 16
FFT2D	2'139,078,656	284,435
FFT setup	1'935,642,304	189
BITREV	4'293,918,720	8996
FFT1D	2'360,365,376	127230
Corner turn	4'294,959,104	4465
LPF	24,576	22,225

Although the algorithm's execution time is limited by the size of the image. It is interesting to do the comparative analysis of time between both core arrangements, in the conclusions section important results of this work are provided.

Our first criterion taken into consideration when the performances of the parallel systems are analyzed is the speedup used to express how many times a parallel program works faster than a sequential one, where both programs are solving the same problem.

The most important reason of parallelization a sequential program is to run the program faster.

Using the speedup equation $S = \frac{T_s}{T_p}$ where T_s is the sequential time and T_p is the parallel time was obtained the results of the Table 2. See Fig. 13.

Table 2. Speedup

Cores	Speedup
FFT2D	7520.448102
FFT setup	10241493.67
BITREV	477314.2197
FFT1D	18551.95611
Corner turn	961916.9326
LPF	1.105781777

Figure 14 shows different images processed with a slight variation in the interpretation of the human eye.

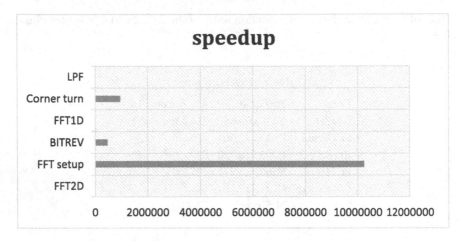

Fig. 13. Speedup of Epiphany III.

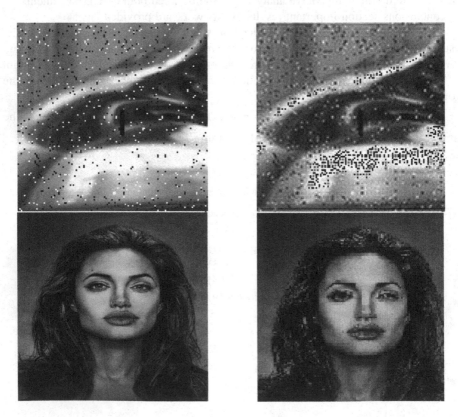

Fig. 14. Other images tested with Epiphany III

7   Conclusions

The algorithm of the fast Fourier transform (FFT) is applied to an image contaminated with Gaussian noise. This algorithm is tested on arrays of 2, 4, 16 cores executed in parallel.

When applied to a kernel (sequential execution), comparing the response time of the execution is irrelevant.

The execution time is reduced considerably when applied on 2, 4, 16 cores.

In this way, the many-core architecture is used to execute the wide data demand for the mathematical calculation required in the image processing.

Although the execution time varies according to the size of the image, this is limited by the internal memory capacity of the system; it is important to mention that the execution time will be increased over larger images.

Know the transfer times between pass by message and packet networks.

Compare the Gaussian filter with the average arithmetic filter or mid-point filter.

Acknowledgement. We appreciate the facilities granted for the completion of this work to the Instituto Politécnico Nacional through the Secretaria de Investigación y posgrado (SIP) with the SIP 20180023, 20180824 project, Unidad Interdisciplinaria de Ingeniería y Ciencias Sociales y Administrativas y Centro de Investigación y Desarrollo de Tecnología Digital. Likewise, to the Program of Stimulus to the Performance of the Researchers and the Program of Stimulus to the Teaching Performance (EDD) and COFAA.

References

1. Gonzalez, R.C., Woods, R.E.: Digital Image Processing, 3rd edn. Pearson Education, London (2008)
2. Camarena: Progress in Pattern Recognition, Image Analysis. Computer Vision (2009)
3. Grama, A., Gupta, A., Karypis, G., Kumar, V.: An Introduction to Parallel Computing Design and Analysis of Algorithms, 2nd edn. Pearson Addison Wesley, Boston (2003)
4. Burger, T.: Intel Multi-Core Processors. Quick Reference Guide. http://cachewww.intel.com/cd/00/00/23/19/231912_231912.pdf
5. Wentzlaff, D., et al.: On-chip interconnection architecture of the tile processor. IEEE Micro **27**, 15–31 (2007)
6. Kalray's MPPA: User's Guide. http://www.kalray.eu/products/mppa-many-core/mppa-256/
7. Adapteva: The Parallella Board. User's Guide. http://www.adapteva.com/parallella-board/
8. INTEL: Intel Xeon Phi Coprocessor. User's Guide. http://www.ssl.intel.com/content/dam/www/public/us/en/documents/datasheets/xeonphi-coprocessor-datasheet.pdf
9. INTEL: The Single-Chip-Cloud Computer. User's Guide. http://www.intel.com/content/dam/www/public/us/en/documents/technologybriefs/intel-labs-single-chip-cloud-rticle.pdf
10. Benini, L., Micheli, G.: Networks on chips: a new SoC paradigm. Computer **35**, 70–78 (2002)
11. Scherson, I.D., Youssef, A.S.: Interconnection Networks for High-Performance Parallel Computers. IEEE Computer Society Press (1994)
12. Teodoro, A.S., Miguel, A.M.R.: Factors influencing many-core processor. cicomp (2014)
13. Wittwer, T.: An Introduction to Parallel Programming, 1st edn. VSSD, Leeghwaterstraat 42, 2628 CA Delft, The Netherlands (2006)

14. Dongarra, J., et al.: Sourcebook of Parallel Computing. Morgan Kaufmann Publishers, Burlington (2003)
15. Hwang, K., Xu, Z.: Scalable Parallel Computing. McGraw Hill, New York (1998)
16. Yaniv, S.: Scalable Parallel Multiplication of Big Matrices, 6 February 2014. http://www.adapteva.com/white-papers/scalable-parallel-multiplication-of-big-matrices/
17. Cannon, L.E.: A cellular computer to implement the Kalman filter algorithm. DTIC Document. Technical report (1969)
18. Adapteva: Epiphany Technical Reference Documents. User's Guide, 6 February 2014. http://www.adapteva.com/all-documents
19. Camarena, J.G., Gregori, V., Morillas, S., Sapena, A.: Fast detection and removal of impulsive noise using peer groups and fuzzy metrics. J. Vis. Commun. Image Represent. **19** (1), 20–29 (2008)
20. Plataniotis, K.N., Venetsanopoulos, A.N.: Color Image Processing and Applications (2000)
21. Vajda, A.: Programming Many-Core Chips. Springer, Heidelberg (2011). https://doi.org/10.1007/978-1-4419-9739-5
22. Diaz, J., Muñoz-Caro, C., Nino, A.: A survey of parallel programming models and tools in the multi and many-core era. IEEE Trans. Parallel Distrib. Syst. **23**(8), 1369–1386 (2012)
23. Lena. https://www.google.com.mx/search?q=lena+noise+gaussian&tbm=isch&tbo=u&source=univ&sa=X&ved=0ahUKEwjXhe7Az7YAhVIIqwKHckJDnEQsAQISQ&biw=1600&bih=807

Amdahl's Law Extension for Parallel Program Performance Analysis on Intel Turbo-Boost Multicore Processors

Amilcar Meneses-Viveros[1]([⊠]), Mireya Paredes-López[2],
and Isidoro Gitler[2]

[1] Computer Science Department, Cinvestav-IPN, Mexico City, Mexico
ameneses@cs.cinvestav.mx
[2] Mathematics Department, Cinvestav-IPN, Mexico City, Mexico

Abstract. In last years the use of multicore processors has been increased. This tendency to develop processors with several cores obeys to look for better performance in parallel programs with a lower consumption of energy. Currently, the analysis of performance of speedup and energy consumption has taken a key role for applications executed in multicore systems. For this reason, it is important to analyze the performance based on new characteristics of modern processors, such as Intel's turbo boost technology. This technology allows to increase the frequency of Intel multicore processors. In this work, we present an extension of Amdahl's law to analyze the performance of parallel programs running in multicore processors with Intel turbo boost technology. We conclude that for cases when the sequential portion of a program is small, it is possible to overcome the upper limit of the traditional Amdahl's law. Furthermore, we show that for parallel programs running with turbo boost the performance is better compare to programs running in processors that does not have this technology on.

Keywords: Amdahl's law extension · Performance analysis · Turbo-Boost
Multicore processors

1 Introduction

In last years the use of multicore processors has been increased [1]. Since its commercial appearance, in 2007 with two cores processors, manufacturers have incorporated processors from 2, 4, 6 up to 32 cores. Nowadays, it is more common to see processors with more cores or greater cache memory capacities than processors with frequencies higher than 3.2 GHz. This tendency to increase processors that do not exceed this frequency limit obeys to take care of the energy consumption when these processors execute instruction flows [2–5].

The variants of the designs of the processors are not only in the number of cores they support, also in the internal architecture of interconnection between cores and in the organization of cache memory levels, SO virtualization mechanisms and the use of virtual cores for Take advantage of processor downtime. There are processors with 2 or

© Springer Nature Switzerland AG 2019
M. Torres et al. (Eds.): ISUM 2018, CCIS 948, pp. 87–96, 2019.
https://doi.org/10.1007/978-3-030-10448-1_8

even 3 levels of cache memory. It also influences the access mechanisms to the main memory, either symmetrically or asymmetrically [2–7].

Other technologies that have been implemented in multi-core processor architecture refer to frequency variations. This technique appeared in the AMD processors in 2007 [2, 3], where the core that were not used were put in an idle state, which implies a reduction in the frequency, which in turn has an impact on the processor's energy consumption. The frequency change has also been incorporated when a processor is running. Changes in frequency affect increases or decreases in the base frequency in which the processor cores work.

In the case in which the processors decrease their frequency is based, it is sought that the processors reduce their energy consumption. For example AMD Opteron multicore processors determine, through the temperature sensor, to decrease the frequency of their cores if they determine that the server has exceeded an upper limit of temperature [2, 3, 7].

The frequency increase has been managed to increase the efficiency of program execution. Technologies such as Intel's Turbo Boost and AMD's Turbo Core are clear examples of this. In these cases, the processors increase their base frequency when they detect a stream of instructions [2–5, 8].

It is observed that the decrease in frequency directly infers in the reduction of energy. Manufacturers such as AMD have incorporated the use of neural networks as part of the frequency control of their processors to find optimal solutions for the problem of having better execution times with reasonable energy consumption [8]. However, a general analysis model is needed to execute programs in processors that increase their frequencies. In this paper we present the analysis of the execution of parallel programs in processors with Intel Turbo Boost Technology [4, 5]. The analysis is proposed by making an extension to the Amdahl model for the case of parallel programs that run at the most with p threads in a multicolored processor of p-cores. The model is validated with the execution of multiplication of $N \times N$ square matrices, when the processor has Turbo Boost enabled and de-enabled. It is observed that, in effect, the parallel programs that are executed with the enabled Turbo-Boost run in less time than the programs that do not have it enabled. One result that seems interesting and will be discussed in detail, is that there are cases in which the traditional upper acceleration limit of Amdahl's Law is exceeded (when the inherently sequential section of the program tends to zero) when programs run and the multi-core with Turbo Boost enabled.

This document is organized in six sections. Section 2 presents the work related to the acceleration models and extensions to the Amdahl's law. Then a brief explanation of the traditional Amdahl's law is given in Sect. 3. Section 4 presents the acceleration model for the case of Intel processors that incorporate Turbo Boost technology. Then, a section of experiments to validate the model is presented. Finally, the conclusions are presented.

2 Related Work

Since the appearance of Amdahl's work in 1967 [9], works have been developed that serve as the basis for establishing metrics or indicators for the execution of parallel programs. You can mention important works such as Gustafson-Barsis [10] and

Karp-Flatt [11]. Unlike Amdahl, Gustafson-Barsis establishes the behavior of the parallel program from the sequential region of the parallel program [10]. Karp and Flatt establish the sequential experimental region of a parallel program based on the speedup generated by the program [11].

Since 2008, several works have been presented with extensions and analyzes on the Amdahl Law, showing the benefits of multi-core processors. Many of these works were aimed at explaining the improvements in performance, but also to explain the benefits in saving energy [12–17].

In 2015, Moreland et al. they present a revision of metrics for large-scale parallel performance, however the factor of change of frequency in their analysis is not included [18].

In 2017, Vernet et al., proposed an extension to Amdahl's law for Intel processors with Turbo Boost [20], however this work only considered frequency change in the portion of the computation that runs in parallel and we observe that the frequency increase occurs when the processor receives instruction stream, regardless of whether this stream corresponds to the sequential or parallel part.

All these works have in common that they extend Amdahl's model. As you can see, the extensions have been dedicated to exploring the behavior of energy consumption and metrics have been given for performance and the frequency change used by the new processor architectures is only consider in [20]. In this work the change of frequency is incorporated in the Amdahl's model, in particular for Intel processors with Turbo Boost technology.

3 Amdahl's Law

In 1967, Gene M. Amdahl presented an analysis to evaluate the convenience of parallelizing a program based on its sequential execution. According to Amdahl [9, 19], the execution time of a sequential program for a problem size of n is given by

$$T(n, 1) = \sigma(n) + \varphi(n), \tag{1}$$

where $\sigma(n)$ refers to the serial portion of the computation and $\varphi(n)$ denotes the portion of the computation that can be executed in parallel.

Following the same principle, the execution time for a program running on a multicore processor is denoted by Eq. 2, where p refers to the number of cores in the multicore processor and $k(n, p)$ refers to the overhead related to the inter communication between processors.

$$T(n,p) = \sigma(n) + \frac{\varphi(n)}{p} + \kappa(n,p). \tag{2}$$

Hence, the definition of the speedup of a parallel program is the ratio between sequential execution time and parallel execution time denoted by inequality 4, assuming that $k(n, p) > 0$ in inequality 3.

$$\Psi(n,p) \leq \frac{\sigma(n) + \varphi(n)}{\sigma(n) + \frac{\varphi(n)}{p} + \kappa(n,p)}, \tag{3}$$

$$\Psi(n,p) \leq \frac{1}{f + (1-f)/p}, \quad \text{where } f = \frac{\sigma(n)}{\sigma(n) + \varphi(n)}. \tag{4}$$

Where f is the sequential portion of the program execution. From inequality 4, it can be seen that the maximum speedup when $f \to 0$ is

$$\lim_{f \to \infty} \Psi(n, p) = p. \tag{5}$$

It's means, when $f = 0$, the program is fully parallel.

4   Amdahl's Law Extension

Since our case study are multicore processors with variable frequency and based on Amdahl's law previous definition of speedup (Eq. 4), we present an extension for the speedup for these specific processors. This variation basically consists of taking into account the variation of frequency of the processors in the Amdahl's law speedup formula as follows in Eq. 6, where $T_{off}(n, 1)$ and $T_{on}(n, p)$ refers to the sequential execution time without having any variation in frequency and the parallel execution time with variation in frequency, respectively. Moreover, H refers to the ratio between the increased frequency and the base frequency of the multicore processor.

$$\Psi(n, p) = \frac{T_{off}(n, 1)}{T_{on}(n, 1)} = \frac{\sigma(n) + \varphi(n)}{\frac{\sigma(n)}{H} + \frac{\varphi(n)}{pH} + \frac{\kappa(n,p)}{H}}. \tag{6}$$

Since $k(n, p)$ is always greater than or equal to zero, then we can remove it from (6) to get the next inequality

$$\Psi(n, p) \leq \frac{\sigma(n) + \varphi(n)}{\frac{\sigma(n)}{H} + \frac{\varphi(n)}{pH}} = H\left(\frac{\sigma(n) + \varphi(n)}{\sigma(n) + \frac{\varphi(n)}{p}}\right). \tag{7}$$

Replacing the following $f = \frac{\sigma(n)}{\sigma(n) + \varphi(n)}$, inequality 7 turns into inequality 8:

$$\Psi(n, p) \leq \frac{H}{f + (1-f)/p}. \tag{8}$$

For example, Figs. 1 and 2 show the speedup for three different values of f: $f = 0.2$, $f = 0.1$ and $f = 0.02$, which refers to the sequential proportion for Amdahl's law. Because $H = 1$ correspond to traditional Amdahl's law Fig. 1, shows the traditional speedup for Amdahl's law. In this case, the p value (number of processors) is the upper limit of the traditional Amdahl's law. Figure 2, shows the speedup for the extension of Amdahl's law for $H = 1.14$.

Figure 1 shows the speedup of a parallel program without presenting variation in the frequency (traditional Amdahl's law) and Fig. 2 presents the speedup of a parallel

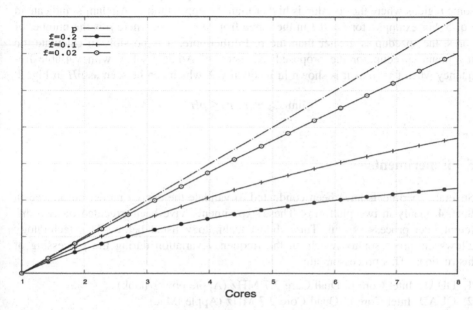

Fig. 1. Speedup with $H = 1$ for various values of f. This case is equivalent to the speeduo reported by the traditional Amdahl law.

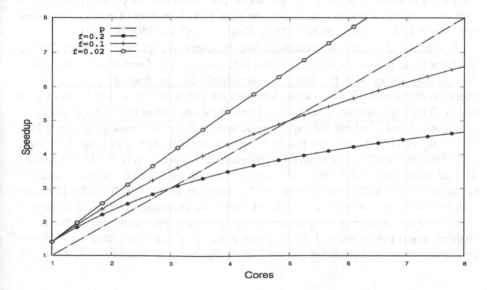

Fig. 2. Speedup with $H = 1.4$ for various values of f.

program by using $H = 1.4$. The H value was taken assuming that the processor used increments its frequency from 2.7 GHz to 3.1 GHz:

$$H = 3.1 \text{ GHz}/2.7 \text{ GHz} = 1.14.$$

In Fig. 2, it can be observed that when for a frequency value $H = 1.14$, there are some regions where the speedup is higher than the upper limit of Amdahl's, indicate in Eq. 5. For example, for $f = 0.1$ in the range from $p \in [1, 5]$, where p is the number of cores, the speedup is greater than the p. Furthermore, it is possible to calculate the maximum speedup for the proposed extension of Amdahl's law with variable frequency when $f \to 0$ as it is shown in inequality 9, which can be seen as pH in Fig. 2.

$$\lim_{f \to \infty} \Psi(n, p) \leq pH. \tag{9}$$

5   Experiments

Several experiments have been conducted to validate the energy model introduced in Sect. 4, manly in two platforms. These experiments have been executed on two different Intel processors with Turbo boost technology listed below. This technology allows the processor to switch on the frequency variation during the processing of instructions. This processors are

1. DUAL: Intel Core i5 Dual Core 2.7 MHz (Apple power book).
2. QUAD: Intel Core i5 Quad Core 2.7 MHz (Apple iMac).

To test the proposed model, part of the Linpack benchmark was used, specifying the multiplication of double precision in square matrices. It is very known that the complexity of this task is $O(n^3)$ and stresses the processor, also the parallel part exceeds 98% of execution time with matrices greater than 1500. The sizes of matrices that were tested were $1500 \times 1500, 2000 \times 2000, 3000 \times 3000$ and 3500×3500.

Figures 3 and 4 show the execution time of matrix multiplication in Intel Core i5 Dual and Quad processors with the Turbo Boost on and off. Continuous lines present the execution times with the Turbo Boost turned off. The dashed lines present the execution of the multiplication of matrices with the Turbo Boost enabled. It can be seen that in all the experiments, the execution times are shorter when the Turbo Boost is on.

Figures 5 and 6 present the experimental speedup of matrix multiplication in Intel Core i5 dual core and quad core test processors. It is observed that in spite of the sizes of matrices, the acceleration behavior is maintained. The speedup is divide sequentially with the Turbo Boost Off by the parallel execution with the Turbo Boost on. The idea is to compare what is the improvement of the programs running with Turbo Boost on with respect to the sequential case without increasing frequency. In Figs. 5 and 6 it is seen that there is an mayor speedup in the sequential case with the Turbo Boost enabled, this is due to the fact that sequential execution with the active Turbo Boost consumes less time, as shown in graphs 3 and 4. Furthermore, it can be seen that for all

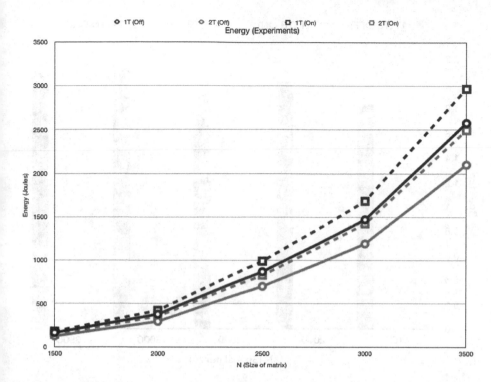

Fig. 3. Execution time for matrix multiplication on Intel Core i5 dual core with Turbo Boost enabled and disabled. Base frequency is 2.7 GHz, and Turbo Boost increase to 3.1 GHz. Thus $H = 1.4$.

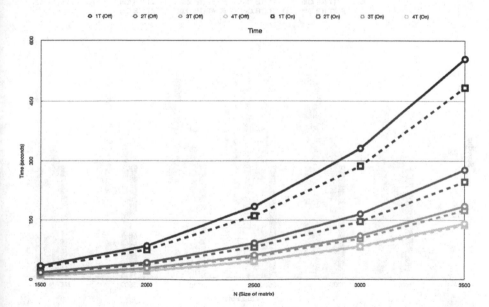

Fig. 4. Execution time for matrix multiplication on Intel Core i5 quad core with Turbo Boost enabled and disabled. Base frequency is 2.7 GHz, and Turbo Boost Increase to 2.8 GHz. Thus, $H = 1.037$.

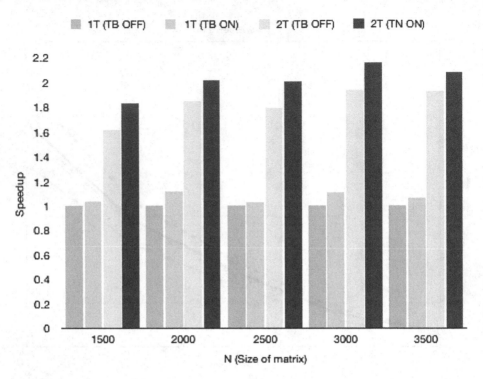

Fig. 5. Speedup for matrix multiplication on Intel Core i5 dual core with Turbo Boost enabled and disabled. Base frequency is 2.7 GHz, and Turbo Boost increase to 3.1 GHz. Thus, $H = 1.4$.

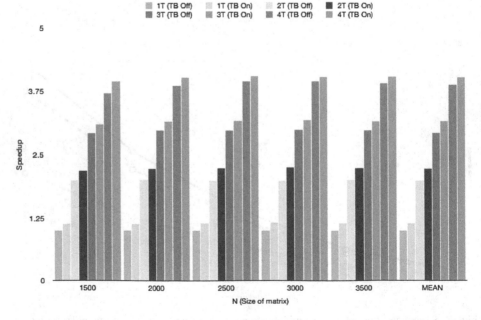

Fig. 6. Speedup for matrix multiplication on Intel Core i5 quad core with Turbo Boost enabled and disabled. Base frequency is 2.7 GHz, and Turbo Boost increase to 2.8 GHz. Thus, $H = 1.037$.

the parallel cases, the acceleration exceeds the traditional limit estimated by Amdahl, Eq. 5, and that they are maintained according to the new estimate, inequality 9.

6 Conclusions

In this paper an extension to the model proposed by Amdahl for acceleration has been presented, considering the behavior offered by Intel's Turbo Boost technology to increase frequencies. This model is a correction to model proposed by Verner and Mendelson [20]. In our model the increase of frequency is in sequential and parallel part. It is noted that the acceleration limit, Eq. 5, calculated by Amdahl's Law is no longer met and must now be adjusted by a scalar value that determines when the frequency is increased, inequality 9.

Experiments were performed on two platforms with Intel Core i5 processors. One with a dual core processor and another with a quad core processor. The processes that were run was the multiplication of matrices in double precision. This problem reduces the sequential part f to less than 0.001, so the problem is highly parallel.

The execution time of the inherently sequential region of a program remains the key knowledge to determine the acceleration that can be obtained, as indicated by Amdahl in his 1967 work [9].

Acknowledgment. The authors thank the financial support given by the Mexican National Council of Science and Technology (CONACyT), as well as ABACUS: Laboratory of Applied Mathematics and High-Performance Computing of the Mathematics Department of CINVESTAV-IPN. Their also thank Advance Studies and Research Center of National Polytechnic Institute (CINVESTAV-IPN), for encouragement and facilities provided to accomplish this publication.

References

1. Fuller, S.H., Miller, L.E.: Computing performance: game over or next level? Computer **44**, 31–38 (2011). The National Academies Press
2. Le Sueur, E., Heiser, G.: Dynamic voltage and frequency scaling: the laws of diminishing returns. In: Proceedings of the 2010 International Conference on Power Aware Computing and Systems, pp. 1–8 (2010)
3. Conway, P., Hughes, B.: The AMD Opteron northbridge architecture. IEEE Micro **27**(2), 10–21 (2007)
4. Rotem, E., Naveh, A., Ananthakrishnan, A., Weissmann, E., Rajwan, D.: Power-management architecture of the intel microarchitecture code-named sandy bridge. IEEE Micro **32**(2), 20–27 (2012)
5. Charles, J., Jassi, P., Ananth, N.S., Sadat, A., Fedorova, A.: Evaluation of the Intel® Core™ i7 Turbo Boost feature. In: IEEE International Symposium on Workload Characterization, IISWC 2009. IEEE, pp. 188–197 (2009)
6. Carro, L., Rutzig, M.B.: Multi-core systems on chip. In: Bhattacharyya, S., Deprettere, E., Leupers, R., Takala, J. (eds.) Handbook of Signal Processing Systems, pp. 485–514. Springer, Boston (2010). https://doi.org/10.1007/978-1-4419-6345-1_18

7. Cho, S., Melhem, R.G.: On the interplay of parallelization, program performance, and energy consumption. IEEE Trans. Parallel Distrib. Syst. **21**, 342–353 (2010)
8. Stegailov, V., Vecher, V.: Efficiency analysis of Intel and AMD x86_64 architectures for Ab initio calculations: a case study of VASP. In: Voevodin, V., Sobolev, S. (eds.) Russian Supercomputing Days, vol. 793, pp. 430–441. Springer, Cham (2017). https://doi.org/10.1007/978-3-319-71255-0_35
9. Amdahl, G.M.: Validity of the single processor approach to achieving large scale computing capabilities. In: Proceedings of the Spring Joint Computer Conference, 18–20 April 1967, pp. 483-485. ACM (1967)
10. Gustafson, J.L.: Reevaluating Amdahl's law. Commun. ACM **31**(5), 532–533 (1988)
11. Karp, A.H., Flatt, H.P.: Measuring parallel processor performance. Commun. ACM **33**(5), 539–543 (1990)
12. Hill, M.D., Marty, M.R.: Amdahl's law in the multicore era. Computer **41**(7), 33–38 (2008)
13. Woo, D.H., Lee, H.-H.S.: Extending Amdahl's law for energy-efficient computing in the many-core era. Computer **41**(12), 24–31 (2008)
14. Basmadjian, R., de Meer, H.: Evaluating and modeling power consumption of multi-core processors. In: Proceedings of 3rd International Conference on Future Energy Systems: Where Energy, Computing and Communications Meet, pp. 1–10. ACM (2012)
15. Londoño, S.M., de Gyvez, J.P.: Extending Amdahl's law for energy-efficience. In: 2010 International Conference on Energy Aware Computing (ICEAC), pp. 1–4. IEEE (2010)
16. Sun, X.-H., Chen, Y.: Reevaluating Amdahl's law in the multicore era. J. Parallel Distrib. Comput. **70**(2), 183–188 (2010)
17. Isidro-Ramirez, R., Viveros, A.M., Rubio, E.H.: Energy consumption model over parallel programs implemented on multicore architectures. Int. J. Adv. Comput. Sci. Appl. (IJACSA) **6**(6), 252–259 (2015)
18. Moreland, K., Oldfield, R.: Formal metrics for large-scale parallel performance. In: Kunkel, J.M., Ludwig, T. (eds.) ISC High Performance 2015. LNCS, vol. 9137, pp. 488–496. Springer, Cham (2015). https://doi.org/10.1007/978-3-319-20119-1_34
19. Quinn, M.J.: Parallel Programming in C with MPI and OpenMP. McGraw-Hill Education Group, New York (2003)
20. Verner, U., Mendelson, A., Schuster, A.: Extending Amdahl's law for multicores with Turbo Boost. IEEE Comput. Archit. Lett. **16**, 30–33 (2017)

Applications and HPC

Traffic Sign Distance Estimation Based on Stereo Vision and GPUs

Luis Barbosa-Santillan[✉], Edgar Villavicencio-Arcadia,
and Liliana Barbosa-Santillan

University of Guadalajara, Periférico Norte N° 799,
Núcleo Universitario los Belenes, 45100 Zapopan, Jalisco, Mexico
{francisco.barbosa,edgar.villavicencio}@alumno.udg.mx

Abstract. Recognition, detection, and distance determination of traffic signs have become essential tasks for the development of Intelligent Transport Systems (ITS). Processing time is very important to these tasks, since they not only need an accurate answer, but also require a real-time response. The distance determination of traffic Signs (TS) uses the greatest number of computational resources for the disparity map calculations based on the Stereo Vision method. In this paper, we propose the acceleration of the disparity map calculation by using our parallel algorithm, called Accelerated Estimation for Traffic Sign Distance (AETSD) and implemented in the Graphics Processors Unit (GPU), which uses data storage strategies based on their frequency of use. Furthermore, it carries out an optimized search for the traffic signal in the stereoscopic pair of images. The algorithm splits the problem into parts and they are solved concurrently by the available massive processors into the stream processors units (SM). Our results show that the proposed algorithm accelerated the response time 141 times for an image resolution of 1024×680 pixels, with an execution time 0.04 s for the AETSD parallel version and 5.67 s for the sequential version.

Keywords: Traffic sign · Stereo vision · Parallel processing

1 Introduction

Intelligent transport systems proposals have been numerous in recent years. The application areas of these systems extend beyond autonomous vehicles, to the incorporation of intelligent driver support systems. Currently, there are many proposals for recognition systems of traffic signals, which varies with the type of algorithms that are used, their advantages and disadvantages, the response time and the precision they reach (Miura et al. 2000; De la Escalera et al. 2003; Maldonado-Bascón et al. 2007). In Gudigar et al. (2016) the authors make a critical review of the algorithms used for segmentation, detection and automatic recognition of traffic signals in a total of 44 published works. According to the review it was found that the processing time is related not only to the hardware and software used, but also to the size of the image and its complexity (which may vary in the different available datasets). Stallkamp et al. (2012) compared several machine learning algorithms for traffic signal classification with the human performance and found that were very similar in results. The different

M. Torres et al. (Eds.): ISUM 2018, CCIS 948, pp. 99–109, 2019.
https://doi.org/10.1007/978-3-030-10448-1_9

proposals have evidenced that automatic recognition of traffic signs has been tackled successfully from numerous approaches (Paclík et al. 2000; Hsu and Huang 2001; Fleyeh et al. 2007; Maldonado et al. 2010; Pazhoumand-Dar and Yaghoobi 2013; Souani et al. 2014). Shi et al. (2017) recently made a proposal for an accelerated version of the traffic signal detection implemented in FPGA, achieving a response time of 126.58 fps in 1920 × 1080 size images; demonstrating that parallel approaches achieve feasible response times for real-time tasks.

Once the traffic signs have been recognized, it is possible to obtain additional information that could provide aid to the driver, such as the priority that must give to each traffic signal according to their distance from the vehicle. One of the most-used methods to determine this distance is the Stereo Vision method, whose main disadvantage is the greater computational cost involved for the calculations in the treatment of the images and formulas used to obtain the disparity map. This causes intelligent transport systems (ITS) applications that use this type of algorithm to be less functional, since their processing times are insufficient for tasks where results are needed in real time (Romdhane et al. 2016). Therefore, the present work focuses on determining the 3D depth of the traffic signal by means of a parallelized version of the stereo vision method, starting from a scene in which the traffic signal has been previously recognized. Section 2 presents the theoretical bases that support the article, Sect. 3 discusses the proposed method, Sect. 4 reports results obtained, and Sect. 5 presents the conclusions.

2 Related Work

In this section, the fundamentals of the two main topics related in this work; the background of parallel processing, the disparity method and their relationship in determining the depth of 2D objects in a picture (distance) are explained.

2.1 Parallel Processing

Traditionally the solutions to problems using a computer has been approached with algorithms that describe a problem through a series of logical and orderly steps analogous to human thinking, so most programming languages, as well as the hardware, were designed at first to work with sequential tasks. The current trend of programs and applications that require a greater number of instructions, for their operation, as well as shorter response times, had been based on increasing the frequency of the processors clock, which has a limit that has already been reached, with serious heating problems. For these reasons it has been necessary to change the programming paradigm based on the resolution of tasks in parallel, which implies greater effort and complexity in design, as well as new hardware with parallel physical resources in which the program can be implemented. The Graphics Processor Unity (GPU's) has proven to be the most successful hardware for parallel applications.

Parallel programming allows the execution of a task to be accelerated by using several processors that work together on a portion of the problem. The programmer must define and assign tasks to each processor, and the data that they will have access to.

One of the challenges that arise when using this approach is the proper use and management of resources between the multitude of processors that demand access to the data to carry out their task.

The GPU cards were initially conceived for video acceleration, being used mostly in the video game industry, although later they were found to be suitable architectures to implement parallel algorithms in a multitude of applications with real-time response requirements such as applications in aeronautics, economy, military applications, ITS applications, etc.

2.2   Disparity and Distance Determination

The correspondence of images, is a process by which an attempt is made to identify the same spatial characteristic (matrix or mask of $N \times N$ pixels) in both images of the stereo system. This is one of the most computationally expensive tasks. This process, which is simple for humans, is enormously complex in terms of computation, since for a pixel or characteristic in one image, there may be a multitude of candidates in the other.

There are different algorithms which can be used to find the disparity map (Shi et al. 2017). In this work the algorithm of absolute difference is used (see Eq. 1) because it is the algorithm that implies a lower computational cost.

$$AD = \sum_{[i,j] \in R} abs[f(i,j) - g(i,j)] \tag{1}$$

The success of correlation based methods, depends on the window used to capture the structure that surrounds the point being studied to establish correspondence. A window that is too small, may not capture enough of the image structure, and may be too sensitive to noise, while a too large one is less sensitive to noise but is subject to possible variations in intensity between the two images of the stereoscopic pair. The cameras that make up the stereo system have different angles, the same point is projected in distinct locations, looking for the highest correspondence peak to identify the same point in the corresponding space for each pixel of the right image in the left image.

The determination of the traffic signal's distance to the vehicle is obtained based on the disparity found in the sub-region that contains the signal, according to the following Eq. 2:

$$Z_0 = \lambda + \frac{\lambda * \Delta x}{X_L - (X_R + \Delta X)} \tag{2}$$

where:

Δx = Cameras' distance
λ = Focal length
X_L = The horizontal coordinate of the traffic signal on the left image
X_R = The horizontal coordinate of the traffic signal on the right image
Z_0 = Depth

See Fig. 1, for a graphic description.

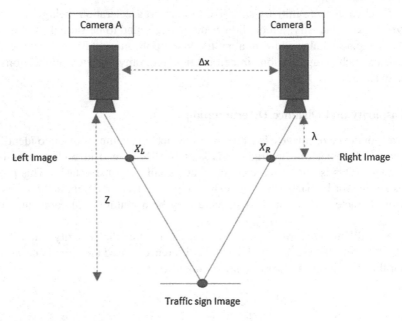

Fig. 1. Vision stereo model.

An alternative to minimize the distraction of the driver when consulting the proximity of the traffic signals, is relating its proximity to an increase in the intensity of color (red), which warns of its proximity in a graphical, immediate and intuitive way.

3   Accelerated Estimation for Traffic Sign Distance (AETSD)

The parallel algorithm was programmed within the Nsight platform using CUDA SDK V7 and implemented on the NVIDIA brand GeForce GTX 780 card. The execution of the sequential version was carried out using an AMD FX-8370 processor with 7.7 GB RAM and a speed of 1400 MHz.

The database used to test the proposed approach, was created within the University Center of Economic and Administrative Sciences of the University of Guadalajara, where 10 traffic signs were selected, and 10 stereoscopic samples were taken (left photo and right photo) at 10, 15 and 20 m away, thus obtaining a dataset of 600 images, each with a size of 1024 × 680. The optical axes of the two lenses of the cameras were placed parallel to each other, and the straight line joining the two optical centers was also parallel to each horizontal line of the traffic sign to respect an epipolar restriction, see Fig. 1.

Also, additional stereoscopic images were taken, but without respecting the epipolar restriction, because in real situations, variations in the alignment of the cameras can occur, as in the case of streets with camber or irregularities in the road.

The general scheme of the Stereo Vision parallelized algorithm is shown in a diagram (Fig. 2). During the first block of the diagram all the variables used within the concurrent routine are declared in internal registers, which have an advantage over the global memory and shared memory regarding to the speed of access to the data, for this reason, the pixels of the right image are stored on them, since the right image pixels are the data most frequently utilized during the correlating task of the images, as described in strategy two. As a second step, the indexes of each thread were established, considering the height and width of the image, so that each pixel is linked to a single processor inside the GPU. During the third step, the position of the pixel is determined within the image, depending on its position. The processor linked to that pixel will decide to end its routine or to save the information in the shared memory and internal registers following strategies number two and three. Finally, the correspondence of both images is calculated according to the method proposed in strategy 1.

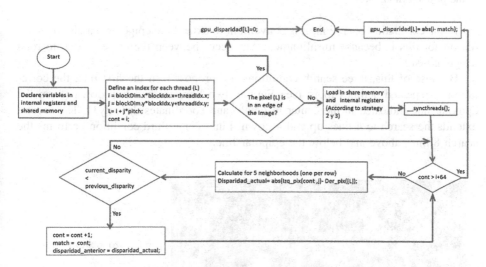

Fig. 2. Diagram of the process for kernel calculations.

The three strategies to make efficient the use of the Gforce GTX 780 card's resources, as well as to accelerate the processing, needed to determine the distance to the traffic sign are described below:

Strategy 1: Performing the correlation on each pixel of the homologous image is the most expensive part of the algorithm. To improve the response time of the correlation task, the search for the maximum correspondence of the neighborhood of a pixel on the right image with coordinates Der_pix (dx1, dy1) starts in the left image from the same coordinate (dx1, dy1), making a stride, which is determined experimentally, through three options; the first with a size of 30, the second of 60 and finally the third of 120 steps, see Fig. 3.

a) Left image   **b) Right image**

Fig. 3. Figure (b) shows a neighborhood of the pixel Der_pix (dx1 = 780, dy1 = 340), and in figure (a) this neighborhood is compared with another 60 neighborhoods of equal size, starting from the same coordinate (780, 340) but on the left image, making a left to right path of 60 steps to the position (840, 340).

In the correlation operation, it is convenient to extend the epipolar search, the main reason for this is because misalignment can occur between the cameras due to road irregularities.

Because of this, three search conditions are proposed, in the first one, the correlation is repeated 4 times more (see Fig. 4), two lines up and two down (from the epipolar line indicated in the center in green, and coordinates dx1, dy1). The second extends the search to 4 lines up and 4 down. Finally, the third condition performs the search 8 lines above and below the epipolar line.

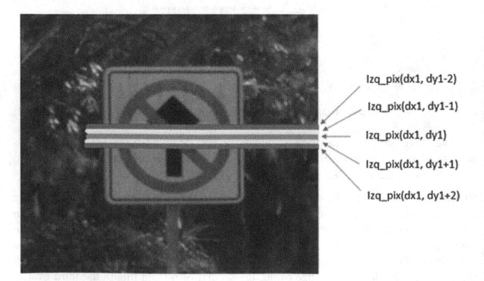

Fig. 4. Searching for the best match, using 4 additional lines to the epipolar line. (Color figure online)

Strategy 2: To accelerate the access to the pixels of the right image, a neighborhood (3 × 3) of the pixel to be correlated in internal records of the thread is loaded. All of them in unsigned char variables, given that they have a byte, being able to save any shade of gray (0–255), copying them from the global memory of the GPU. Thereby reducing the access time to the data. Figure 5 shows the assignments of each of the gray tones of the neighborhood in internal registers (unsigned char) in each multi-processor. The data are taken from the image stored in a vector named gpu_der its size is 696,320 items of global memory (the pitch refers to the width of the image and "*l*" is the index that identifies each processor).

deai11=gpu_der[l-pitch-1];	*deca1=gpu_der[l-pitch];*	*dead11=gpu_der[l-pitch+1];*
deci1=gpu_der[l-1];	*dece=gpu_der[l];*	*decd1=gpu_der[l+1];*
debi11=gpu_der[l+pitch-1];	*decb1=gpu_der[l+pitch];*	*debd11=gpu_der[l+pitch+1];*

Fig. 5. Pixel's neighborhood names of gpu_*der[l]* (in green). (Color figure online)

Strategy 3: To reduce the access time to the pixels of the left image, they are loaded into shared memory as described below.

The number of pixels that will be loaded by each thread will depend on the chosen window's size, to determine the ideal size, three varied sizes are tested (3, 7, 11).

Storing the 7 lines of the left image that are used in the search is used as an example: first, all the line's threads in parallel load their associated pixel, plus three pixels up and three down from their index, obtaining a total of 7 pixels for each thread. Finally, they wait for all the threads to finish, before continuing with the program, by using the following code:

```
tile[0][threadIdx.x] = gpu_izq[l − 3 * pitch];
tile[1][threadIdx.x] = gpu_izq[l − 2 * pitch];
tile[2][threadIdx.x] = gpu_izq[l − pitch];
tile[3][threadIdx.x] = gpu_izq[l];
tile[4][threadIdx.x] = gpu_izq[l + pitch];
tile[5][threadIdx.x] = gpu_izq[l + 2 * pitch];
tile[6][threadIdx.x] = gpu_izq[l + 3 * pitch];
__syncthreads();
```

Strategy 4: The architecture implemented on the GPU for the analysis of the 1024 × 680 images, consisted of grouping the processors in rows of the same length as the image, i.e., each block contains 1024 processors (block dimension BLOCK_X = 1024, BLOCK_Y = 1) corresponding to a row of the image, having in total 680 blocks, which makes efficient the use of shared memory per block, and ensures that each processor has access to sufficient information to complete its task, working as a team with the neighboring processors as shown in strategy 3.

The dimension of the grid of blocks is calculated with Eqs. 3 and 4:

$$\text{grid.x} = (\text{ANCHO} + \text{BLOCK\_X} - 1)/\text{BLOCK\_X} \qquad (3)$$

$$\text{grid.y} = (\text{ALTO} + \text{BLOCK\_Y} - 1)/\text{BLOCK\_Y} \qquad (4)$$

Equations 3 and 4 consider the width and height of the image to obtain the dimension of the block grid. In the case of our 1024×680 pixel image, a grid.x = 1, grid.y = 680 is obtained, completely covering all the pixels with an associated thread.

4   Results and Discussion

To evaluate the proposed algorithm, a stereoscopic pair of synthetic images was created, with the purpose of limiting the vertical variation of the traffic signals in both images.

Table 1 shows the response times for the GPU and the CPU to get the disparity map of the pair of stereoscopic images. In this test, a window size of 3×3 pixels was

Table 1. GPU and CPU processing time.

Processor type	Time (seconds)	Window size	Horizontal search	Vertical search
GPU	0.09	3×3	1024	1
CPU	10.68	3×3	1024	1
GPU	0.02	3×3	120	1
CPU	2.38	3×3	120	1
GPU	0.02	3×3	60	1
CPU	1.23	3×3	60	1
GPU	0.0000001	3×3	10	1
CPU	0.21	3×3	10	1
GPU	0.23	3×3	1024	3
CPU	29.30	3×3	1024	3
GPU	0.04	3×3	120	3
CPU	6.52	3×3	120	3
GPU	0.02	3×3	60	3
CPU	3.36	3×3	60	3
GPU	0.01	3×3	10	3
CPU	0.58	3×3	10	3
GPU	0.34	3×3	1024	5
CPU	48.32	3×3	1024	5
GPU	0.06	3×3	120	5
CPU	10.74	3×3	120	5
GPU	0.04	3×3	60	5
CPU	5.67	3×3	60	5
GPU	0.01	3×3	10	5
CPU	0.95	3×3	10	5

used. In addition, the vertical search around the epipolar line was enlarged, as well as the sizes of horizontal paths.

Due to the characteristics of the images of the stereoscopic pair used in this test, it was found that when there are no irregularities in the street or a possible misalignment in the cameras, it is not necessary to extend the search on the vertical axis, because the window that contains part of the traffic signal in the right image will be found on the same epipolar line in the left image. In addition, it was found that a horizontal path of 60 steps was enough to find the homologous window of the right image in the left image, but not in the case of the horizontal route limited to 10 steps, since it had problems with the traffic signals that were closer to the camera, which may have a greater shift to 60 steps on the horizontal axis. A complete horizontal travel of the image (1024 steps) consumes more time, reaching up to 48.32 s for the CPU and 0.34 s for the GPU.

Figure 6a shows the disparity map found in case of a horizontal 60 step path, as well as the distance obtained to each signal, while Fig. 6b shows the disparity with a path of only 10 steps. As can be seen in Fig. 6b, the two closest signals do not present the same aspect observed in the signals of Fig. 6a, concluding that it was not possible for the algorithm to reach the sub-region of interest, and consequently presenting a problem for the distance determination to those signals.

a   b

Fig. 6. Disparity maps found with different horizontal size search.

In (Stallkamp et al. 2012), a parallel approach was used to carry out the tasks of detection and traffic signals recognition on 1920 × 1080 images, obtaining times of 0.008 s. The method proposed here solves the task to get the distance in a time of 0.04 s with images of 1024 × 680, which in total gives a time of 0.048 s, in comparison with (Souani et al. 2014), where the authors obtain a processing time of 0.957 s for the three tasks, in an image of only 288 × 384 pixels.

5 Conclusions

In this paper, the Accelerated Estimation for Traffic Sign Distance (AETSD) method has been presented. This method can assist a car driver through images taken during the journey, where, in the case where a traffic sign appears and is identified, the stereoscopic pair is processed in parallel, sending a visual feedback that alerts the driver to the signal that has priority by intensifying its color according to the proximity.

Because, in this type of application, a result is only considered useful if it is provided in real time, several strategies were implemented in the handling and processing of the data, achieving a minimal time of 0.04 s per scene, in comparison with the 5.67 obtained by the CPU. The strategies consisted of the efficient management of shared memory and internal registers. It was also possible to accelerate the algorithm due to the coordinated collaboration of as many threads as pixels presented in the image.

In addition to the epipolar search of the maximum correlation on the stereoscopic pair, 4 more were added because of the possible misalignments of the cameras due to irregularities in the road that the car travels. As a future work it is suggested that a greater number of tests is used to define the ideal search size, based on a set of images taken in different road conditions, as well as defining the window size that offers the most efficient correlation for this application.

References

De la Escalera, A., Armingol, J., Mata, M.: Traffic sign recognition and analysis for intelligent vehicles. Image Vis. Comput. **21**(3), 247–258 (2003)

Fleyeh, H., Dougherty, M., Aenugula, D., Baddam, S.: Invariant road sign recognition with fuzzy ARTMAP and Zernike moments. In: IEEE Intelligent Vehicles Symposium, Istanbul, Turkey, pp. 31–36 (2007)

Gudigar, A., Chokkadi, S., Raghavendra, U.: A review on automatic detection and recognition of traffic sign. Multimed. Tools Appl. **75**, 333–336 (2016)

Hsu, S.-H., Huang, C.-L.: Road sign detection and recognition using matching pursuit method. Image Vis. Comput. **19**(3), 119–129 (2001)

Miura, J., Kanda, T., Shirai, Y.: An active vision system for real-time traffic sign recognition. In: Proceedings of the IEEE Intelligent Transportation Systems, pp. 52–57 (2000)

Maldonado-Bascón, S., Lafuente-Arroyo, S., Gil-Jimenez, P., Gómez-Moreno, H., López-Ferreras, F.: Road-sign detection and recognition based on support vector machines. IEEE Trans. Intell. Transp. Syst. **8**(2), 264–278 (2007)

Maldonado, S., Acevedo, J., Lafuente, S., Fernández, A., López-Ferreras, F.: An optimization on pictogram identification for the road-sign recognition task using SVMs. Comput. Vis. Image Underst. **114**(3), 373–383 (2010)

Romdhane, N.B., Mliki, H., El Beji, R., Hammami, M.: Combined 2D/3D traffic signs recognition and distance estimation. In: IEEE Intelligent Vehicles Symposium (IV) (2016)

Paclík, P., Novovicová, J., Pudil, P., Somol, P.: Road sign classification using Laplace kernel classifier. Pattern Recogn. Lett. **21**(13–14), 1165–1173 (2000)

Pazhoumand-Dar, H., Yaghoobi, M.: A new approach in road sign recognition based on fast fractal coding. Neural Comput. Appl. **22**(3–4), 615–625 (2013)

Stallkamp, J., Schlipsing, M., Salmen, J., Igel, C.: Man vs. computer: benchmarking machine learning algorithms for traffic sign recognition. Neural Netw. **32** (2012). http://www.sciencedirect.com/science/article/pii/S0893608012000457

Souani, C., Faiedh, H., Besbes, K.: Efficient algorithm for automatic road sign recognition and its hardware implementation. J. Real-Time Image Process. **9**(1), 79–93 (2014)

Shi, W., Li, X., Yu, Z., Overett, G.: An FPGA-based hardware accelerator for traffic sign detection. IEEE Trans. Very Large-Scale Integr. (VLSI) Syst. **25**, 1362–1372 (2017)

The Use of HPC on Volcanic Tephra Dispersion Operational Forecast System

Agustín García-Reynoso[1(✉)], Jorge Zavala-Hidalgo[1],
Hugo Delgado-Granados[2], and Dulce R. Herrera-Moro[1]

[1] Centro de Ciencias de la Atmosfera,
Universidad Nacional Autónoma de México, Mexico City 04510, Mexico
agustin@atmosfera.unam.mx
[2] Instituto de Geofísica, Universidad Nacional Autónoma de México,
Mexico City 04510, Mexico

Abstract. High Performance Computing (HPC) was used to estimate the tephra dispersion forecast in an operational mode using the Popocatepetl volcano as base case. Currently it is not possible to forecast a volcanic eruption, which can occur at any time. In order to reduce the human intervention for obtaining immediate ash deposition information, the HPC was used to compute a wide spectrum of possible eruptions and dispersion scenarios; information obtained from previous eruptions and meteorological forecast was used to generate the possible scenarios. Results from the scenarios are displayed in a web page for consultation and decision-making when a real eruption occurs. This work shows the methodology approach used to forecast the tephra dispersion from a possible eruption, the computing strategy to reduce the processing time and a description of products displayed.

Keywords: Ash dispersion · Tephra · Popocatépetl · Forecast

1 Introduction

Volcanic eruptions can produce tephra clouds affecting health (e.g. $PM_{2.5}$ ambient concentrations increment), economic activities (e.g. airport closing and delays), infrastructure (e.g. additional weight on roof by ash) and ecosystems (e.g. ash deposition in water bodies and plant leaves) [1]. In order to reduce adverse effects, an alert and preparation actions have to be taken in advance. This is possible by using a tephra dispersion forecast, because after the release the ash can take from minutes to hours before a point of interest has been reached, therefore a set of prevention actions can be taken in advance.

The implementation of an operational forecast system requires a large amount of computational resources that can be provided by High Performance Computing (HPC) systems. This requirement is accomplished by the following task: meteorological forecast, dispersion and deposition forecast, and visualization task. A description of the case study, methods and equipment is presented in the following sections.

© Springer Nature Switzerland AG 2019
M. Torres et al. (Eds.): ISUM 2018, CCIS 948, pp. 110–117, 2019.
https://doi.org/10.1007/978-3-030-10448-1_10

1.1 Case Study

The Popocatépetl volcano was used as case study to develop a forecast system. Information about volcanic activity, tephra characteristics and plume height were available [2–5]. The volcano is located around 60 km from Mexico Megacity, a constant eruptive activity has been observed since 1994, this activity also includes some degassing processes and eruptions from small to larger ones.

The government of Mexico has a major concern about the adverse effects from the tephra clouds produced during the eruptions. The material released has adverse effect on public health and infrastructure. A forecast system can provide timely useful information for decision making in the risk and environmental area.

2 Methods

The general procedure considered the following steps: implementation and setting up of the meteorological forecast model; identification of the geographical influence area; volcanic eruptions parameter scenarios development; tephra dispersion and deposition model implementation; non-parametric optimization for operational process and results visualization.

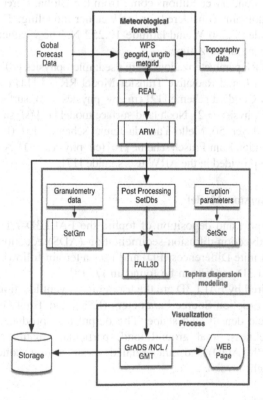

Fig. 1. Forecast system flow diagram. Meteorological forecast in upper level, ash dispersion in the middle part and visualization and storage in bottom part.

Figure 1 shows the general procedure for ash dispersion forecast. The Weather Research Forecast model (WRF) [6] was used for the meteorological forecast, the Fall3D [7] for ash dispersion-sedimentation and NCL libraries [8] for visualization in a web page.

The strategy for forecast a volcanic ash dispersion consists of the following steps. A 56-h weather forecast is generated, the first 12 h are used for spinning up the WRF model, subsequently 108 scenarios are performed corresponding to 3 different heights (3, 5 and 10 km) and for the following 36 forecast hours. Each scenario ran for 8 h after the starting time in order to obtain the dispersion and sedimentation within the studied region. Thus the last scenario started at 48 forecast hour and after 8 h of dispersion simulation ended (56 forecast hour). In each scenario the eruption lasted one hour.

In the next section a description of model parameters for WRF and Fall3d and optimization methodology are presented.

2.1 Meteorological Forecast Model

The meteorological forecast was obtained by the Weather Research and Forecasting (WRF) model system, the core used was the Advance Research WRF (ARW). This meteorological model is used for operational and research applications. It can be used in a multiple core hardware and is an open source software.

The initial and boundary conditions come from the Global Forecast System Center [9]. There are two domains considered for the weather modeling. The domain's center is located at longitude 98.586 W and latitude 19.252 N. The weather forecast is set up to run for 56 h starting at 00 Z time.

The following WRF parameterizations were used: microphysics [10] (mp_physics = 8), Long-wave Radiation Rapid Radiative Transfer Model RRTM [11] (ra_lw_physics = 1), short wave radiation Goddard scheme [12] (ra_sw_physics = 2), surface layer ETA similarity [13] (sf_sfclay_physics = 2), Noah land surface model [14] (sf_surface_physics = 2), planetary boundary layer 50 Mello-Yamada-Janjic scheme [15] (bl_pbl_physics = 2), cumulus parameterization Kain-Fritsch scheme [16] (cu_physics = 1). A detailed description of these schemes are provided in the ARW users guide [17].

2.2 Tephra Dispersion Model

To model the transport and deposition of tephra the FALL3D-7.1 was applied. This model solves the advection-diffusion-sedimentation (ADS) equations set by using an explicit scheme of Finite Differences (FD) and uses a terrain-following grid. A detailed description of FALL3D model can be found in [7, 18].

Input data required by FALL3D are the topography, vent location, eruption starting time and duration, Eruption Source Parameters (ESP), and Total Grain-Size Distribution (TGSD), particle density and shape. The output data produced by FALL3D are tephra ground thickness, total ground load, particulate matter air concentrations, aerosol optical depth (AOD) and other related variables (e.g. concentrations at predefined relevant flight levels).

The computational domain for ash dispersion is discretized considering 100 by 100 cells, each cell is around 4 km lateral length and it has 27 vertical levels (500 m thickness) from 500 m to 13500 m. Model parameterizations used are: the vertical turbulence by the Kv similarity theory, the horizontal turbulence model is constant with a value of 1000 m²/s and the option Ganser for the particle setting velocity model [19]. The topography data is obtained from the WRF model.

An important input for any ash dispersion forecast model is the emission source, the problem in this case is the impossibility to forecast the starting time, duration and intensity of volcanic eruptions. In order to resolve that, an analysis of previous eruptions was made to identify the characteristics of the possible events that may occur [20–22]. Previous events can be described as one hour of emission under three cases: eruption height columns 3 km, 5 km and 10 km. These emissions are assigned to the crater, which is located at −98.6246 W, 19.0231 N with a height of 5,160 m above mean sea level.

The TGSD considers a Gaussian distribution with 19 classes and a mean value $\Phi = 4.75$, standard deviation (σ) $\Phi = 1$ with a rage from to −1 to 9.7 (Φ), density range from 1000 to 2000 kg/m³ and sphericity (ψ) from 0.89 to 0.91. The granulometry was obtained from previous field works [3].

The eruptive column was set to the Suzuki type with $A = 10$ and $\lambda = 5$. The mass flow rate was estimated from column height and wind field by following Woodhouse [23]. A consideration of an eruption that last for one hour was used.

The Cornell model [24] was used in order to consider the aggregation effects. The main mode of the aggregates was 2Φ, the density was 350 kg/m³. For all the simulations there was no gravity current effect.

The FALL3D model can run in serial or parallel mode, for this case the parallel mode was used in order to take advantage of the multiple processors available in the hardware.

2.3 Hardware Description

A tower workstation used to implement the forecast system has 2 processors: Intel Xeon E5-2640v2 eight cores, 20 M cache, 95 w and 64 GB in memory, with centos operating system.

2.4 Optimization

A set of tasks was performed in order to develop the tephra forecast in a reasonable time in the hardware. Three different configurations on the meteorological domain were used and presented in Table 1.

Table 1. Domain strategies used for the WRF model

	Case 1		Case 2		Case 3	
Domain	1	2	1	2	1	2
East-west	100	151	100	144	80	79
South North	80	126	80	123	80	79
Cell size km	20	4	20	6.66	20	6.66

The FALL3D has the advantage for selecting the number of cores and the number of granulometry bins that are computed per core. Thus the machine has 16 cores and there are 19 bins in the granulometry. The following 25 configurations (see Table 2) for the FALL3D model were used.

Table 2. Groups and cores used in FALL3D parallel execution.

Case	Cores	Groups	Case	Cores	Groups	Case	Cores	Groups
1	11	11	10	9	9	19	12	12
2	10	10	11	12	6	20	12	2
3	10	5	12	15	5	21	14	14
4	10	2	13	12	3	22	15	15
5	9	3	14	6	3	23	13	13
6	8	2	15	12	4	24	16	8
7	8	4	16	14	7	25	16	2

3 Results

Table 3 shows the different computational time for the selected configuration in the WRF model; the third strategy has the lowest computational time.

Table 3. Computational time for different configuration in WRF

Strategy	Computational time 72-h modeling
1	3 h 18 min
2	1 h 52 min
3	1 h 15 min

The FALL3D calculation time depends on the mesh required. In this case we have a domain of 100×100 cells of 4 km, with 27 vertical layers of 500 m height each. The time it takes depends on the number of processors used and the group numbers for the size distribution calculations as shown in Fig. 2; it can be seen that using 11 cores and 11 groups provides the lowest time spend for tephra dispersion.

The final script uses batch runs of 11 cores for the ash dispersion, the total time in operational mode is 11 h 42 min on average.

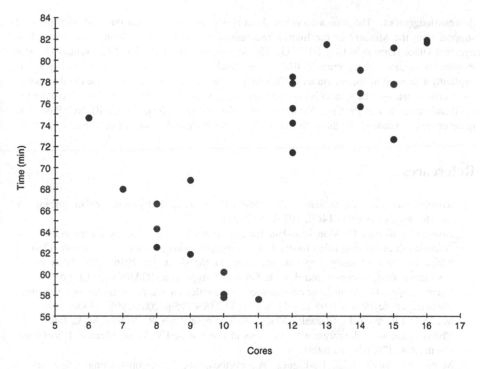

Fig. 2. Time used for computing each scenario

4 Conclusions

An ash forecast system was developed using Popocatépetl volcano as a case study. The models (meteorological and dispersion) and parameters used to perform the ash dispersion were presented. Because currently it is not possible to forecast a volcanic eruption for supporting the decision making process, a set of possible eruption cases were selected from previous studies and modeled in a daily basis. The set of eruptions consist of a combination of three column heights at 36 different moments with every eruption activity lasting one hour.

The use of HPC is a powerful tool for doing risk scenario. In this case for the ash dispersion forecast, operating a workstation with multiple cores was useful for obtaining products in a reasonable time. Using more cores did not improve the performance, while using smaller number of cores per scenario was a way to take advantage of the available processors and performed two scenarios at the same time.

Future work can be done in order to improve the performance of the system by using current technologies such as Intel latest processors version v3 or other architectures. The visualization process also can be parallelized in order to reduce operational time.

Acknowledgement. The forecast system described above was carried out with the financial support from the Ministry of the Interior (Secretaría de Gobernación) through the Risk Management Office (Dirección General de Gestión de Riesgos) under the Fund for Natural Disaster Prevention (FOPREDEN) grant E.III.02. The final system was designed following needs explicitly expressed by the personnel of CENAPRED in order to have a tool focused in their needs for decision-making. The system is currently operated by the CENAPRED and issued to warn the Civil Defense as well as the Civil Aviation (Dirección General de Aviación Civil). NCEP NOAA, meteorological datasets. We thank to Luisa Molina for the proofreading of this text.

References

1. Rivera Tapia, J.A., Yáñez Santos, A., Cedillo Ramírez, L.: Emisión de ceniza volcánica y sus efectos. Ecosistemas **14**(3), 107–115 (2005)
2. Jimenez-Escalona, J.C., Monsivais-Huertero, A., Avila-Razo, J.E.: Maps risk generations for volcanic ash monitoring using modis data and its application in risk maps for aviation hazard mitigation: case of study Popocatepetl Volcano (Mexico). In: 2016 IEEE International Conference on Geoscience and Remote Sensing Symposium (IGARSS), IEEE (2016)
3. Linares-Lopez, C.: Análisis granulométricos y modales en cenizas emitidas por el Volcán Popocatépetl de 1994 a 1998 (2001). http://132.248.9.195/pd2001/299833/Index.html
4. Martin-Del Pozzo, A.L., Gonzalez-Moran, T., Espinasa-Perea, R., Butron, M.A., Reyes, M.: Characterization of the recent ash emissions at Popocatepetl Volcano, Mexico. J. Volcanol. Geoth. Res. **170**, 61–75 (2008)
5. Martin-Del Pozzo, A.L., Rodríguez, A., Portocarrero, J.: Reconstructing 800 years of historical eruptive activity at Popocatepetl Volcano, Mexico. Bull. Volcanol. **78**, 1–13 (2016)
6. Skamarock, W.C., et al.: A description of the advanced research WRF version 2 (No. NCAR/TN-468+ STR). National Center For Atmospheric Research Boulder Co Mesoscale and Microscale Meteorology Div. (2005)
7. Folch, A., Costa, A., Macedonio, G.: FALL3D: a computational model for transport and deposition of volcanic ash. Comput. Geosci. **35**, 1334–1342 (2009)
8. Brown, D., Brownrigg, R., Haley, M., Huang, W.: The NCAR Command Language (NCL) (version 6.0.0). UCAR/NCAR Computational and Information Systems Laboratory, Boulder, CO (2012). https://doi.org/10.5065/d6wd3xh5
9. NOAA National Centers for Environmental Prediction (NCEP): NOAA/NCEP Global Forecast System (GFS) Atmospheric Model (2011). https://www.emc.ncep.noaa.gov/index.php?branch=GFS
10. Thompson, G., Field, P.R., Rasmussen, R.M., Hall, W.D.: Explicit forecasts of winter precipitation using an improved bulk microphysics scheme. Part II: implementation of a new snow parameterization. Mon. Weather Rev. **136**, 5095–5115 (2008)
11. Mlawer, E.J., Taubman, S.J., Brown, P.D., Iacono, M.J., Clough, S.A.: Radiative transfer for inhomogeneous atmospheres: RRTM, a validated correlated-k model for the longwave. J. Geophys. Res.: Atmos. **102**, 16663–16682 (1997)
12. Chou, M.-D., Suarez, M.: An efficient thermal infrared radiation parameterization for use in general circulation models. NASA Tech. Memo. 104606, vol. 3, 84 p. (1994). (NASA Center for Aerospace Information, 800 Elkridge Landing Rd., Linthicum Heights, MD 21090-2934). http://www.worldcat.org/title/efficient-thermal-infrared-radiation-parameterization-for-use-in-general-circulation-models/oclc/919970577

13. Janić, Z.I.: Nonsingular implementation of the Mellor-Yamada level 2.5 scheme in the NCEP Meso model. US Department of Commerce, National Oceanic and Atmospheric Administration, National Weather Service, National Centers for Environmental Prediction (2001). https://repository.library.noaa.gov/view/noaa/11409
14. Ek, M., et al.: Implementation of Noah land surface model advances in the National Centers for Environmental Prediction operational mesoscale Eta model. J. Geophys. Res.: Atmos. **108** (2003)
15. Mellor, G.L., Yamada, T.: Development of a turbulence closure model for geophysical fluid problems. Rev. Geophys. **20**, 851–875 (1982)
16. Kain, J.S.: The Kain-Fritsch convective parameterization: an update. J. Appl. Meteorol. **43**, 170–181 (2004)
17. Skamarock, W.C., et al.: A description of the advanced research WRF version 2. National Center for Atmospheric Research Boulder Colorado Mesoscale and Microscale Meteorology Division (2005)
18. Costa, A., Macedonio, G., Folch, A.: A three-dimensional Eulerian model for transport and deposition of volcanic ashes. Earth Planet. Sci. Lett. **241**, 634–647 (2006)
19. Ganser, G.H.: A rational approach to drag prediction of spherical and nonspherical particles. Powder Technol. **77**, 143–152 (1993)
20. Granados, H.D., De la Cruz Reyna, S., Tilling, R.I.: The 1994–present eruption of popocatépetl volcano: background, current activity, and impacts. J. Volcanol. Geoth. Res. **1**(170), 1–4 (2008)
21. Quezada-Reyes, A., Lesage, P., Valdés-González, C., Perrier, L.: An analysis of the seismic activity of Popocatepetl volcano, Mexico, associated with the eruptive period of December 2002 to February 2003: looking for precursors. Geol. Soc. Am. Spec. Pap. **498**, 89–106 (2013)
22. Cross, J., Roberge, J., Jerram, D.: Constraining the degassing processes of Popocatépetl Volcano, Mexico: a vesicle size distribution and glass geochemistry study. J. Volcanol. Geoth. Res. **225**, 81–95 (2012)
23. Woodhouse, M., Hogg, A., Phillips, J., Sparks, R.: Interaction between volcanic plumes and wind during the 2010 Eyjafjallajökull eruption, Iceland. J. Geophys. Res.: Solid Earth **118**, 92–109 (2013)
24. Cornell, W., Carey, S., Sigurdsson, H.: Computer simulation of transport and deposition of the Campanian Y-5 ash. J. Volcanol. Geoth. Res. **17**, 89–109 (1983)

High Performance Open Source Lagrangian Oil Spill Model

Andrea Anguiano-García[1(✉)], Olmo Zavala-Romero[1,2],
Jorge Zavala-Hidalgo[1], Julio Antonio Lara-Hernández[1],
and Rosario Romero-Centeno[1]

[1] Centro de Ciencias de la Atmósfera,
Universidad Nacional Autónoma de México, Mexico City, Mexico
andrea_anguiano@ciencias.unam.mx,
{jzavala, rosario}@atmosfera.unam.mx,
julio-lara.hernandez@hdr.mq.edu.au
[2] Department of Radiation Oncology,
University of Miami Miller School of Medicine, Miami, FL, USA
oszl@med.miami.edu

Abstract. An oil spill particle dispersion model implemented in Julia, a high-performance programming language, and Matlab is described. The model is based on a Lagrangian particle tracking algorithm with a second-order Runge-Kutta scheme. It uses ocean currents from the Hybrid Coordinate Ocean Model (HYCOM) and winds from the Weather Research and Forecasting Model (WRF). The model can consider multiple oil components according to their density and different types of oil decay: evaporation, burning, gathering, and exponential degradation. Furthermore, it allows simultaneous modeling of oil spills at multiple locations. The computing performance of the model is tested in both languages using an analogous implementation. A case study in the Gulf of Mexico is described.

Keywords: Julia language · Lagrangian model · Oil spill model
HYCOM · WRF · Julia vs Matlab performance

1 Introduction

The dispersion of oil spills has been of interest for many years [1]. However, after the 2010 Deepwater Horizon accident in the Gulf of Mexico, there has been more research for understanding the processes that determine the fate of oil spills. These efforts include studying, modeling and predicting oil advection, dispersion, impact of using oil dispersants, biodegradation, evaporation, controlled burning, skimming, etc. [2–5]. Other modeled processes include the rise of a buoyant plume, the spill evolution in the oceanic surface boundary layer, and the effect of waves. Currently, most of numerical models studying oil spills are based on Lagrangian modules because these numerical schemes have less diffusivity and can be run off-line with less computational effort.

The simulation of an oil spill can be separated in two stages. First, the vertical evolution of the plume from the deep ocean into ocean layers of different depth,

© Springer Nature Switzerland AG 2019
M. Torres et al. (Eds.): ISUM 2018, CCIS 948, pp. 118–128, 2019.
https://doi.org/10.1007/978-3-030-10448-1_11

including the surface; and second, the horizontal evolution and decay of the plume once it is in a specific layer, which depends on oil properties, presence of bacteria, application of chemical dispersants, and weathering. In the mixed layer, waves and more energetic turbulent processes can also modify the oil decay [1, 6].

The current generation of oil spill models includes the Oil Spill Contingency and Response Model [7], the Spill Impact Model Application Package/Oil Modeling Application Package [8], and the General NOAA Operational Modeling Environment [9], among others. These models have important characteristics in common. For instance, all of them have a basic structure formulated on Lagrangian methods to represent the transport processes, and they use individual algorithms for the fate processes [1].

Spaulding [1] provides a review of the current state of the art of oil spill models. In his work, the author summarizes key points learned in the design of these models: (1) the lagrangian-particle-based strategy to represent the oil allows the model to account for the temporally and spatially variation of the oil, and this strategy is amenable to sensitivity testing of results; (2) the use of tools for post-processing and visualization is essential; (3) the model should undergo validation against spill events; (4) the model needs to consider its potential use to assess the impact of response options. At the same time, the dominant driver for the transport of particles is the ocean currents and using a larger number of particles will, in general, improve the accuracy of the models. This constant search for simulating large amounts of particles, demands high computational power and efficient algorithms. Finally, the main challenges in the state-of-the-art modules are to better represent complex processes, such as the marine snow and the rising plume, as well as to improve the speed of computational algorithms while making the model user friendly.

Julia is a high-level and high-performance dynamic programming language for numerical computing that provides a sophisticated compiler, distributed parallel exe-cution, numerical accuracy, and an extensive mathematical function library [10]. It is an open source project (https://julialang.org/) with over 500 contributors and is available under the MIT License. Julia features optional typing, multiple dispatch and good performance achieved using type inference and just-in-time (JIT) compilation, implemented using LLVM. Matlab is a commercial software that contains multiple tools for linear algebra, engineering, machine learning, plotting, etc. Matlab uses standard packages of linear algebra, and is well suited for matrix arrays and numerical computations.

High performance computing comprises not only parallel processing in clusters and GPUs, but also the development of efficient programming languages as well as the development of optimal sequential implementations of demanding algorithms. In this work, an open source Lagrangian oil spill model implemented in Julia and Matlab is described. The performance of the proposed model is analyzed through the outlined implementations.

2 Proposed Open Source Lagrangian Oil Spill Model

Software Architecture

The proposed lagrangian model was programmed in three different manners: the first code was developed in Julia; the second was implemented in Matlab using structures for storing data, and the third was also implemented in Matlab but following object oriented programming, using classes to store data.

The main stages followed by the model at each time step are:

- Read velocity fields (wind and ocean currents).
- Release particles according to the simulation setup (e.g. spill location and timing, number of particles, oil groups, oil decays).
- Interpolate velocities to the position and timing of each particle.
- Move particles (advection and turbulent-diffusion).
- Eliminate particles according to the specified oil decays (biodegradation, evaporation, burning, and gathering).

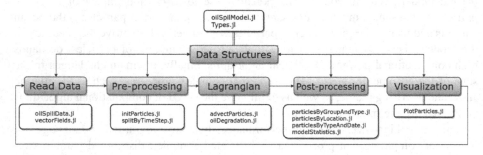

Fig. 1. Main components and associated files of the proposed oil spill model implemented in Julia.

The software architecture for all implementations follow these main steps. Figure 1 shows the modules of the Julia implementation together with the files associated with each module. A more detailed explanation of each module is available at the GitHub repository https://github.com/AndreaAnguiano/Oilspill_model-.

For both programming languages, Matlab and Julia, the same modules were created. Meticulous care was taken to make all implementations analogous. The main difference between the two Matlab implementations is the *Data Structures* module. In one case the information and status of particles is stored using structures and in the second case the information is stored in classes.

The scope of this work is to compare the performance of two programming languages, widely used in the scientific computing community, with the proposed oil spill model. The current implementations of the model run sequentially, but a parallel implementation would be valuable. In the ongoing model, the most expensive steps are reading the data and particle advection (interpolation and Runge-Kutta scheme). A straightforward parallel version will split the number of particles being advected by the number of processing units (PU), reducing the execution time of the model and enhancing the forecasted oil spill by using more particles in the simulation. Adjustments in the *Read Data* and *Pre-processing* modules are required to achieve the suggested parallelization scheme; the other modules can be reused. It should be mentioned that a shared memory model must be guaranteed to achieve speedups of a parallel version, if a GPU is used to parallelize the evolution of the particles, sending data to the GPU (vector fields of currents and winds) can become the bottleneck of the model.

Lagrangian Scheme

A 2nd order Runge-Kutta scheme in space and time (Fig. 2) is used to compute surface and subsurface 2D displacements of oil particles due to advection and turbulent-diffusion. In this study, advection of surface oil is a function of surface ocean currents and the wind multiplied by a constant (3.5%), deflected due to Coriolis force [11]. Advection of subsurface oil is only due to subsurface ocean currents. Wind and/or ocean velocities are interpolated to the location of each particle using bi-linear and tri-linear interpolation methods. To represent sub-grid dispersion unresolved by the hydrodynamic model, turbulent-diffusion is considered by adding random velocities v' (Eq. 1) during the calculation of particle displacements.

$$v' = VR \qquad (1)$$

In Eq. 1 v' is the turbulent-diffusion velocity, V is the interpolated velocity from ocean currents and wind, and R is a random number with uniform distribution from $-a$ to a, the dispersion coefficient. The value of a is defined by the user to control the degree of turbulent-diffusion [12]. Displacements of each particle are computed by multiplying the velocity of the particle (advection + turbulent-diffusion) times a time step dt defined by the user, using a 2nd order Runge Kutta scheme. For the study case in this manuscript, $dt = 3600$ s.

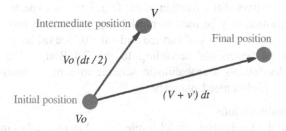

Fig. 2. 2nd order Runge-Kutta scheme. The circles represent the positions of an oil particle, *Vo* is the velocity interpolated to the initial position, *V* is the velocity interpolated to the intermediate position, *v'* is the turbulent-diffusion velocity, and *dt* is the time step.

Wind and Ocean Velocities

Previously stored wind and ocean velocities are required as inputs for the oil spill model. For the case study presented in this manuscript, winds come from simulations carried out with the Weather Research and Forecasting (WRF) model, which is run in the supercomputing center of the Center of Atmospheric Sciences at the UNAM. The ocean currents come from the year 2010 of a 20-year reanalysis of the Gulf of Mexico obtained using the HYbrid Coordinate Ocean Model (HYCOM). This reanalysis is available for download from the HYCOM webpage (https://hycom.org/dataserver/ gom-reanalysis). Additionally, wind data are spatially interpolated to the ocean model grid.

Simulation Time and Spill Locations
The simulation period is set by defining not only the initial and final day of the spill, but also the last day of the simulation because some oil remains in the ocean after the spill ends. Additionally, a probabilistic scheme for the temporal release of particles is considered to avoid rounding and therefore bias in the number of released particles. For the location of spills, several positions can be specified in terms of latitude and longitude. Particles will be randomly released around these locations, following a Gaussian distribution with a standard deviation equal to a user-defined radius in kilometers.

Oil Groups
Since a mixture of oil can be subdivided into different oil groups according to their density [13], the spill model was designed to consider as many groups as specified by the user. Each group is defined with a specific relative abundance and a specific exponential degradation rate. For instance, the first component may be assumed less dense and more abundant if a super light oil spill is simulated. Additionally, a higher exponential degradation rate could also be assigned to the first oil groups.

Oil Decay
Simulations of surface spills may include oil decay due to evaporation, burning, collection, and/or exponential degradation. Evaporation is the main natural process involved in the removal of oil from sea surface [14]. Burning and collection refers to human actions for mitigating the spill. For sub-surface simulations, only exponential degradation may be considered. The user sets the degree of exponential degradation by indicating the time in days that a fraction of oil (e.g. 95%) is expected to be degraded. This type of degradation may be used to model any degradation process following an exponential decay. The quantities of surface and sub-surface oil, as well as the amount of evaporated oil, are calculated according to the Oil Budget Calculator [2]. The removal of particles follows a probabilistic scheme to avoid rounding and therefore bias in the number of eliminated particles.

Performance Considerations
The architecture of the Lagrangian model implemented in Julia takes into consideration multiple performance tips described in the Julia language main website. The most important are: to avoid using global variables by modularizing the code in multiple functions; to reduce memory allocations by not using containers with abstract types and declaring types of each variable inside structures and functions; to pre-allocate arrays; to maximize the use of vectorized operations; and to access arrays in the proper order.

Case Study

The proposed model was used to simulate the 2010 Deepwater Horizon oil spill. The number of oil barrels spilled, the amount of oil that was evaporated, collected, and burned was obtained from the Oil Budget Calculator [2]. This simulation generates one particle for every two barrels of oil, it has a time step of one hour, and is configured to start on April 22nd and end on November 1st of 2010. It is configured to simulate 8 different types of oil at three depths (surface, 400 m and 1100 m), and the location of the spill is set at 28.73°N, 88.36°W. This simulation does not make any reinitialization of the particles positions from satellite data, as it has been proposed by Liu et al. [15]. Figure 3 shows the amount of oil at the surface integrated through time, with barrels of oil as units, in a logarithmic scale. This figure only shows the third type of oil that was simulated, with an exponential decay of 4.5 days.

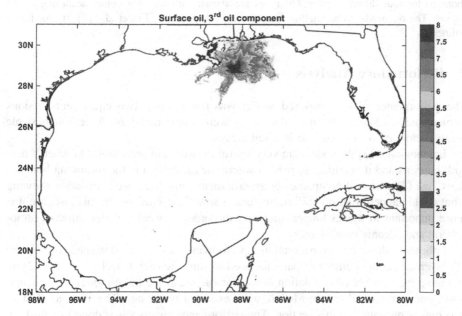

Fig. 3. Cumulative concentration of oil at the surface from a simulation of the 2010 Deepwater Horizon oil spill. The oil component displayed has an exponential decay of 4.5 days.

To assess the model performance, modeled trajectories were compared with the oil distribution mask from satellite images provided by Liu et al. [15]. The comparison shows a good agreement between the model simulation and satellite estimates. It is important to mention that the main forcing moving the oil is the ocean currents, using currents from other ocean models could produce different results. Figure 4 shows the oil spill distribution in four different dates; in the upper row, the oil masks at the surface obtained from the MODIS satellite are shown, and in the bottom row are the results from the model simulation. The different colors indicate the type of oil being simulated.

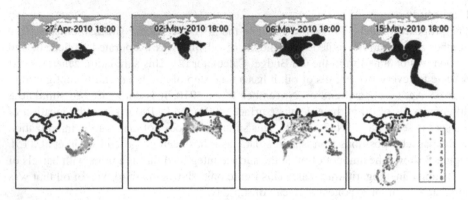

Fig. 4. Oil distribution comparison between satellite images (top) and the numerical simulation (bottom) for four different dates. Oil types are shown with different colors according to the legend. The oil masks from satellite images were adapted from Liu et al. [15]. (Color figure online)

3 Performance Analysis

The performance of the proposed model was tested using two equivalent versions implemented in Matlab. Both Matlab codes were programmed as efficient as possible using vectorized operations and indexed arrays.

Lagrangian oil spill models are very useful in two main scenarios: (1) when a new spill happens and it is critical to predict where the oil will go in the following hours or days, and (2) when oil companies or environmental agencies need scenarios showing what could happen if an oil spill occurs under specific conditions. In this last case it is more important to model longer times, on the order of weeks, under different atmospheric and oceanic conditions.

Following these two considerations, performance tests were designed as follows: (1) by changing the number of particles used to simulate each barrel of oil, and (2) by changing the number of simulation days. For each test, the three model implementations, one in Julia and two in Matlab, were executed two times. The average of these two runs is presented in this section. The performance analysis was done in a desktop computer with an Intel Core i7-6700 processor, 16 GB of DDR4 RAM, and a GeForce GTX 1080 GPU. Model parameters are summarized in Table 1.

Table 1. Model parameters considered for the performance tests.

Parameter	Value	Parameter	Value
Wind contribution	0.035	Depths	0, 100, 1000 m
Evaporation	On	Spill location	28.73° N, 88.36° W
Burn	On	Visualization	Off
Biodegradation	On	Save output	Off
Collection	On	Runge Kutta	2nd order
Number of oil components	8	Start date	04/22/2010

The performance comparison when the number of particles per barrel is modified is presented in Fig. 5. The execution time for all the implementations increases proportionally with the number of particles per barrel of oil. The total number of particles created for the first scenario (1 particle per barrel) is in the order of 5×10^5, while for the last scenario (10 particles per barrel) is in the order of 5×10^6. The Matlab implementation using classes was only tested up to 5 particles per barrel because of its long execution times (4.6 h for 5 particles) and because the amount of RAM was depleted.

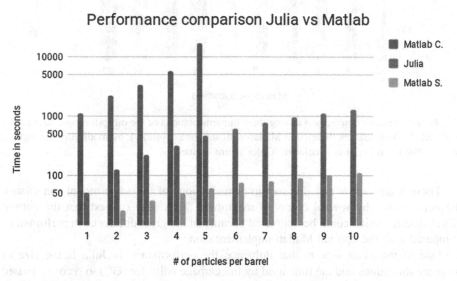

Fig. 5. Model performance comparison between three implementations: with Julia (red), Matlab using classes (blue) and Matlab using structures (yellow), by modifying the number of particles per barrel. (Color figure online)

The largest speedup obtained between the fastest Matlab implementation and Julia implementation is 11. This first test shows that different implementations of the same model can influence the performance more than the programing language used. A deeper analysis, using profiler tools of both languages, shows that the main difference between the performance of the two Matlab versions is the time needed for searching values inside arrays of data structures and searching inside arrays of objects. Searching inside structures is much faster than searching inside classes instances. In the case of the Julia implementation, the largest amount of time is used for the interpolation of currents and winds in the Runge Kutta method. To perform 2D interpolations the *interpolations* package is used.

For the second performance test, the number of days simulated varies from 2 to 20. The time for all implementations is shown in Fig. 6. For this test, the largest speedup obtained between Matlab (using data structures) and Julia is 3.5.

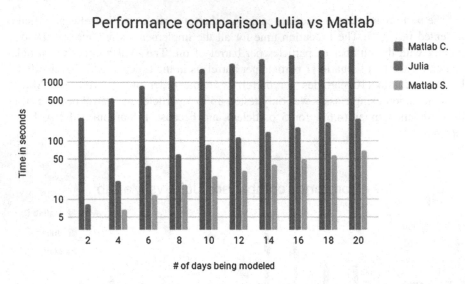

Fig. 6. Performance comparison among three implementations of the oil spill model: using Julia (red), Matlab with classes (blue), and Matlab with structures (yellow), by modifying the number of days that the oil spill is simulated. (Color figure online)

These results show that different implementations of the same model can change the performance by several orders of magnitude. They also suggest that the current Julia implementation could be optimized because of the great difference in performance compared with the optimal Matlab implementation.

One of the main aspects that influence the performance in Julia is the size of memory allocations and the time used by the garbage collector (GC) to recover unused objects. Julia provides information about these two important factors with the *@time* macro for the execution of any program, in this case the Lagrangian oil spill model. The amount of memory allocated by a program in Julia can vary greatly, depending on the implementation of the software, as described in the *performance tips* section of the documentation.

Table 2 shows the amount of memory that was allocated (in gigabytes) and the percentage of time used by the GC. These results were obtained when executing the implementation of the Lagrangian model in Julia for the first test, varying the amount of particles used to simulate each barrel of oil.

Table 2. Memory allocation and percentage of time used by the garbage collector (GC).

Particles per barrel	1	2	3	4	5	6	7	8	9	10
Percentage of GC time	49%	59%	66%	69%	73%	74%	77%	79%	79%	80%
Memory allocation (GB)	32.1	54.6	80.6	102	124	146	168	189	211	234

The large amount of memory allocations happens for two main reasons: the large amount of data read in every time step, with information of the currents and winds, and the way Julia allocates memory when copying data from one array to another variable.

4 Conclusions and Future Work

In this work, a new open source oil spill model implemented in Julia is described. The model is based on a Lagrangian algorithm for tracking particles and can consider multiple oil components and different processes of oil decay. It is initialized using oceanic currents from the HYCOM model and wind data from the WRF model, and it allows the simultaneous simulation of spills in various locations. The proposed implementation is compared with two implementations using the Matlab programming language, one based on classes and the other on structures. All the implementations are free to use and are available for download at https://github.com/AndreaAnguiano/Oilspill_model- (Julia version), https://github.com/AndreaAnguiano/OilSpill_vStruct (Matlab using structures), and https://github.com/olmozavala/oilspill (Matlab using classes).

The main conclusion of this study is that Julia, a young programming language that is being updated very fast, is not yet as mature as Matlab. In multiple occasions there is conflict between packages and the system can stay in an unstable condition. Julia contains many packages to solve the same problem, which makes it hard to decide which one is the best option. However, Julia is free, its community is growing rapidly, faster and better libraries are being created as well as improved tools for debugging and profiling, which makes it one of the best programming languages for scientific computing nowadays.

Another result that is relevant is the importance of efficient implementations, no matter the programming language been used. Comparing the best times of both programing languages, our results show that Matlab performs 10 times faster than Julia with the proposed single core implementations. Yet comparing between the two analogous Matlab implementations, their difference in performance is very large, the code that uses structures is up to 250 times faster than the one that uses classes, while Julia's performance is between these two.

In future work we plan to test the use of multiple cores in a single processor, as well as to execute the models in parallel using multiple processors in a cluster. Additionally, it is important to reduce the size of allocated memory by Julia, which requires a deeper knowledge of this programming language.

Acknowledgments. This work was funded by the CONACYT-SENER-Hidrocarburos grant 201441. This is a contribution of the Gulf of Mexico Research Consortium (CIGoM).

References

1. Spaulding, M.L.: State of the art review and future directions in oil spill modeling. Mar. Pollut. Bull. **115**, 7–19 (2017)
2. OBCS: Oil Budget Calculator: Deepwater Horizon. Books LLC (2012)

3. Liu, Z., Liu, J., Zhu, Q., Wu, W.: The weathering of oil after the Deepwater Horizon Oil spill: insights from the chemical composition of the oil from the sea surface, salt marshes and sediments. Environ. Res. Lett. **7**, 035302 (2012)
4. Beyer, J., Trannum, H.C., Bakke, T., Hodson, P.V., Collier, T.K.: Environmental effects of the Deepwater Horizon oil spill: a review. Mar. Pollut. Bull. **110**, 28–51 (2016)
5. Özgökmen, T., et al.: Over what area did the oil and gas spread during the 2010 Deepwater Horizon Oil spill? Oceanography **29**, 96–107 (2016)
6. Guo, W., Wang, Y.: A numerical oil spill model based on a hybrid method. Mar. Pollut. Bull. **58**, 726–734 (2009)
7. Reed, M., Ekrol, N., Rye, H., Turner, L.: Oil Spill Contingency and Response (OSCAR) analysis in support of environmental impact assessment offshore Namibia. Spill Sci. Technol. Bull. **5**, 29–38 (1999)
8. Spaulding, M., Kolluru, V., Anderson, E., Howlett, E.: Application of three-dimensional oil spill model (WOSM/OILMAP) to Hindcast the Braer spill. Spill Sci. Technol. Bull. **1**, 23–35 (1994)
9. Beegle-Krause, J.: General NOAA oil modeling environment (Gnome): a new spill trajectory model. In: International Oil Spill Conference Proceedings, vol. 2001, pp. 865–871 (2001)
10. Bezanson, J., Edelman, A., Karpinski, S., Shah, V.B.: Julia: a fresh approach to numerical computing. SIAM Rev. **59**, 65–98 (2017)
11. Samuels, W.B., Huang, N.E., Amstutz, D.E.: An oil spill trajectory analysis model with a variable wind deflection angle. Ocean Eng. **9**, 347–360 (1982)
12. Döös, K., Rupolo, V., Brodeau, L.: Dispersion of surface drifters and model-simulated trajectories. Ocean Model. **39**, 301–310 (2011)
13. Reddy, C.M., et al.: Composition and fate of gas and oil released to the water column during the Deepwater Horizon oil spill. Proc. Natl. Acad. Sci. **109**, 20229–20234 (2011)
14. Berry, A., Dabrowski, T., Lyons, K.: The oil spill model OILTRANS and its application to the Celtic Sea. Mar. Pollut. Bull. **64**, 2489–2501 (2012)
15. Liu, Y., Weisberg, R.H., Hu, C., Zheng, L.: Trajectory forecast as a rapid response to the Deepwater Horizon Oil spill. In: Geophysical Monograph Series, pp. 153–165. American Geophysical Union, Washington, D. C. (2011)

Fast Random Cactus Graph Generation

Joel Antonio Trejo-Sánchez[1(✉)], Andrés Vela-Navarro[2],
Alejandro Flores-Lamas[3], José Luis López-Martínez[4],
Carlos Bermejo-Sabbagh[2], Nora Leticia Cuevas-Cuevas[2],
and Homero Toral-Cruz[5]

[1] CONACyT-Centro de Investigación en Matemáticas,
Sierra Papacal, Yucatán, Mexico
joel.trejo@cimat.mx
[2] Tecnológico Nacional de México-I.T. Mérida, Periférico Poniente Mérida,
Mérida, Mexico
[3] Centro de Investigación Científica y de Educación Superior de Ensenada,
Baja California, México
[4] Universidad Autónoma de Yucatán, Tizimín, Yucatán, Mexico
[5] Universidad de Quintana Roo, Chetumal, Quintana Roo, Mexico

Abstract. In this article, we propose a fast algorithm for generating a cactus graph. Cacti has important applications in diverse areas such as biotechnology, telecommunication systems, sensor networks, among others. Thus, generating good random cacti graphs it is important for simulation of the diverse algorithms and protocols. In this paper, we present an efficient parallel algorithm to generate random cactus. To the best of our knowledge, this algorithm is the first parallel algorithm to generate random cacti graphs.

Keywords: Parallel algorithms · Graph generation · Cacti graphs

1 Introduction

Generation of random graphs is crucial for many applications including database applications, biotechnology, social networks analysis, and others. The most common model for the generation of random graphs is the Erdös-Rényi model. This model initially distributes randomly a set of n disconnected nodes. Then the algorithm iteratively connects pair of nodes until the graph is connected. There exists several class of graphs very useful for the research community. An interesting class of graph is the cactus graph.

A graph $K = (V_K, E_K)$ is a cactus (plural: cacti) if every edge of E_K belongs to at most one cycle (any pair of cycles has at most one vertex in common). These graphs have important applications in telecommunication networks, location problems, practical computer networks, and in biotechnology. Since the 1980s, cacti attracted the attention of the research community when it was found out that some NP-hard computational problems for arbitrary topologies admit polynomial time solutions in cacti. For instance, in [4–6] authors present algorithms in cacti. Thus, generating cacti graphs shall be of interest to the research community working in these problems. Figure 1 shows an example of a cactus graph.

© Springer Nature Switzerland AG 2019
M. Torres et al. (Eds.): ISUM 2018, CCIS 948, pp. 129–136, 2019.
https://doi.org/10.1007/978-3-030-10448-1_12

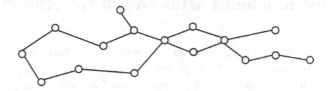

Fig. 1. A cactus graph with two cycles

In this paper, we present an algorithm for the generation of random cacti graphs. Our algorithm generates a random graph considering the Erdös-Rényi model. First, we describe the sequential version of the algorithm. This algorithm is implemented in R programming language using the igraph package. We show experimentally that, as the number of nodes increases, the execution time of our algorithm grows significantly. Later, we provide a parallelization of the sequential version of our algorithm. We show that using the same number of nodes, the parallel version of our algorithm decreases the execution time in proportion as the number of cores using for its execution.

The paper is organized as follows. Section 2 presents a review of related work on graph generation. Section 3 describes the proposed sequential algorithm. Section 4 proposed the parallelization of our sequential method. Section 5 considers the experimental evaluation of our algorithms. Finally, Sect. 6 presents the conclusions and formulates the main lines for future work.

2   Related Work

There exist several models to generate random graphs. We describe some of the more representative models; the Erdös-Rényi and the Barabási and Albert model.

Erdös-Rényi [2] receives as input an integer n that represents the set of vertices, and a set of edges distributed with certain probability; i.e. two vertices are connected with a probability p. Figure 2 presents an example of n vertices randomly distributed and there exists a connection between any pair of vertices x, y with probability p.

Barabási-Albert [3] considers the self-organizing property of complex networks to generate a random graph. They prove that in such networks the probability that any pair of vertices are connected decreases exponentially as the number of vertices in the

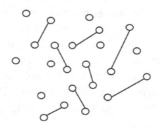

Fig. 2. Vertices randomly distributed, connections performed with probability p

network increases. The Barbási-Albert proposes to construct a graph considering a subset of vertices with high degree, and one subset of vertices with low degree. For a new vertex, it has greater probability to be connected in high degree vertices that in low degree vertices. Figure 3 shows an example random Barbási-Albert graph.

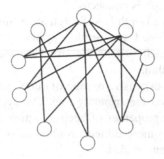

Fig. 3. Vertices randomly distributed with Barbasi-Albert model

Although there exist some generators of random trees, and other class of graphs, to our knowledge there is no random cactus generator. Now, we present an algorithm to generate random cactus. First we present the idea behind the algorithm, later we propose a parallization method to improve the execution time of our algorithm.

3 Proposed Algorithm

Now, we describe our sequential algorithm for generation of cactus graph. Our algorithm is very simple, it receives as input an integer representing the number of vertices of the cactus and the probability p. Pseudocode 1 presents the general idea of our algorithm SEQRANDOMCACTUS(n, p).

SEQRANDOMCACTUS(n, p)·

Input: Integer n, probability p

Output: Cactus graph K

1· G← ERDOSRENYI(n, p)
2· T← DFS(G)
3· K ← CREATECYLES(T)
4· Return K

Pseudocode 1. Algorithm to compute a random cactus graph.

Now, we describe deeply our algorithm. The first step of our algorithm computes a random Renyi random graph with n vertices and a probability p of connect vertices u and v for any vertices u, v in G. In this step, we must ensure that the graph is connected; i.e. that the there exists a path between any pair of vertices u and v. Any traverse algorithm like the breadth first search (BFS) or depth first search (DFS) [1] can be used to compute if the graph is connected.

The second step performs a Depth First Search algorithm [1]. We use the depth first search over the graph G obtained as a result a spanning tree T. Within the DFS we obtain the depth index of each vertex. We use later such indexes to perform the following steps of the algorithm.

The third step is the most expensive routine of our algorithm. This routine creates a variable number of cycles over the spanning tree. The cycles must guarantee that the resulting graph preserves the properties of been a cacti (every edge belong at most at one cycle). Since, this is the more difficult routine of our algorithm, Pseudocode 2 provides the algorithm to create cycles.

CREATECYCLES(T)·

Input: Tree T with tries = 0

Output: Cactus graph K

1. While (tries < threshold)
2.   (x,y) ← RandomVertices
3.   if (INCONFLIC(x,y))
4.   tries ← tries + 1
5.   return to step 2
6.   else
7.   createEdge(x, y)
8.   K ← T ∪(x,y)
9. return K

Pseudocode 2. Algorithm to compute a random cactus graph.

The CREATECYCLES routine proceed as follows. The algorithm selects a pair of random vertices x and y. Then, the algorithm verifies that after create the edge (x, y) in T, the new graph $K \leftarrow T \cup (x, y)$ is a cactus; i.e. that after connecting x and y, there is no edge belonging to two or more cycles. The function INCONFLIC(x,y) performs a traversal path from x to y and determines if there exist an edge (a, b) that belongs to a cycle; in such a case, the edge (x, y) is in conflict, because after connecting the edge, (a, b), will belong to two cycles. Figure 4 shows that there is no conflict after connecting random vertices 5 and 8. Figure 5 shows two cases when attempting to connect vertices. The first case, encounter a conflict for edge (7, 8); the second case has no conflict after connecting edge (1, 2).

The time complexity of our algorithm is $O(N^2)$. The step one (Erdos Renyi) takes $O(N)$, step two (DFS) takes $O(N+M)$, where M is the number of edges; step four, **CREATECYCLES,** takes $O(N^2)$ since the tries required to create the cycles. Thus, the time complexity is $O(N^2)$.

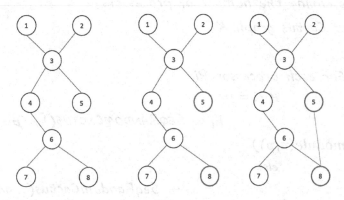

Fig. 4. Connecting edge (5, 8) after validating there is no conflict between those edges.

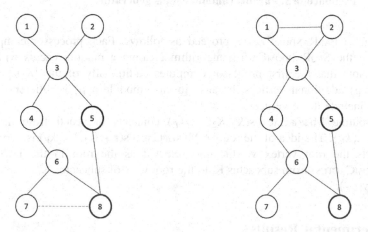

Fig. 5. The case on the left shows that there exists conflict if we connect edge (7, 8), because the edge (6, 8) belongs to a cycle in the path 7-6-8.

4 Parallel Algorithm for the Cactus Graph Generation

Now, we describe the parallel algorithm to generate a cactus graph. The pseudocode 3 describe our algorithm PARRANDOMCACTUS.

ParRandomCactus(n, p)·

Input: Integer n representing the number of nodes· Integer p representing the number of processors·

Output: Cactus graph K

1. *For each processor Pi*
2. *if (i = 0)*
3. $K_i \leftarrow SeqRandomCactus(\lceil n/p \rceil + module(n, p))$
4. *else*
5. $K_i \leftarrow SeqRandomCactus(\lceil n/p \rceil)$
6. $K \leftarrow MergeCactus(K_1, K_2, ..., k_P)$
7. *Return K*

Pseudocode 3. Parallel random cactus generator.

Algorithm PARRANDOMCACTUS proceed as follows. Each processor computes an instance of the SEQRANDOMCACTUS algorithm creating a random cactus with $\lceil n/p \rceil$ vertices. Note that the first processor computes additionally of the $\lceil n/p \rceil$ vertices, $module(n, p)$ additional vertices, because in case $module(n, p)$ is different of 0, no processor include those vertices.

The routine MERGECACTUS($K_1, K_2, ..., k_P$) connects the cacti from the subset $\{K_1, K_2, ..., k_P\}$. The idea of the routine MERGECACTUS($K_1, K_2, ..., k_P$) is very simple. It connects the root vertex v_i (the one selected as the root in the DFS of the SEQRANDOMCACTUS) from subcactus K_i to the root v_{i+1} of subcactus K_{i+1} creating the edge (v_i, v_{i+1}).

5 Experimental Results

We perform the experiments using a PC with Ubuntu 17.10 Operating System, with an AMD A8-6410 processor with four cores, with 8 GB of RAM. Our code is implemented using multi-core processing with multi-core R programming language (a similar manner to OpenMP in C). We test our algorithm running twelve experiments sequential and parallel. Table 1 (respectively Tables 2 and 3) presents the results of performing four cacti graph with 20 vertices (respectively 50 and 100) each one. Notice that the parallel version outperforms the cacti generation over the sequential version.

Table 1. Cacti generation with 20 vertices

Number of vertices	Sequential	Parallel
20	6 s	2 s
20	6 s	2 s
20	6 s	2 s
20	5 s	1.5 s

Table 2. Cacti generation with 50 vertices

Number of vertices	Sequential	Parallel
50	20 s	3 s
50	20 s	3 s
50	17 s	3 s
50	18 s	3 s

Table 3. Cacti generation with 100 vertices

Number of vertices	Sequential	Parallel
100	68 s	10 s
100	73 s	8.5 s
100	67 s	8.5 s
100	71 s	8.5 s

6 Concluding Remarks

In this paper, we present a fast algorithm to generate random cactus graph. Cacti graphs are very useful since many combinatorial NP-hard problems, admit polynomial solution under this topology. To our knowledge no previous random cactus graph generation exists.

We implement our algorithm using a DFS to generate a MST and connecting arbitrary edges to create cycles. The sequential version of our algorithm is time consuming, but we show experimentally that the parallel multi-core version of our algorithm outperforms the execution time of the sequential version.

As future work we propose studying other approaches to parallelize our algorithm, like MPI and GPU programming. Additionally, another line of work consists in defining a cleverer approach to the sequential version, to reduce the execution time of such version.

References

1. Thomas, H.: Introduction to Algorithms. MIT Press, Cambridge (2009)
2. Erdös, P., Rényi, A.: On random graphs I. Publicationes Mathematicae **6**, 290–297 (1959)
3. Barabási, A.L., Albert, R.: Emergence of scaling in random networks. Science **286**(5439), 509–512 (1999)
4. Trejo-Sánchez, J.A., Fernández-Zepeda, J.A.: A self-stabilizing algorithm for the maximal 2-packing in a cactus graph. In: 2012 IEEE 26th International Parallel and Distributed Processing Symposium Workshops & PhD Forum (IPDPSW), pp. 863–871. IEEE, May 2012
5. Trejo-Sánchez, J.A., Fernández-Zepeda, J.A.: Distributed algorithm for the maximal 2-packing in geometric outerplanar graphs. J. Parallel Distrib. Comput. **74**(3), 2193–2202 (2014)
6. Flores-Lamas, A., Fernández-Zepeda, J.A., Trejo-Sánchez, J.A.: Algorithm to find a maximum 2-packing set in a cactus. Theor. Comput. Sci. **725**, 31–51 (2018)

Theoretical Calculation of Photoluminescence Spectrum Using DFT for Double-Wall Carbon Nanotubes

A. P. Rodríguez Victoria[1(✉)], Javier Martínez Juárez[1],
J. A. David Hernández de la Luz[1], Néstor David Espinosa-Torres[2],
and M. J. Robles-Águila[1]

[1] Centro de investigaciones en Dispositivos Semiconductores (CIDS) del
ICUAP, Benemérita Universidad Autónoma de Puebla (BUAP),
Col. Jardines de San Manuel, Av. San Claudio y 14 Sur Cd. Universitaria,
Edificios IC5 y IC6, 72570 Puebla, Puebla, Mexico
angelj3236p@hotmail.com, angelj3236@gmail.com
[2] Instituto de Energías Renovables (IER-UNAM), Xochicalco, Azteca,
62588 Temixco, Morelos, Mexico

Abstract. Using DFT theory, we calculated theoretically photoluminescence (PL) spectra of double-walled carbon nanotubes (DWCNTs). Using the super-computer (LNS) tool, the photoluminescence spectra for eight double-walled nanotubes were calculated with the Gaussian09 software; the DWCNTs built are of the armchair/armchair type, (3,3)/(2,2), (6,6)/(3,3), (8,8)/(4,4), (10,10)/(5,5), (12,12)/(6,6), (14,14)/(7,7), (16,16)/(8,8) and (18,18)/(9,9). The calculations were obtained taking into account different DWCNT lengths ranging from 4.9 Å to 23.4 Å when changing the chirality (n, m) of the double-walled carbon nanotubes, as well as we considered the increase in their inter-radial distance ranging from $0.18 \leq d_R \leq 0.62$ nm. The objective of this work focuses on investigating the DWCNTs PL considering different atomic arrangements. The calculation was performed at a DFT level in which we used the Generalized Gradient Approximation (GGA) to establish the molecular geometries and the fundamental state energies. To obtain the results of the PL spectra, the DWCNTs were optimized in their ground state, with the hybrid function CAM-B3LYP, which is a mixed functional exchange and correlation and the base set that was used is the 6–31 G.

Keywords: Photoluminescence · DWCNT · Spectrum · DFT
Radial distance

1 Introduction

The double-walled carbon nanotubes (DWCNTs) have attracted considerable attention due to their mechanical, optical and electrical properties [1, 2]. The DWCNTs are studied due to the recognition of their optical properties which may be superior to those of the single wall carbon nanotubes (SWCNTs) and multiple wall carbon nanotubes (MWCNTs). Nowadays, there are controversial discussions about the ability to emit

© Springer Nature Switzerland AG 2019
M. Torres et al. (Eds.): ISUM 2018, CCIS 948, pp. 137–146, 2019.
https://doi.org/10.1007/978-3-030-10448-1_13

photoluminescence (PL) signal from the DWCNTs, in this context, it is found in the scientific literature works about this topic, such is the case of the Okazaki et al. one which reports that a decrease between the inter-walls distances of the two concentric SWCNTs forming the DWCNT, improves the interaction between the inner and outer SWCNTs, resulting in an significant reduction of the DWCNTs PL [3]. In addition, Koyama et al., found that the relative intensity of the steady-state PL from the inner walls in DWCNTs is ∼700 times weaker than that of SWCNTs [4].

On the other hand, other authors such as Kishi et al. reported that the PL is mainly emitted from inner-walls in most of the DWNTs (∼90%), [5] and Iakoubovskii et al. demonstrated that the DWCNTs exhibit strong PL in their experiments [6]. Recently, Muramatsu et al. observed bright PL from the inner SWCNTs of synthesized DWCNTs using a theory about the peapod-driven DWCNTs [7].

Experimentally there are several separation techniques in order to obtain the isolated DWCNTs, for example, such one which uses ultra-centrifugation density gradient (DGU) [8], another one uses catalytic chemical vapor deposition (CCVD) of CH_4 on a solid solution Mg1 -XCoxO that contains Mo oxide [9].

With the aforementioned motivations, we aim our work to obtain results which will contribute to elucidate the controversies about the origin of the DWCNTs PL considered as an unusual nano-material, supporting our results with experimental results reported in previous references.

To obtain theoretical photoluminescence spectra, we designed eight DWCNTs, in which we vary their chirality indices, diameter and axial length. We label each structure according to the DWCNTs own chirality, that is, the smallest structure is (3,3)/(2,2), thus labeling them consecutively (6,6)/(3,3), (8, 8)/(4,4), (10,10)/(5,5), (12,12)/(6,6), (14,14)/(7,7), (16,16)/(8,8) and (18,18)/(9,9); the first pair of chiral indices corresponds to the external nanotube (outer) and the second one to the internal nanotube (inner). The two concentric SWCNTs are of the armchair type.

The diameters theoretically obtained for the outer nanotube lie in ∼0.6 nm ≤ d_{ext} ≤ 2.5 nm and for the inner nanotube in ∼0.3 nm ≤ d_{int} ≤ 1.3 nm, and the value for the inter-walls distances lies in ∼0.18 nm ≤ dint ≤ 0.62 nm. Figure 1 shows the DWCNTs in which the parity of the chirality indices of the inner nanotube is both even and odd. We perform this classification for a better comfort and simplicity in the analysis of results.

The computational calculations are performed by using DFT theory, where the one-to-one relationship between the electronic density $\rho(\vec{r})$ and its associated wave function $\Psi(\vec{r}_1, \vec{r}_2, \vec{r}_3, \ldots \vec{r}_n)$ has been demonstrated [10].

From the numerical point of view the manipulation of a poly-electronic wave function is a complex matter, because the wave function of the N electrons is a function of 3 N variables, however the density $\rho(\vec{r})$ is easier to handle since it is a function of only three variables, regardless of the number of electrons in the system.

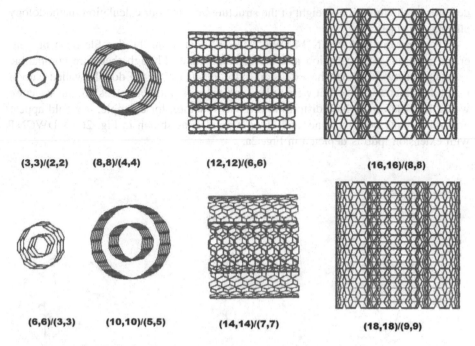

(3,3)/(2,2)   (8,8)/(4,4)   (12,12)/(6,6)   (16,16)/(8,8)

(6,6)/(3,3)   (10,10)/(5,5)   (14,14)/(7,7)   (18,18)/(9,9)

Fig. 1. The DWCNTs with even and odd parity of the chiral indices of the inner nanotube.

2 Computational Details

The DWCNTs were designed using Nanotube Modeler software, which is a program to generate XYZ position coordinates for the atoms forming the carbon nanotubes structure and other types of Nano-structures [11].

The spatial coordinates of the atoms that make up the DWCNTs are created using purely geometric criteria; energy calculations are not performed in this step; this facilitates the design work of our structures; the generated geometries can be seen using a viewer program, in our case we use the SPARTAN'14 program to do which accepts the extension of the file (.xyz) that is generated in Nanotube Modeler program previously.

Once we have visualized the DWCNT by using SPARTAN'14 the next stage consists in exporting the generated structure to Gaussian 09 program, which is the software where the computational calculations were made with the help of Supercompute LNS (National Laboratory of the Southeast, México); The mean reasons why we use SPARTAN'14, is due to the compatibility of extensions, because Gaussian 09 does not accept the extensions .xyz generated from Nanotube Modeler even though it has a visualizer. The basic unit of execution is a processing core. Each standard calculation node has 24 cores (2 sockets Intel Xeon E5−2680 v3 at 2.5 Ghz with 12 cores per socket) and 128 GB of shared RAM. For the calculation of the double-walled nanotubes, 3 nodes are used, that is, 72 cores, 120 to 100 GB of RAM were used for each calculation. The processing time for each calculation is between 80 h and 10 h depends on the molecular weight of the structure, making our calculation methodology efficient and fast.

To export the SPARTAN'14 DWCNT file to Gaussian 09, this file must be generated with an .pdb extension and the reason is that although there are compatible extensions between them, the extension .pdb does not alter the double-walled carbon nanotube structure, since if it were to be exported with another extension, the structure would have defects, which distort the original structure, for example, it would appear bonds that unite both the inner and outer nanotubes as shown in Fig. 2b. A DWCNT with extension .pdb is depicted in Fig. 2a.

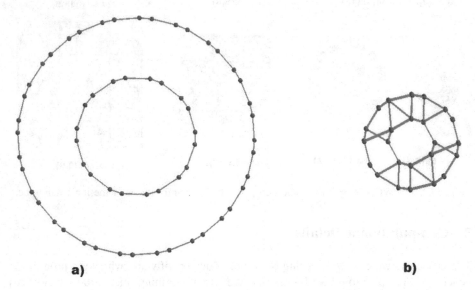

a)   b)

Fig. 2. (a) A DWCNT with extension .pdb and (b) A DWCNT with another type of extension is distorted.

The Density Functional Theory better known as DFT is used in this work, this theory calculates the energy of the atoms representing their kinetic energy as a functional of their electronic density, and combines the result with the classic expressions of the interactions core-electron and electron-electron [12].

Our Generalized Gradient Approximation (GGA) calculations are semilocal approximations because they consider not only the value of the density at each point but also the value of its gradients.

The first step to obtain the photoluminescence (PL) spectra, consists in the relaxation of the structures, which was carried out with DFTB (Density Functional Tight Binding) method which is based on a tight-binding model (TB). They work on the principle of treating the electronic wave functions. The elements of the Hamiltonian matrix are approximated by analytical functions (it is not necessary to calculate integrals), with this model the structures were optimized.

To generate the UV/VIS spectra, the DWNTCs were optimized in their ground state, with the hybrid function CAM-B3LYP [13] which is a mixed functional exchange and correlation that has the qualities of the hybrid B3LYP functional and the load transfer correction of excited states and the base set that was used is 6–31 G [10, 14, 15].

The next step consisted of the TD-SCF calculation with the same hybrid function and base set, CAM-B3LYP-6-31G [13], the calculation includes the singlet states and was performed for two excited states.

3 Discussion and Results

Our analysis of the photoluminescence spectra for the eight double-walled carbon nanotubes will be classified in two parts, that is, we first analyze the inner nanotubes that have an even chirality, namely (3,3)/(2,2), (8,8)/(4,4), (12,12)/(6,6) and (16,16)/(8,8) hereupon we analyze the second set of structures with odd chiral indices inner nanotubes (6,6)/(3,3), (10,10)/(5,5), (14,14)/(7,7) and (18,18)/(9,9), for reasons of abbreviation of nomenclature we take the first chiral index of the inner SWCNT and we rename the structures as DWCNT2, DWCNT4, DWCNT6, DWCNT8, the same consideration was done for the odd chiral index structures.

Table 1 shows theoretically obtained data. We tabulate the length of the DWCNTs, as well as their inter-walls radial distance, the internal and external diameters of the tubes, the energy band gap Eg and the maximum emission peak energy.

Table 1. Data of the DWCNTs with inner nanotube even chirality indices.

Structure	No. of atoms	(n,n)/(m.m)	Length (Å)	D_{ext} (Å)	D_{int} (Å)	Inter-walls distance (Å)	Energy gap (eV)	Max. peak (eV)
DWNTC2	69	(3,3)/(2,2)	4.923	6.785	3.14	1.8225	2.38	0.453
DWNTC4	239	(8,8)/(4,4)	11.098	10.856	5.428	2.714	1.747	0.382
DWNTC6	539	(12,12)/(6,6)	17.229	16.283	8.142	4.0705	1.545	0.821
DWNTC8	863	(16,16)/(8,8)	20.933	21.711	10.856	5.4275	1.057	0.148

Figure 3 shows the photoluminescence spectra of the DWCNTs with even chirality indices, such spectra display that as the chirality indices increase, they shift towards lower energies, that is, there is roughly a tendency that the inner diameter of the DWCNT is inversely proportional to the maximum intensity peaks energy of PL, with the exception of the DWCNT6 structure, whose maximum peak shifts to higher energy such behavior is in agreement with experimental results reported by Okazaki et al., so when decreasing the inter-walls radial distance it makes that their interaction is strong which results in a reduction of the PL intensity (quenching effect) of the DWCNTs [3]. This result is an outstanding contribution of our work. It is worthy to point out that for designing armchair/armchair DWCNTs it exists a minimum inter-wall radial distance, such distance according to our analysis it results of around 1.8 Å, below this value the DWCNT structure coalesces, by virtue of this situation, it was not possible to design the (4,4)/(2,2) structure because it violated this restriction.

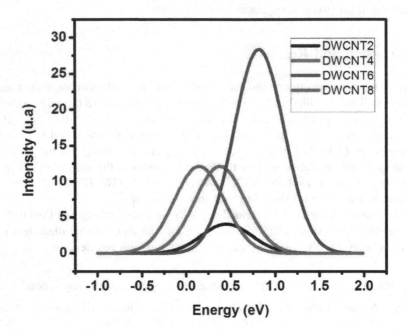

Fig. 3. PL spectra for double-walled carbon nanotubes with inner nanotubes even chirality indices.

To find PL signal in the DWCNT is needed that for the internal diameter (D_{int}), it must be limited to lie at $\sim 3 \text{ Å} \leq D_{int} \leq 11 \text{ Å}$, such request is similar to that experimentally reported in the range of $\sim 4 \text{ Å} \leq D_{int} \leq 10 \text{ Å}$ [3]; These bounded values of the parameter D_{int} are very important in the formulation of the hypothesis about the origin of the DWCNT PL that it comes from the inner tube [8].

Figure 4 displays a graph of the inter-walls distance versus maximum intensity peak in which an exponential type adjustment was made to observe the emission behavior of PL, for the structures DWCNT2 and DWCNT4 such adjustment fits well, but for the DWCNT8 it is roughly good. In case of DWCNT6 it moves away from the adjustment, such behavior demands a deeper study which is a topic of future work.

For the case of DWCNTs with odd chirality indices of the inner nanotube they are labeled as DWCNT3, DWCNT5, DWCNT7 and DWCNT9. Table 2 lists the characteristic parameters of DWCNTs for which their lengths lie in the range from 6 Å to 23.5 Å.

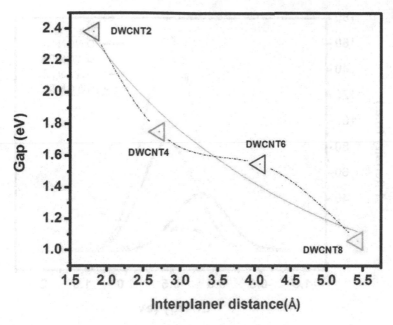

Fig. 4. Inter-wall distance vs. maximum intensity peak for DWCNTs with inner nanotubes even chirality indices.

Table 2. Data of the DWCNTs with inner nanotubes odd chirality indices.

Structure	No. Of atoms	(n,n)/(m,m)	Length (Å)	D_{ext} (Å)	D_{int} (Å)	Inter-walls distance (Å)	Energy gap (eV)	Max. peak (eV)
DWNTC3	107	(6,6)/(3,3)	6.194	8.142	4.071	2.0355	1.76	0.166
DWNTC5	389	(10,10)/(5,5)	14.768	13.57	6.785	3.3925	1.619	0.371
DWNTC7	629	(14,14)/(7,7)	17.777	18.998	9.499	4.7495	1.48	0.533
DWNTC9	1079	(18,18)/(9,9)	23.393	24.425	12.213	6.106	0.84	0.519

Unlike the previous even chirality indices DWCNTs, we deal now with DWCNTs which have a larger internal diameter D_{int}, it widens somewhat the limit of the range of tube diameters obtained experimentally, however they even meet the requirement of small diameters for the emission of photoluminescence (Fig. 5).

Figure 6 exhibits the inter-walls distance versus maximum PL Peak, an adjustment of the exponential type was also made, as can be observed in the figure, the DWCNT3, DWCNT5 and DWCNT7 fit so well not so the DWCNT7 structure. By comparing both even chirality indices and odd chirality indices DWCNTs it leads to that the even chirality indices DWCNTs display a major dispersion in relation to the correlation PL and inter-walls distance.

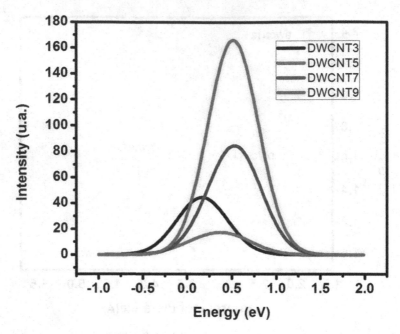

Fig. 5. PL spectra for DWCNTs with inner nanotubes odd chirality indices.

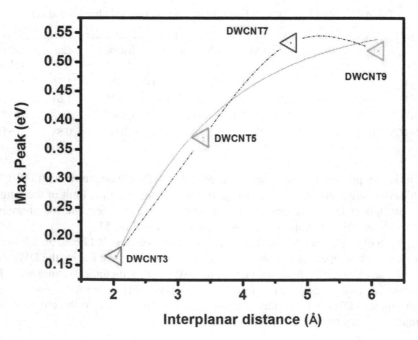

Fig. 6. Inter-walls distance graph vs peak of DWCNTs with inner nanotubes odd chirality indices.

4 Conclusions

We have studied by using DFT theory different DWCNTs structures of type armchair/armchair through considering even and odd chirality indices for the inner and outer tubes. We focused on obtaining the UV/vis spectra considering the influence of the parity of the chirality indices and the inter-walls distance.

We found that there is a minimum inter-walls radial distance of the order of 1.8 Å, below this value the DWCNT structure coalesces. The PL spectra for DWCNTs with even chirality indices of the inner nanotubes shift to regions of lower energies such behavior is contrary to that of DWCNTs with odd chirality indices inner tubes for which PL spectra shift to regions of higher energy. In general the maximum PL peaks for DWCNTs with even chirality indices inner tubes decrease when increasing the inter-walls distance and for DWCNTs with odd chirality indices inner tubes increase when increasing the inter-walls distance. Our predictions in the UV/vis spectra are in good agreement with those experimentally reported for these type of DWCNTs structures in the literature.

Acknowledgment. "The authors thankfully acknowledge the computer resources, technical expertise and support provided by the Laboratorio Nacional de Supercómputo del Sureste de México". This work has also been partially supported by Project 100145955-VIEP2018. NDET is grateful for the Posdoctoral Scholarship provided by CONACYT with Project No. 229741.

References

1. Wei, C., Cho, K., Srivastava, D.: Tensile strength of carbon nanotubes under realistic temperature and starin rate. Phys. Rev. B **67**, 115407 (2003). https://doi.org/10.1103/PhysRevB.67.115407
2. Charlier, J.C., Michenaud, J.P.: Energetics of multilayered carbon tubules. Phys. Rev. Lett. **70**, 1858 (1993). https://doi.org/10.1103/PhysRevLett.70.1858
3. Okazaki, T., et al.: Photoluminescence quenching in peapod-derived double-walled carbon nanotubes. Phys. Rev. B **74**, 153404 (2006). https://doi.org/10.1103/PhysRevB.74.153404
4. Koyama, T., Asada, Y., Hikosaka, N., Miyata, Y., Shinohara, H., Nakamura, A.: Ultrafast exciton energy transfer between nanoscales coaxial cylinders: intertube transfer and luminescence quenching in double-walled carbon nanotubes. ACS Nano **5**(7), 5881–5887 (2011). https://doi.org/10.1021/nn201661q
5. Kishi, N., Kikuchi, S., Ramesh, P., Sugai, T., Watanabe, Y., Shinohara, H.: Enhanced photoluminescence from very thin double-wall carbon nanotubes synthesized by the zeolite-CCVD method. J. Phys. Chem. B **110**(49), 24816–24821 (2006). https://doi.org/10.1021/jp062709j
6. Iakoubovskii, K., Minami, N., Ueno, T., Kazaoui, S., Kataura, H.: Optical characterization of double wall carbon nanotubes: evidence for inner tube shielding. J. Phys. Chem. C **112**(30), 11194–11198 (2008). https://doi.org/10.1021/jp8018414
7. Muramatsu, H., et al.: Bright photoluminescence from the inner tubes of "peapod"-derived double-walled carbon nanotubes. Small **5**(23), 2678–2682 (2009). https://doi.org/10.1002/smll.200901305

8. Yang, S., Parks, A.N., Saba, S.A., Ferguson, P.L., Liu, J.: Photoluminescence from inner walls in double-walled carbon nanotubes: some do, some do not. Nano Lett. **11**, 4405–4410 (2011). https://doi.org/10.1021/nl2025745

9. Flahaut, E., Bacsa, R., Peigney, A., Laurent, C.: Gram-scale CCVD synthesis of double-walled carbon nanotubes. Chem. Commun. 1442–1443 (2003). https://doi.org/10.1039/b301514a

10. Becke, A.D.: Density-functional thermochemistry. III. The role of exact exchange. J. Chem. Phys. **98**, 5648 (1993). https://doi.org/10.1063/1.464913

11. www.jcrystal.com/products/wincnt/

12. Dirac, P.A.M.: Note on exchange phenomena. Proc. Camb. Phil. Soc. **26**, 376 (1930). https://doi.org/10.1017/S0305004100016108

13. Yanai, T., Tew, D.P., Handy, N.C.: A new hybrid exchange-correlation functional using the Columb-attenuating method (CAM-B3LYP). Chem. Phys. Lett. **393**, 51–57 (2004). https://doi.org/10.1016/j.cplett.2004.06.011

14. Liu, J., et al.: Science **280**, 1253 (1998). https://doi.org/10.1126/science.280.5367.125

15. Lee, C., Yang, W., Parr, R.G.: Development of the colle-salvetti correlation-energy formula into a functional of the electron density. Phys. Rev. B **37**, 785 (1988). https://doi.org/10.1103/PhysRevB.37.785

Computational Study of Aqueous Solvation of Vanadium (V) Complexes

Francisco J. Melendez[1](✉), María Eugenia Castro[2],
Jose Manuel Perez-Aguilar[1], Norma A. Caballero[3], Lisset Noriega[1],
and Enrique González Vergara[2]

[1] Lab. de Química Teórica, Centro de Investigación, Depto. de Fisicoquímica,
Facultad de Ciencias Químicas, Benemérita Universidad Autónoma de Puebla,
Edif 105-I, San Claudio y 22 Sur, Ciudad Universitaria, Col. San Manuel,
72570, Puebla, Mexico
francisco.melendez@correo.buap.mx
[2] Centro de Química, Instituto de Ciencias, B. Universidad Autónoma de Puebla,
Complejo de Ciencias, ICUAP, 22 Sur y San Claudio, Ciudad Universitaria,
72570 Puebla, Mexico
[3] Facultad de Ciencias Biológicas, Benemérita Universidad Autónoma de
Puebla, 22 Sur y San Claudio, Ciudad Universitaria, 72570 Puebla, Mexico

Abstract. Vanadium complexes are of great biological interest due to their antidiabetic and anticancer properties. Analyses of the aqueous solvation effects using explicit models in the octahydrated complexes of vanadium (V) linked to the tridentate ONO Schiff base ($VL·(H_2O)_8$), are performed. Here, **L** is the Schiff base 1-(((5-chloro-2-oxidophenyl)imine)methyl)naphthalen-2-olate. The complexes **VL1**, **VL2**, **VL3** and **VL4**, include the functional groups ^+NH $(CH_3CH_2)_3$, $−CH_2CH_2CH_3$, and $−CH_2CH_2CH_2CH_3$, respectively. The explicit model is used to examine the effects of water molecules in the first solvation shell that surrounds the bis-peroxo-oxovanadate ion (two molecules per oxygen atom in the $[VO(O_2)_2·(H_2O)]^-$). Computational calculations are performed using density functional theory (DFT)/M06-2X. A complete basis set (CBS) using correlation-consistent Dunning basis sets from double-ξ to quadruple-ξ is used. The solvation energies are analyzed in order to propose possible complex structures as the most relevant species in biological-like systems. The results indicate that, by including explicit water molecules in the first solvation shell, a particular stabilization trend in the octahydrated complexes $(VL1–VL4)·(H_2O)_8$ is observed with $VL1·(H_2O)_8 < VL3·(H_2O)_8 < VL4·(H_2O)_8 < VL2·(H_2O)_8$. Our results indicate that the complex $VL3·(H_2O)_8$, substituted with $−CH_2CH_2CH_3$, presents the most stable ΔG^{Solv} and hence, it might represent the more likely species in biological-like environments.

Keywords: Vanadium (V) complexes · Explicit solvation · Density functionals

M. Torres et al. (Eds.): ISUM 2018, CCIS 948, pp. 147–156, 2019.
https://doi.org/10.1007/978-3-030-10448-1_14

1 Introduction

Vanadium (IV) and (V) complexes are of biological interest due to their properties as antidiabetic and anticancer agents [1, 2]. Schiff bases have been used for the synthesis of a variety of metal-based compounds, including vanadium in its different oxidation states. In the present work, the ONO tridentate Schiff base 1-(((5-chloro-2-oxido-phenyl)imino)methyl)naphthalen-2-olate (**L**) and the oxide-V(V) complexes are studied: **VL1**, **VL2**, **VL3**, and **VL4** that include the functional groups $-^{+}NH(CH_3CH_2)_3$, $-CH_2CH_2CH_3$ and $-CH_2CH_2CH_2CH_3$, respectively (Fig. 1). These complexes have showed high anticancer activity in MCF-7 cells, which are a common cellular line used in the study of breast cancer [3]; however, their coordination chemistry and structural stability in biological environment remains unclear. In order to understand how the solvation energy values change in the Schiff base (**L**) when it is linked to the $[VO_2]^+$ ion, which form part of the V(V) complexes that display anticancer properties, we carried out a theoretical study using Density Functional Theory (DFT) [4], in gas phase and in solvation-like phase using a different number of water molecules (from 1 to 8). The explicit solvation energies values were estimated using the Complete Basis Set (CBS) limit [5] utilizing the Dunning correlation consistent basis sets [6], which has been applied for energy predictions. In this work, we predicted the solvation energies with explicit solvation model with the aim of understanding the stabilizing details of the vanadium complexes in the context of a biological-like environment.

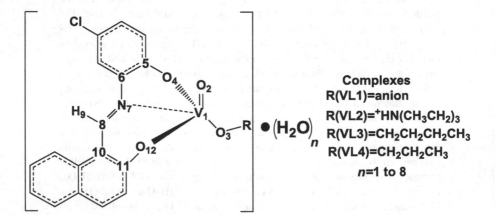

Fig. 1. Numbering convention for the **L**, **VL1–VL4** and (**VL1–VL4**)·(**H₂O**)₈ systems.

2 Computational Methodology

Optimization and vibrational frequencies were calculated to assure the global minimum of ground state structures by DFT theory using the M06-2X functional. The starting point geometries for the calculations were taken from the crystallographic Data Center

(CCDC) with the references code ccdc 1032429, 1028790, and 1052671 for **VL2–VL4** respectively. The cc-pVDZ basis set [6] was used for the C, H, N, O, and Cl atoms, whereas the LanL2DZ basis set was used for the V atom [7]. Vanadium atoms use an effective core potential (ECP) that replaces the core electrons with a pseudopotential.

The calculations were carried out in gas phase as well as considering the solvent effect by adding to the complexes eight water molecules, *i.e.*, two water molecules per oxygen atom in the complex formed by the $[VO(O_2)_2 \cdot (H_2O)]^-$ and Schiff base. The M06-2X [8] and the B3LYP [9] DFT functionals were used for the optimization calculations and the CBS estimations, respectively.

The Dunning correlation consistent basis sets, cc-pVDZ, cc-pVTZ, cc-pVQZ [6], and Ahlrichs TZVP [10] were used for the C, H, O, N, and Cl atoms, whereas the LanL2DZ [7] was use for the V atom. In both cases we extrapolated to the complete basis set (CBS) limit [5], for the gas phase and the explicit solution-like phase.

The extrapolated function for obtaining the CBS limit energy values for the **(VL1–VL4)·(H₂O)₈** complexes, has the following exponential from:

$$A(x) = A(\infty) + Be^{-(x-1)} + Ce^{-(x-1)^2} \tag{1}$$

where x is the cardinal number corresponding to the basis set (2, 3, 4 for DZ, TZ and QZ) and $A(\infty)$ is the estimated CBS limit for δ when $x \to \infty$.

All calculations were carried out using the Gaussian09 program [11].

3 Results

3.1 Optimization

The **VL1–VL4** complexes were optimized with the goal of knowing the most stable conformations in the ground state. These complexes were built from the tridentate ONO Schiff base **L** linked to the $[VO2]^+$ ion bound to different functional groups. The **VL2–VL4** complexes were synthesized by Ebrahimipour *et al.* [3] and contained the respective Schiff base **L**. In the case of the **VL1** complex, it was built from the Schiff base **L** linked to $[VO_2]^+$ ion.

Selected parameters for the **VL1–VL4** complexes calculated with the M06-2X and the cc-pVDZ, and with the LANL2DZ basis sets are shown in Table 1.

In order to evaluate the effect of the aqueous solvation on the electronic and free energies, the $[VO_2]^+$ ions in the **VL1–VL4** complexes were surrounded by eight water molecules in the first solvation shell, in increments of two water molecules at each step to obtain a total of eight molecules corresponding to four steps. The complexes 1-(((5-chloro-2-oxidophenyl)imine)methyl)naphthalen-2-olate-di-oxido-vanadate (V)·(H₂O)₈ **(VL1·(H₂O)₈)**, triethylammonium-1-(((5-chloro-2-oxidophenyl)imino)methyl)naph-thalene-2-olate-di-oxido-vanadate(V)·(H₂O)₈ **(VL2·(H₂O)₈)**, 1-(((5-chloro-2-oxidophe nyl)imino)methyl)-naphthalen-2-olate-propoxido-oxido-vanadium(V)·(H₂O)₈ **(VL3· (H₂O)₈)**, and 1-(((5-chloro-2-oxidophenyl)imino)methyl)-naphthalen-2-olate-butoxido

Table 1. Selected parameters for the optimized **VL1–VL4** complexes at the M06-2X/cc-pVDZ and LANL2DZ level of theory in gas phase. Bond lengths are in (Å) and angles are in (°).

Parameter	VL1	VL2	VL3	VL4
O4–C5	1.261	1.324	1.333	1.334
O12–C11	1.265	1.303	1.315	1.317
N7–C8	1.337	1.299	1.299	1.296
N7–C6	1.369	1.411	1.409	1.407
Cl–C	1.731	1.750	1.747	1.747
V1–O4	2.058	1.920	1.870	1.855
V1–O12	1.969	1.899	1.858	1.859
V1–O3	1.579	1.641	1.749	1.742
V–O2	1.578	1.584	1.551	1.552
V1–N7	2.191	2.191	2.14	2.186
C10–C8–N7	126.5	125.3	124.4	124.1
C8–N7–C6	119.3	121.2	122.8	122.7
C10–C11–O12	123.4	123.7	122.7	123.0
C6–C5–O4	118.2	117.9	116.8	117.0
N7–C6–C5	112.3	111.4	110.9	110.9
C8–C10–C11	119.6	119.3	118.9	119.2
O2–V1–O3	110.9	107.1	107.4	105.4
O2–V1–N7	115.3	100.6	94.2	92.9
O3–V1–O4	92.5	92.0	90.1	94.4
O3–V1–O12	97.4	96.2	96.0	96.5
O12–V1–N7	80.1	80.3	81.2	80.0
O4–V1–N7	74.6	76.3	77.2	76.6
O12–V1–O4	152.7	144.5	135.3	136.6
O3–V1–N7	133.3	151.8	157.9	161.5

oxidovanadium (V)·(H$_2$O)$_8$ (**VL4**·(**H$_2$O**)$_8$) were fully optimized in gas phase and also including the water molecules using the M06-2X/cc-pVDZ theory level. The optimized structures in gas phase, including four and eight water molecules are shown in Fig. 2.

The selected parameters for the (**VL1–VL4**)·(**H$_2$O**)$_8$ complexes are shown in Table 3. Numbering convention is according to Fig. 1.

As seen in Table 2, the parameters for the hydrated (**VL1–VL4**)·(**H$_2$O**)$_8$ complexes change slightly when compared to the values obtained in the gas phase calculations, however, these conformational changes do not modify the distorted squared pyramid structure of the vanadium coordination sphere and their overall geometry. In Fig. 3 the energies obtained from the optimized complexes containing 0 to 8 water molecules (in increments of two) in the first solvation shell display a decreasing trend in their energy values. As shown, the **VL2** complex consistently displays the lowest energy values.

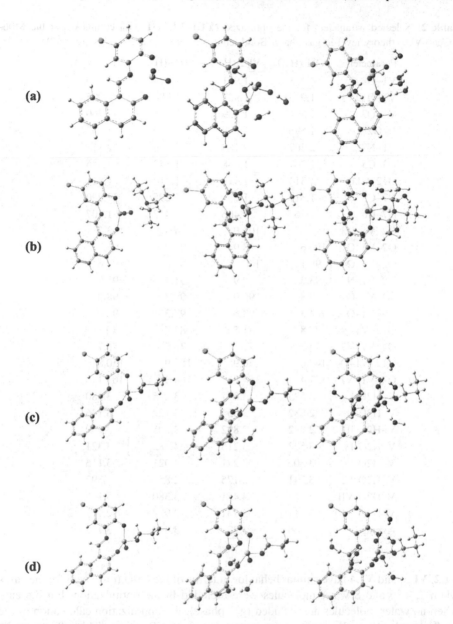

Fig. 2. Vanadium (V) complexes linked to the **VL** Schiff base (left) without water molecules, (center) four water molecules and (right) eight water molecules: **(a) VL1, (b) VL2, (c) VL3,** and **(d) VL4**.

Figure 4 shows the related CPU time spent during the optimization of the complexes when different numbers of water molecules were included, from 0 to 8. It can be seen that the **VL1** complex used more CPU time than the other complexes, especially for the case when 8 water molecules were included in the optimization. Complexes

Table 2. Selected parameters for the optimized (**VL1–VL4**)·(**H₂O**)₈ complexes at the M06-2X/cc-pVDZ theory level in gas phase. Bond lengths are in (Å) and angles are in (°).

Parameter	VL1·(H$_2$O)$_8$	VL2·(H$_2$O)$_8$	VL3·(H$_2$O)$_8$	VL4·(H$_2$O)$_8$
V1–O4	2.078	1.951	1.924	1.910
V1–O12	1.923	1.927	1.884	1.905
V1–O3	1.597	1.639	1.743	1.760
V–O2	1.596	1.599	1.570	1.562
V1–N7	2.207	2.189	2.116	2.115
O4–C5	1.267	1.338	1.342	1.346
O12–C11	1.314	1.312	1.312	1.321
N7–C8	1.311	1.289	1.295	1.290
N7–C6	1.36	1.406	1.412	1.407
O2–V1–O3	107.6	105.0	104.3	103.2
O2–V1–O12	100.6	98.9	97.9	96.7
O2–V1–O4	99.1	100.7	101.8	103.6
O2–V1–N7	93.2	89.9	91.4	95.7
O3–V1–O4	93.8	96.9	95.7	98.8
O3–V1–O12	104.3	98.6	97.3	96.6
O12–V1–N7	79.8	81.5	82.7	80.7
O4–V1–N7	73.7	77.2	78.5	76.7
O12–V1–O4	147.6	150.9	152.9	150.8
O3–V1–N7	157.4	164.8	164.2	161.1
V–H2O I	3.523	3.077	3.225	3.380
V–H2O II	2.882	3.054	3.122	3.136
V–H2O III	2.882	2.892	3.205	3.190
V–H2O IV	3.523	3.215	4.782	3.321
V–H2O V	3.302	3.271	4.021	3.116
V–H2O VI	3.241	3.125	2.859	3.392
V–H2O VII	3.167	4.451	3.380	3.135
V–H2O VIII	3.611	2.731	2.929	2.707
Average	3.266	3.227	3.440	3.172

VL2, **VL3**, and **VL4** have similar behavior in terms of the CPU time spent for the cases when 2, 4, 6 and 8 water molecules were included in the optimization. For the case when no water molecules are included (gas phase), the optimization calculation of the **VL2** complex was the most expensive in terms of CPU time. This effect can be attributed to the particular geometry of the **VL2** complex were intramolecular electrostatic interactions play a more significant role.

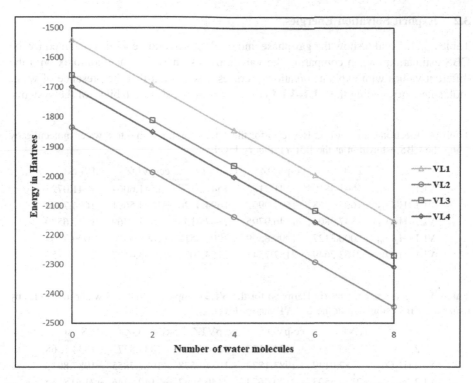

Fig. 3. Energies for the **VL1–VL4** complexes (in Hartrees) for the cases with different number of water molecules (increments of two) added to the system.

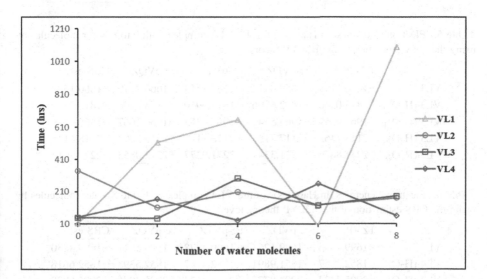

Fig. 4. CPU time (in hours) for the **VL1–VL4** optimizations when different numbers of water were included, from 0 to 8 water molecules.

3.2   Explicit Solvation Energies

Tables 3, 4, 5 and 6 show the gas phase and explicit solvation energies obtained by the CBS estimation. When comparing the values in gas phase for each complex with the different values with explicit solvation energies it is evident that the presence of water molecules surrounding the **VL1–VL4** complexes increases the stability of the systems,

Table 3. Electronic energies (in Hartrees) for the **VL1** complex with 0 to 8 water molecules by using the CBS estimation at the B3LYP theory level.

	TZVP	cc-pVDZ	cc-pVTZ	cc-pVQZ	CBS est.
VL1	−1541.4810	−1541.2185	−1541.5157	−1541.6064	−1541.0727
VL1·$(H_2O)_2$	−1694.4268	−1694.0903	−1694.4620	−1694.5691	−1694.7174
VL1·$(H_2O)_4$	−1847.3803	−1846.9795	−1847.4153	−1847.5369	−1847.6580
VL1·$(H_2O)_6$	−2000.3127	−1999.8599	−2000.3512	−2000.9370	−2000.7704
VL1·$(H_2O)_8$	−2153.2649	−2152.7541	−2153.3030	−2153.4497	−2153.1455

Table 4. Electronic energies (in Hartrees) for the **VL2** complex with 0 to 8 water molecules by using the CBS estimation at the B3LYP theory level.

	TZVP	cc-pVDZ	cc-pVTZ	cc-pVQZ	CBS est.
VL2	−1834.6737	−1834.3157	−1834.7148	−1834.8277	−1834.2568
VL2·$(H_2O)_2$	−1987.6149	−1987.1873	−1987.6578	−1987.7855	−1987.8913
VL2·$(H_2O)_4$	−2140.5503	−2140.0634	−2140.5937	−2140.7346	−2140.8154
VL2·$(H_2O)_6$	−2293.5056	−2292.9592	−2293.5490	−2293.7037	−2293.9386
VL2·$(H_2O)_8$	−2446.4510	−2445.8432	−2446.4954	−2446.6644	−2446.3160

Table 5. Electronic energies (in Hartrees) for the **VL3** complex with 0 to 8 water molecules by using the CBS estimation at the B3LYP theory level.

	TZVP	cc-pVDZ	cc-pVTZ	cc-pVQZ	CBS est.
VL3	−1660.1129	−1659.8112	−1660.1514	−1660.2519	−1660.1527
VL3·$(H_2O)_2$	−1813.0546	−1812.6766	−1813.0940	−1813.2108	−1813.3390
VL3·$(H_2O)_4$	−1965.9959	−1965.5543	−1966.0355	−1966.1667	−1966.2681
VL3·$(H_2O)_6$	−2118.1462	−2117.7156	−2118.2171	−2118.3294	−2118.6115
VL3·$(H_2O)_8$	−2271.8876	−2271.3341	−2271.9277	−2272.0853	−2271.7613

Table 6. Electronic energies (in Hartrees) for the **VL4** complex with 0 to 8 water molecules by using the CBS estimation at the B3LYP theory level.

	TZVP	cc-pVDZ	cc-pVTZ	cc-pVQZ	CBS est.
VL4	−1699.4386	−1699.1253	−1699.4778	−1699.5811	−1699.4830
VL4·$(H_2O)_2$	−1852.3787	−1851.9891	−1852.4197	−1852.5398	−1852.6618
VL4·$(H_2O)_4$	−2005.3224	−2004.8727	−2005.3633	−2005.4976	−2005.5939
VL4·$(H_2O)_6$	−2158.2732	−2157.7626	−2158.3144	−2158.4616	−2158.7123
VL4·$(H_2O)_8$	−2311.2134	−2310.6472	−2311.2534	−2311.4139	−2311.0846

Table 7. Solvation energies (in Hartrees) for the **VL1–VL4** complexes at the M062X/cc-pVDZ theory level.

Complexes	$\Delta G^{solvation} = (G_{water\ molecules} - G_{Gas})$			
	VL1	VL2	VL3	VL4
$(H_2O)_2$	−152.9408	−152.5423	−152.8264	−152.8253
$(H_2O)_4$	−305.7808	−305.3273	−305.6623	−305.6600
$(H_2O)_6$	−458.2867	−458.1162	−458.1517	−458.4981
$(H_2O)_8$	−611.4505	−610.8981	−610.9336	−610.9279

i.e., more favorable energy values are obtained with differences around −610 Hartrees in all the systems.

In Table 7 the explicit solvation free energies for the **VL1–VL4** complexes are shown. When comparing the values in this table, it can be seen that there is an augmented stabilizing effect due to the inclusion of the water molecules, meaning that the solvation-like free energies for each complex has more negative values. From this analysis we observed the following trend: **VL1·(H₂O)₈ < VL3·(H₂O)₈ < VL4·(H₂O)₈ < VL2·(H₂O)₈**. These results shows that the **VL3·(H₂O)₈** complex, that is, when in the VL1 structure, the $-CH_2CH_2CH_3$ group is introduced, presents the most stable ΔG^{Solv}. Our results suggests that, from the systems considered in this study, the structure of the **VL3·(H₂O)₈** complex, could represent the most probable structure in biological-like conditions.

4   Conclusions

The effect of aqueous solvation on the different vanadium-based complexes was evaluated using explicit water molecules. The structures of the **VL·(H₂O)₈** complexes were optimized in a stepwise fashion (by adding two water molecules at a time until a total of eight were included in their first solvation shell) using the M06-2X theory level and the cc-pVDZ and LANL2DZ basis sets. The estimated energies values for the **(VL1–VL4)·(H₂O)₈** complexes were calculated under the Complete Basis Set (CBS) limit approach, using the DFT with different Dunning correlation consistent basis sets. This methodology allowed us to predict the explicit solvation-like energies for these complexes with adequate precision. Based on the results presented here, it is possible to assume that the **VL·(H₂O)₈** complexes are significantly stabilized by the solvent as showing by the continuous inclusion of the explicit water molecules. From the solvation-like free energy calculations, we suggests that the **VL3·(H₂O)₈** complex might be the most probable entity in biological-like environments. Further calculations by also using implicit solvation models should be used as an interesting test for analyzing the solvent effect in the different complexes beyond the first solvation shell. Another interesting perspective to this work will be to further analyze the conformational flexibility of the different substituents: $-^+NH(CH_3CH_2)_3$, $-CH_2CH_2CH_3$, and $-CH_2CH_2CH_2CH_3$.

References

1. Pessoa, J.C., Etcheverry, S., Gambino, D.: Coord. Chem. Rev. **301-302**, 24–48 (2015)
2. Bernard, D.: Anticancer Res. **24**, 1529–1544 (2004)
3. Ebrahimipour, S.Y., et al.: Polyhedron **93**, 99–105 (2015)
4. Hohenberg, P., Kohn, W.: Inhomogeneous electron gas. Phys. Rev. **136**, B864–B871 (1964)
5. Peterson, K.A., Woon, D.E., Dunning Jr., T.H.: Benchmark calculations with correlated molecular wave functions. IV. The classical barrier height of the H+H2 → H2+H reaction. J. Chem. Phys. **100**, 7410–7415 (1994)
6. Dunning Jr., T.H.: J. Chem. Phys. **90**, 1007–1023 (1989)
7. Jeffrey, H.P., Wadt, W.R.: J. Chem. Phys. **82**, 299–310 (1985)
8. Zhao, Y., Truhlar, D.G.: Theor. Chem. Acc. **120**, 215–241 (2008)
9. Becke, A.D.: J. Chem. Phys. **98**, 5648–5652 (1993)
10. Schaefer, A., Horn, H., Ahlrichs, R.: J. Chem. Phys. **97**, 2571–2577 (1992)
11. Frisch, M.J., et al.: Gaussian 09, Revision A.02 Gaussian Inc.: Wallingford (2009)

3D Image Reconstruction System
for Cancerous Tumors Analysis Based
on Diffuse Optical Tomography with Blender

Marco Antonio Ramírez-Salinas[1]($\boxtimes$), Luis Alfonso Villa-Vargas[1]($\boxtimes$),
Neiel Israel Leyva-Santes[1]($\boxtimes$),
César Alejandro Hernández-Calderón[1]($\boxtimes$),
Sael González-Romero[1]($\boxtimes$), Miguel Angel Aleman-Arce[2]($\boxtimes$),
and Eduardo San Martín-Martínez[3]($\boxtimes$)

[1] Centro de Investigación en Computación, Instituto Politécnico Nacional,
Av. Juan de Dios Bátiz, Esq. Miguel Othón de Mendizábal
Col. Nueva Industrial Vallejo Del. Gustavo A. Madero,
07738 Mexico City, Mexico
{mars, lvilla}@cic.ipn.mx,
israel.leyva.santes@gmail.com, hdzces@gmail.com,
sael.gonzalez13@gmail.com
[2] Centro de Nanociencias y Micro y Nanotecnologías del Instituto Politécnico
Nacional, Av. Luis Enrique Erro S/N, Delegación Gustavo A. Madero,
07738 Mexico City, Mexico
maleman@ipn.mx
[3] Centro de Investigación en Ciencia Aplicada y Tecnología
Avanzada del Instituto Politécnico Nacional,
Calzada Legaria No. 694 Col. Irrigación, Del. Miguel Hidalgo,
11500 Mexico City, Mexico
maguilarme@ipn.mx

Abstract. There are different studies that allow detecting the presence of cancer cells in a patient; however, the time it takes to obtain a correct diagnosis is critical for these cases. This work presents the design and construction of a prototype as first approach for a microtomograph based on Diffuse Optical Tomography (DOT). Diffused Optical Tomography is a technique that uses light from the Near Infrared Region (NIR) to measure tissue's optical properties that has become relevant for the medical field due to it being a non-invasive technique. The main goal of this device is to be able to detect and analyze cancerous tumors by measuring diffuse photon densities in turbid media. As a first phase of the development, this project integrates an image acquisition mechanism, an image processing interface at software level developed with Blender to exploit a GPU architecture to optimize the execution time.

Keywords: Microtomography · Diffused Optical Tomography
Blender · 3D reconstruction

© Springer Nature Switzerland AG 2019
M. Torres et al. (Eds.): ISUM 2018, CCIS 948, pp. 157–166, 2019.
https://doi.org/10.1007/978-3-030-10448-1_15

1 Introduction

Medical imaging is a discipline that provides a visual representation of internal human body through multiple techniques or processes. Some examples are magnetic resonance, mammography or ultrasound; these techniques or processes can be classified in invasive or non-invasive.

The invasive processes are those which chemically or mechanically attack the body. These processes can modify the cellular structure or drill to tissue, and it produce secondary effects in human body. On the other hand, the non-invasive processes are the opposite to invasive processes, since these processes protect the integrity of organisms.

The non-invasive techniques in medical imaging used to obtain data from the interior of the organism do not disturb the cellular structure of the organ or tissues, that is, the test signals do not modify the tissue under study at any level. By contrast, X-ray tomography is an invasive technique because it can alter the cells genetically.

Medical imaging has been proof to be useful for the analysis of malignant agents in the human body, as a support tool to obtain a clinical diagnostic. This discipline uses a different mechanical and computational tools for acquire and process the images. The mature tools provide high-quality images although some have problems or inconveniences, as shown in [1].

Some medical imaging tools have been studied and developed for several years which can generate images with a considerable percentage of accuracy, and facilitate the reconstruction in 3D images, but the problem is the low quality. Tools with highest quality are more expensive and in some cases has been demonstrated that affect the organism with secondary effects.

Nowadays, medical imaging is essential in the detection, analysis, staging and restaging of diseases such as cancer. This technique has permitted guiding treatments, establishing procedures, monitoring the spread of cancer cells by the body and knowing the response to medications. The optical tomography is of recent development and has demonstrated efficacy for obtaining data of physiological aspects, unlike the techniques of X-ray tomography and magnetic resonance that deliver anatomical information [2, 3].

Optical tomography is based on the use of laser beams as a probe inside human tissues; the information is obtained by applying a laser source in one or different locations around the object of interest, the emitted light is detected in one or multiple positions to establish certain characteristics of the tissue [4].

Recently, some tools and methods have begun to be studied and developed as result of its low or null affected to human body. For example, fluorescence-based methods that use chemical compounds for generate luminescence in the internal tissues, capturing the luminescence making use of special cameras. Although the chemical compounds are introduced in human body, it doesn't produce secondary effects and the process of get information (images of luminescence) is a non-invasive method.

1.1 Diffuse Optical Tomography

Diffuse optical Tomography (DOT) is a non-invasive technique [5] adopted to obtain images with physiological tissue information. It uses a Near InfraRed (NIR) spectrum laser; the light penetrates the tissue and with the help of sensors, as photodiodes or CCD cameras, the emerging light is detected in different locations. The data collected, in combination with image reconstruction algorithms, are applied to determine the intrinsic optical properties of the tissue [6]. DOT includes the optical fluorescence tomography, a method to obtain images from the distribution of a fluorophore *in vivo*. The instrument is designed to illuminate large parts using an optically expanded laser beam; fluorescent light from the tissue surface is detected using a CCD camera [7]. Despite DOT is a recently created method, it has been considerate as the method with more number of advantages over other mature methods and it starts to be used for cancer imaging and brain functional imaging as show in [8].

The main goal of medical imaging studies is to develop tools that provide high resolution images of the human body without causing tissue damages, accessible and inexpensive. In this sense, DOT use drivers with high precision optics but compared to mature methods, as X-ray computed tomography, the resulting costs are low. Additionally, DOT needs a mechanical system to generate, get and process the information from the fluorescence. For this reason, it is coupled with a microtomograph which accomplish these functions.

A study involving approximately 2000 women observed that about 85% of the breast lesions could be detected by DOT with an effective cost-benefit which collects physiological information as main advantages. Nevertheless, it is still used as a complementary technique in combination with traditional techniques such as X-ray CT or MRI [9–11]. This is why there is an urgent need to develop algorithms capable of reconstructing the tissue under study in a virtual way, improving the reliability of the DOT results, being able to set aside the use of invasive techniques.

With this in mind, and because it is a non-destructive method capable of analyzing the same object, microtomography has become widely used in different research fields such as biomechanical engineering, tissue engineering, material characterization, cardiovascular systems, among other [12, 13].

1.2 Fluorescence-Based Method

These methods get information by using chemical compounds with the capability of emitting chemiluminescence throughout tissue within human body, facilitating the quantification of the luminous intensity as long as the chemiluminescence endures. By definition, the application of chemical compound is an invasive process; nevertheless, this doesn't represent a danger for the study object because the chemical compounds used in these methods do not produce secondary effects, and the processes used to obtain the information are non-invasive process, so it is possible to say that is a non-invasive method [14].

In this work it is used Fluorophore to generate the chemiluminescence needed to take the required measurements. The following list shows the process to generate the chemiluminescence using Fluorophore.

1) Application of Fluorophore in tissue.
2) Excitation using a laser.
3) Capturing information using a video camera.

In the second stage (Excitation) a photon of energy is supplied by a laser and absorbed by the fluorophore, generating the chemiluminescence. The excited state has a limit time of duration: 1–10 ns. During this time the cameras get all the possible information from the chemiluminescence [15].

A great advantage of the luminescence technique is that it is a clean light source (there are no other background light emissions) and the images can be acquired without light filters.

This article presents the preliminary results corresponding to the first desing stage of an optical microtomograph developed at the Computing Research Center of the National Polytechnic Institute of Mexico. The microtomograph design is based on the DOT technique, having as a main goal the capacity to detect and analyze cancerous tumors by measuring diffuse densities of photons in turbid media, to subsequently obtain a manipulable 3D model of the sample, with the capacity to perform simulations.

This paper is organized as follows. Section 2 describe the hardware design of the device. Section 3 the algorithm developed for 3D reconstruction is given. Section 4 shows the results obtained. Finally, Sect. 5 presents the conclusions of this project.

2 Microtomograph Design

The microtomograph is designed as a structure made with aluminum supports and acrylic walls, in such a way as to prevent the passage of external light. Inside, at the top, there is a monochromatic 48 fps video camera, with a 3-megapixel lens and a spectral range between 400 and 1000 nm (VIS + NIR). A white LED lamp with diffuse lighting in the form of a ring is coupled to the camera. At the bottom of the structure there is a laser driver with wavelength range from 766 to 1532 nm, a pulse width equal to 70 ps, and an output power of 400 mW. Finally, just above the lasser, there is a base to place the tissue sample. Figure 1 shows the structural design of the microtomograph,

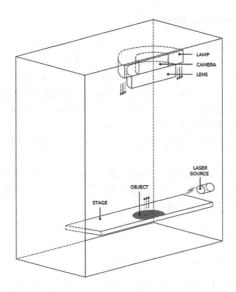

Fig. 1. Structural design of the microtomograph.

where it is possible to see the components distribution. It has a stage used to put a sample object (in this case a mouse that represent a human tissue); there is a laser source which its main goal is to excite the fluorophore within the tissue to produce the chemiluminescence. At the top, there is a camera with special lens to get an image set of the tissue with the fluorophore reacting.

2.1   Operation of the Microtomograph

Initially, a sample of tissue is placed at the base of the microtomograph to which fluorophore should previously have been applied. The internal lighting is controlled in its entirety by the LED lamp, which allows coalibrar luminous intensity as required. Once this is done, the laser is used to irradiate the parts of the tissue to be analyzed, thereby exiting the fluorophore during the time lapse in which the images are captured with the monochromatic camera. This method has a short time for testing, since the fluorophore has a reduced lifetime on the tissue.

3   Methodology for 3D Reconstruction

Nowadays, different algorithms for 3D reconstruction have become more popular and more mature; each algorithm has different properties that characterize it. These properties are used to select the ideal algorithm to provide the whole requirements for a specific application. Some algorithms more popular are: (a) Marching cubes, (b) Point cloud, (c) Delaunay triangulation. In this work it has been chosen the Point cloud algorithm.

3.1   Data Collection

The data acquired by the microtomograph is a set of images that show how the luminescent effect of the fluorophore changes over time. It is possible to analyze the transition that occurs from the low luminosity stage, passing to the maximum luminosity due to laser excitation, and finally returning to its lowest brightness until it is left without luminosity as a result of the degradation effect of the fluorophore. Figure 2 shows this process: the initial state of the fluorophore in the tissue is shown on the left side of the image, as time progresses and the laser excites the tissue, the affected area of the tissue reaches the maximum level of excitation. It will subsequently end up degrading the fluorophore and stop emitting useful information.

In spite of having a set of images, it would be a mistake to apply some 3D reconstruction algorithm such as "Point cloud", since the captured images are at the same depth distance. Our proposal for the 3D reconstruction is as follows:

(a) Collection of a set of images during the excitation period of the fluorophore.
(b) Sweep the set of images pixel by pixel to detect the maximum brightness points of each pixel.
(c) Reconstruction of a reference image from the extracted pixels, placing them at the exact extraction coordinates.
(d) Definition of the depth threshold from the white balance associated with each pixel.

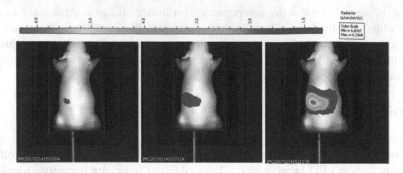

Fig. 2. Evolution of the behavior of the fluorophore with respect to time.

In this initial stage of the project, the necessary elements to operate the microto-mograph are not yet available, so this process was carried out by analyzing the data collection process and simulating the result with a test image with the necessary characteristics to perform a simulation of the reconstruction process. Furthermore, the necessary elements for the images acquisition through the microtomograph are not yet available, so this process is omitted and the reference image has been replaced with a test image that includes the required features to perform a simulation of the 3D reconstruction process.

3.2   Image Segmentation

The depth thresholds defined from the luminescence levels will indicate the depth at which the tissue under study is located. The deeper the tissue is, the luminescence that it generates will be weaker. When the reference image has been obtained, the next step is to start with the reconstruction of the virtual model in 3D, for this the following is necessary:

(a) Decompose the image in pixels and assign each pixel its respective coordinates.
(b) Group the pixels by luminescence intensity.
(c) Plot one node for each pixel, and one layer for each level of luminescence.

In (a), a GPU is used to generate a sweep on the image and to detect the luminosity of each pixel. This process generates a database with the metadata for each pixel, that includes: luminosity level and coordinates (x, y). The deep of the database is equal to the total of pixels in the reference image. The luminosity level is used to select the pixels that belong to a specific area generated by the fluorophore, these pixels and their related metadata are hold into a different database, meanwhile the rest of the pixels are deleted as they not contain a useful information.

In (b), the limits of luminosity are established in different ranges of the radiance produced by the fluorophore. Finally, the metadata related to each pixel is pulled apart in a different database according to its luminosity and the umbral previously defined, where each database represents one slide or level in a point cloud.

3.3 Modeling Test

Figure 3 shows the test image used in this phase of the project. It is a monochromatic image with high contrasting elements. The first test of data processing was performed in Python language and Blender software version 2.79, and the second test was performed in CUDA 9.0 and OpenGL language.

Fig. 3. Image used for modeling 3D tests. https://goo.gl/D9WUrE

To perform the tests of the algorithm designed for 3D reconstruction, an AlienWare desktop model X51 R3 was used, with an Intel Core i7 6700 K processor at 3.4 GHz, with 16 GB DDR4 RAM memory and an Nvidia GTX 960 GPU with 2 GB GDDR5.

4   Results

From the Fig. 4 we obtained a total of 36049 points distributed in 4 levels of luminescence, 2788 for the first level, 5271 in the second level, 11301 for the third and 16689 for the fourth.

Figure 4 shows a 3D model using the virtual nodes generated by Blender, while Fig. 6 shows the result using CUDA and OpenGL. This has been done considering four levels of luminescence; the more levels plotted, the more defined the image is. For the examples, we use different colors for each level from the bottom to the top as follows: red, green, blue and cyan.

In Fig. 4, the top level layer, colored in red, represents the most intense luminescence, while the lower layers represent the darker areas in the original reference image. In this work, a monochromatic camera is used to get the reference image, as result, the most illuminated area will be represented as the darkest (Fig. 3).

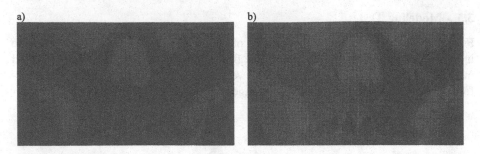

Fig. 4. Model 3D of reference image using blender. (a) three level of luminescence (b) four level of luminescence (Color figure online)

Figure 5 shows the different levels plotted with Blender. Only four levels from the reference image have been plotted, representing around the 40% from the possible reconstruction.

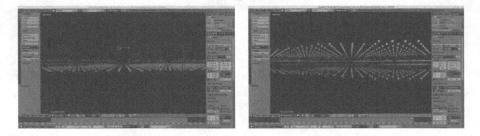

Fig. 5. Different levels of luminescence plotted using nodes.

Fig. 6. Model 3D of reference image using CUDA and OpenGL (Color figure online)

5   Conclusions and Future Work

This work presented a system focused on analysis of cancerous tissues through image acquisition to produce a virtual model with 3D reconstruction. For this, the first stage of the design process includes a microtomograph, that has been built, while the reconstruction algorithm is already implemented, forming the hardware and software layer of the project, respectively. The preliminary results show how the methodology for 3D reconstruction is done using a two-dimensional image. With this methodology it is possible to get as many layers as we want to represent different levels of luminescence. The point cloud algorithm has been chosen because it can be used in a graph for simulation purposes, where each point of the cloud represents node within a graph.

The first tests were performed in Blender and with a Python script; in these tests it was not possible to obtain the expected results. All indicate that, due to the properties of the objects modeled with Blender, it takes a lot of time because Blender only uses the GPU for rendering but not to create an object in its virtual world. To create a series of objects in Blender has to be done sequentially by the CPU, besides considering that the software must to assign physical properties to the object.

Each layer was created in different running because of the time of creation. The first layer lasted up to 4 h approximately; the second layer took around 16 h to be done; for the next layers, more than 24 h were required to finish the task. For the case where CUDA combined with OpenGL, were used to run the test the execution time were reduce considerably: 0.15 s for the whole set of layers.

The advantages of using DOT include: more portability and lower cost compared with other methods; by contrast, DOT only allows a partial reconstruction, since this method only yields a half of the object reconstructed, while the other half remains hidden. With respect to this, the future work must present a solution to this problem.

It will be analyzed the possibility to run the reconstruction process in a real time, this means, to represent the Fluorophore lifetime behavior in real time.

Finally, it is possible to use Blender software to exploit its capabilities for generating renders from the simulations, getting a better graphical representation to understand the Fluorophore behavior.

References

1. Schweiger, M., Gibson, A., Arridge, S.R.: Computational aspects of diffuse optical tomography. Comput. Sci. Eng. **5**(6), 33–41 (2003). https://doi.org/10.1109/mcise.2003.1238702
2. Laal, M.: Innovation process in medical imaging. Procedia - Soc. Behav. Sci. **81**, 60–64 (2013). https://doi.org/10.1016/j.sbspro.2013.06.388. ISSN 1877-0428
3. Erturk, S.M., Johnston, C., Tempany-Afdhal, C., Van den Abbeele, A.D.: Imaging Tools in Human Research. In: Clinical and Traslational Science - Principles of Human Research Chapter 6, pp. 87–104 (2009). Accessed 23 Feb 2009

4. National Research Council (US) and Institute of Medicine (US) Committee on the Mathematics and Physics of Emerging Dynamic Biomedical Imaging. Mathematics and Physics of Emerging Biomedical Imaging. National Academies Press (US), Washington (DC) (1996). Chapter 11, Medical Optical Imaging. https://www.ncbi.nlm.nih.gov/books/NBK232476/

5. Leff, D.R., et al.: Diffuse optical imaging of the healthy and diseased breast: a systematic review. Breast Cancer Res. Treat. **108**(1), 9–22 (2008)

6. Dehghani, H., et al.: Near infrared optical tomography using NIRFAST: algorithm for numerical model and image reconstruction. Commun. Numer. Methods Eng. **25**(6), 711–732 (2008)

7. Stuker, F., Ripoll, J., Rudin, M.: Fluorescence molecular tomography: principles and potential for pharmaceutical research. Pharmaceutics **3**(2), 229–274 (2011). https://doi.org/10.3390/pharmaceutics3020229

8. Konovalov, A.B., Vlasov, V.V.: Analytical representation of the sensitivity functions for high resolution image reconstruction in parallel-plate time domain diffuse optical tomography. In: 2017 Progress Electromagnetics Research Symposium - Spring (PIERS), St. Petersburg, pp. 3487–3494 (2017). https://doi.org/10.1109/piers.2017.8262364

9. Leff, D.R., Warren, O.J., Enfield, L.C., et al.: Breast Cancer Res. Treat. **108**, 9 (2008). https://doi.org/10.1007/s10549-007-9582-z

10. Godavarty, A., Rodriguez, S., Jung, Y.-J., Gonzalez, S.: Optical imaging for breast cancer prescreening. Breast Cancer: Targets Ther. **7**, 193–209 (2015). https://doi.org/10.2147/BCTT.S51702

11. Taka, S.J., Srinivasan, S.: NIRViz: 3D visualization software for multimodality optical imaging using visualization toolkit (VTK) and Insight Segmentation Toolkit (ITK). J. Digit. Imaging: Off. J. Soc. Comput. Appl. Radiol. **24**, 1103–1111 (2011). https://doi.org/10.1007/s10278-011-9362-5

12. Landis, E.N., Keane, D.T.: X-ray microtomography. Materials Characterization **61**(12), 1305–1316 (2010). ISSN 1044-5803, https://doi.org/10.1016/j.matchar.2010.09.012

13. Boerckel, J.D., Mason, D.E., McDermott, A.M., Alsberg, E.: Microcomputed tomography: approaches and applications in bioengineering. Stem Cell Res. Ther. **5**(6), 144 (2014). https://doi.org/10.1186/scrt534

14. Vasquez, K.O., Casavant, C., Peterson, J.D.: Quantitative Whole Body Biodistribution of Fluorescent-Labeled Agents by Non-Invasive Tomographic Imaging. PLoS ONE **6**, e20594 (2011)

15. Johnson, I.D.: Molecular Probes Handbook: A Guide to Fluorescent Probes and Labeling Technologies, Life Technologies Corporation (2010)

Sea-Surface Temperature Spatiotemporal Analysis for the Gulf of California, 1998–2015: Regime Change Simulation

María del Carmen Heras-Sánchez[1],
José Eduardo Valdez-Holguín[2(✉)],
and Raúl Gilberto Hazas-Izquierdo[3]

[1] Departamento de Matemáticas, Universidad de Sonora,
Blvd. Luis Encinas y Rosales s/n, Col. Centro, 83000 Hermosillo,
Sonora, Mexico
carmen.heras@unison.mx
[2] Departamento de Investigaciones Científicas y Tecnológicas,
Universidad de Sonora, Blvd. Luis Encinas y Rosales s/n, Col. Centro,
83000 Hermosillo, Sonora, Mexico
jvaldez@guayacan.uson.mx
[3] Departamento de Investigación en Física, Universidad de Sonora,
Blvd. Luis Encinas y Rosales s/n, Col. Centro, 83000 Hermosillo,
Sonora, Mexico
raul.hazas@unison.mx

Abstract. Aiming to gain insight into probable climate change regime in the Gulf of California, a spatiotemporal simulation of sea surface temperature (SST) for the years 1998–2015 based on monthly satellite images with spatial resolution of 4 km was undertaken. In addition to SST's time series, El Niño Southern Oscillation (ENSO) Multivariate Index (MEI) and monthly standardized SST anomalies (SSTA) for the study area were further taken in consideration. Arrival dates for summer transition, SST $\geq$ 25 °C, showed up 15.5 days earlier for the 2007 to 2015 period, with respect to the 1998–2006 period. In contrast, the winter transition, SST < 25 °C, for such period turned up 3.9 days later, which add up to 20 extra days of summer for this time series. Furthermore, for the later period, the spatial distribution of surface waters with SST > 26 °C covered an extra 10% of the Gulf's area. Additionally, the SST variability showed an annual positive trend of 0.04 °C, 0.72 °C total for the series, according to Theil-Sen trend estimation.

Keywords: Gulf of California · SST · ENSO · MEI

1 Introduction

The Gulf of California has been typified as an evaporation basin with a temperature gradient incrementing toward the Gulf's interior during summer and decreasing during winter, with a net salt and heat gain that is balanced by sea water flux towards the Pacific ocean (Marinone and Lavín 1997; Lavín *et al.* 2014; Gutiérrez *et al.* 2014),

© Springer Nature Switzerland AG 2019
M. Torres et al. (Eds.): ISUM 2018, CCIS 948, pp. 167–181, 2019.
https://doi.org/10.1007/978-3-030-10448-1_16

the latter being the mechanism that significantly influences the SST's variability (Castro *et al.* 1994; Mascarenhas *et al.* 2004). The spatiotemporal SST variability is mainly caused by the annual component (Soto-Mardones *et al.* 1999; Lavín *et al.* 2003).

The Gulf's climate is characterized by two distinct seasons: a warm season with SST temperatures $\geq$ 25 °C, and a cold season with SST temperatures < 25 °C (Soto-Mardones *et al.* 1999; Lavín *et al.* 2003). Temporally-wise, during July, August, and September in particular, the highest SST temperatures and the lowest variability are observed (Soto-Mardones *et al.* 1999; Bernal *et al.* 2001). Spatially-wise, the areas around the large islands and the head of the Gulf show the lowest SST temperatures and the lowest variability in any given year (Soto-Mardones *et al.* 1999).

Conversely, interannual SST variability is related to ENSO events (Herrera-Cervantes *et al.* 2007; Kessler 2006). These episodes cause further seasonal intensification (Baumgartner and Christensen 1985). According to Beier (1997), and Herrera-Cervantes *et al.* (2007), the ENSO signal propagation associated to a standing Kelvin wave trapped along the coast may take about 20 days to traverse from the continent's edge along the Gulf and out by the Baja California Peninsula's coastline. Oceanographic conditions at the mouth of the Gulf are more sensitive to these interannual events (Lavín *et al.* 1997; Soto-Mardones *et al.* 1999; Lavín *et al.* 2014).

Oceanographic conditions on the rest of the Gulf are determined by the surrounding continental mass, forced mainly by the communication to the Pacific Ocean, the wind system and the tides (Lavín *et al.* 1997; Bernal *et al.* 2001). Surface circulation exhibit a distinct North American Monsoon system influence (Roden 1964; Douglas *et al.* 1993; Lavín *et al.* 1997), resulting in a southward flow along the Sonora and Sinaloa coastline during winter-spring, and along the Baja California Peninsula during summer-autumn (Beier 1997; Gutiérrez *et al.* 2004).

Aiming to detect probable climate change regime in the Gulf of California, this work performs a spatiotemporal simulation of monthly SST temperature based on an 18-year series of satellite images.

2 Materials and Methods

2.1 Study Area

The Gulf of California is on average 200 km wide and has a length of 1500 km. Its natural borders are the arid Mexican states of Sonora and Sinaloa on the east, and the equally arid Baja California Peninsula on the west. Its southern edge directly intercommunicates with the Pacific Ocean, but for our purposes we consider a hypothetical boundary running from Cabo San Lucas, B.C.S., to Bahía de Banderas, Nayarit. The total area spans 237,207 km^2 (Fig. 1).

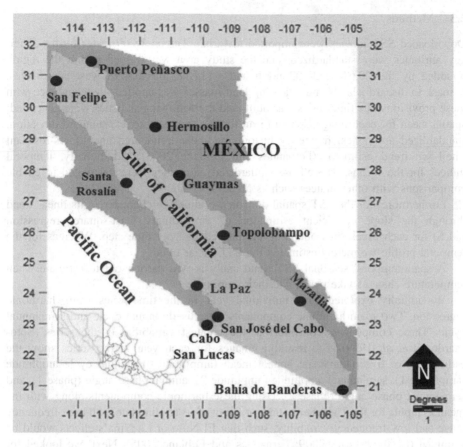

Fig. 1. Study area. Gulf of California

2.2 Data Set

A 216-point Sea-Surface Temperature (SST) time-series was built from monthly mean satellite images from January 1998 through December 2015. Such span was chosen due to the image's quality within the available collection with an approximate 4 km spatial resolution. For different set of analysis, the series was partitioned in two subperiods: 1998–2006, and 2007–2015. Images corresponding to January 1998 to June 2002 were downloaded from NOAA/ERDAPP data server (NOAA-ERDAPP 2015) and from July 2002 to December 2015, images were taken from NASA/Ocean Color Web (NASA-OCW 2016) data set. The data's metadata such as data type, unit of measurement, data rate, beginning and end of the series, Julian day count, datum, and coordinate system necessary for the spatial-temporal analysis are included in the raster files. Additionally, an accompanying MEI index data set was annexed from NOAA/ESRL (NOAA-ESRL 2016).

2.3   Methods

Downloaded SST images were imported to Idris's Terrset 18.09 raster format. Their key attributes were standardized, and the study area was framed within the region bounded by the 20.61 to 32.02 north and −114.98 to −104.98 west coordinates. A mask to discard islands and adjoining land masses was applied. In accordance with these provisions, the time-series was built, and the following statistics were generated: spatial mean for each image, spatial mean for the complete series, standard deviation, standardized anomalies, frequency histogram, linear trend, and an outliers-resistant Theil-Sen trend estimator (Fernandes and Leblanc 2005). Additionally, temporal indices for the means, as well as standardized anomalies were calculated to enable comparisons with other indices such as MEI.

Furthermore, for the SST spatial domain we aimed to characterize its linear trend through the slope coefficient estimation of an ordinary least-squares regression (OLS) for each pixel, thus obtaining the rate change per time step. Whereas for the temporal profile we merely estimated the SST linear trend.

A spatiotemporal seasonal SST trend analysis was carried out to estimate when temperature changes take place, and their amplitude.

We initially explored each individual year in the time-series using harmonic regression. Two main harmonic components were used: annual cycle and semiannual cycle. These components contribute to the greatest variability of the series (Soto-Mardones et al. 1999). The resulting images for each year in the series show the estimations of five parameters: annual mean (amplitude 0), annual cycle amplitude (amplitude 1), semiannual amplitude (amplitude 2), annual phase angle (phase 1), and semiannual phase angle (phase 2). Using these harmonic components along with the mean as inputs for the Theil-Sen estimator, allowed us to eliminate both high-frequency noise and low-frequency variability, such that El Niño or La Niña's effects would be excluded (Eastman et al. 2009; Fernandes and Leblanc 2005). Next, we looked for trends on each of the previous parameters using the Theil-Sen median slope method. The resulting images permitted us to build two RGB constructs for the whole series: one for amplitudes (amplitude 0 in red, amplitude 1 in green, and amplitude 2 in blue), and another for phase angles (phase angle 1 in green, phase 2 in blue, while red still belonged to amplitude 0).

Due to the breadth of data involved, and the complexity of the simulation, it was necessary to make use of high performance computing resources provided by the Área de Cómputo de Alto Rendimiento at Universidad de Sonora.

3   Results

SST mean spatial distribution shows a latitudinal thermal gradient from 27.8 °C in the southeast region of the Gulf to 23.4 °C at the mouth of the Gulf, only the region of the large islands registered SST temperatures < 23 °C (Fig. 2). SST temporal distribution showed a positive linear trend with an approximate 1.38 °C temperature increase for the 18 year series.

Significant cold periods were observed during winter-spring season in 2008 and winter 2011 with the lowest temperatures registered ($\sim$18.3 °C, with SSTA anomaly of <-1.39) corresponding to La Niña events 2007–2008, and 2010–2011.

On the other hand, highest SST temperatures were registered during the summer of 2014 and 2015 with readings above 31.6 °C and SSTA anomaly > 1.78. These maxima correspond to a global warming period that began in May 2014 and continued until December 2015, with waning episodes in October 2014, and January-February 2015 (NOAA/ESRL 2016). In the Gulf the warmest period began in January 2014 and continued until December 2015, losing intensity in September and October 2014 with SSTA anomalies of 0.35 and 0.39, respectively.

Likewise, the SSTA anomalies series show a spatiotemporal linear correlation coefficient r = 0.64 with respect to the MEI index with a one-month delay (lag-1) on the ENSO signal. For both series, the linear trend shows a positive increment, yet the Gulf's SSTA denote greater variability and a rising trend. Correlation is particularly stronger near the southern coasts of Sinaloa, and along the Baja California Sur

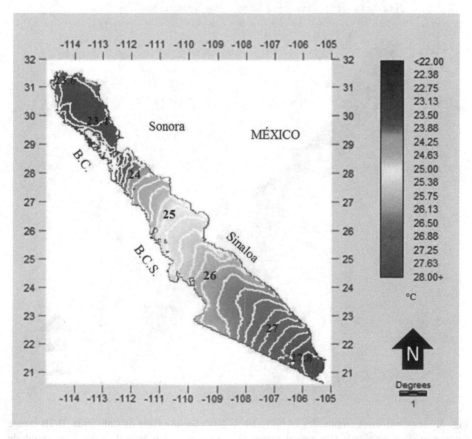

Fig. 2. Average monthly SST for the Gulf of California for the period 1998–2015 with isotherms at 0.2 °C equidistance

coastline. In relation to the observed MEI index for the length of this study, the El Niño events seam to appear during approximately in 35% of the series, La Niña events do 26% of the time, and the remaining 39% of the series doesn't display significant variability. Positive SSTA anomalies account for 30% of the series, negative SSTA 34%, and those less significant anomalies make the remaining 36% of the series, which seem to suggest that Gulf SST is affected by ENSO events 64% of the time, with fluctuating spatial distribution.

Seasonal Trend Analysis
Figure 3 shows an image for the amplitudes. Adjacent same-color areas on the Gulf exhibit a similar trend (Idrisi 2015): regions where the annual mean prevail appear in red tones; those where the annual cycle prevail appear in green tones; those regions where annual and semiannual cycles predominate appear in rose and purple tones; and combinations of the three amplitudes, meaning absence of seasonal trend, appear in

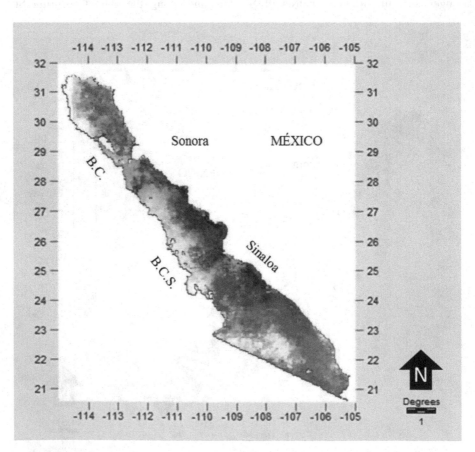

Fig. 3. Seasonal trend amplitudes of SST, 1998–2015 for the Gulf of California. RGB image composite: R = amplitude 0 = annual mean; G = amplitude 1 = annual cycle; B = amplitude 2 = semiannual cycle (Color figure online)

grey and white tones. From the amplitudes' image we created graphs displaying the calculated means from the observed values for every month (Fig. 4a) as well as fitted seasonal curves (Fig. 4b). From the observed values' means we noticed that the lowest mean temperature values correspond to January months for the 2007–2015 subperiod, whereas the months of March–April and November–December for the same period

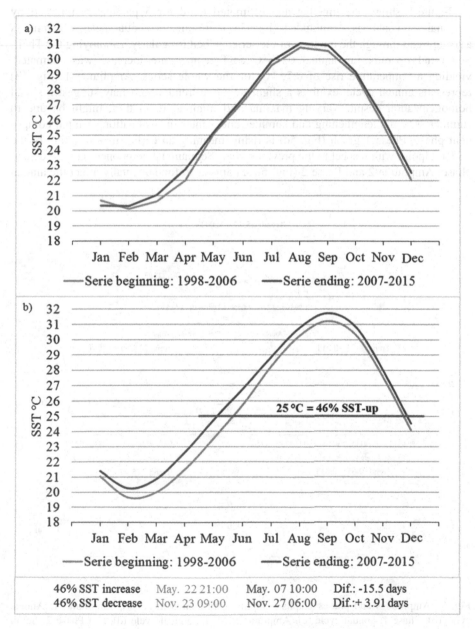

Fig. 4. Observed (a) and fitted (b) seasonal curves with 25 °C line

registered an 0.4 SST difference with respect to the 1998–2006 subperiod. The fitted graphs are associated with the whole series' seasonal trend. In this graph we observed the time the SST intersects the 25 °C threshold which is the assumed temperature signaling the progression from winter to summer and vice versa and corresponds to 46% of the range. From the Fig. 4b, it is apparent that in the second subperiod of the series, summer arrives 15.5 days earlier and winter delays for 3.91 days, see Fig. 4b.

Figure 5 shows the timeline and estimated trend for 5 parameters returned by seasonal trend analysis. Amplitude 0 (Fig. 5a) represents the annual mean, which infers a rising trend through the duration of the series, albeit irregularly. Employing the Theil-Sen trend operator, an annual 0.04 °C SST temperature increase was estimated, yielding a temperature rise of 0.72 °C for the whole series. Amplitude 1 (Fig. 5b) represents annual cycle, exhibits a slight negative trend which may suggest a signal homogenization despite varying maxima and minima. It, in turn, might be due to summer season's lengthening and summer and winter intensification. Annual component phase, Phase 1 graph (Fig. 5c) is rising meaning an earlier manifestation of the SST midpoint with respect to the previous year. Semiannual component amplitude and phase, Amplitude 2 and Phase 2 (Fig. 5d–e) appear to fundamentally affect the annual

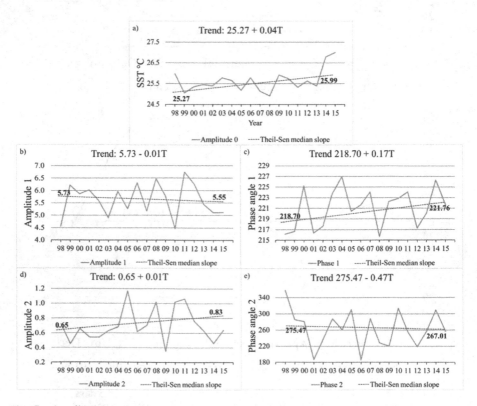

Fig. 5. Amplitudes and phases graphs. Amplitude 0: annual mean (a), Amplitude 1: Annual cycle (b), Phase 1: annual cycle (c), Amplitude 2: Semi-annual cycle (d), and Phase 2: Semi-annual cycle (e)

mean: a rising trend in amplitude apparently due to pronounced summer and winter seasons, whereas a negative phase trend implies a later onset of SST change during the year (Eastman *et al*. 2009).

Monthly climatology shows that SST from December to April (winter) lies about 4 °C below annual mean, although it shows significant fluctuations along the years. May and November display frequent oscillations above and below the annual mean, while summer months exhibit temperatures nearly 4 °C above the annual mean. Figure 6 shows the seasonal climatology that represent winter means, as well as summer means, along with May, November, and annual means.

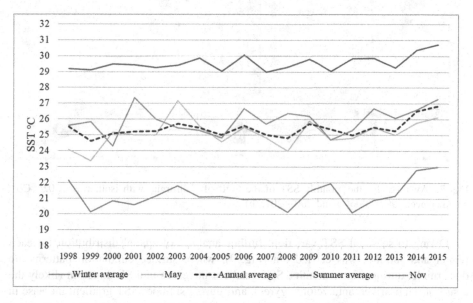

Fig. 6. Seasonal climatology for the whole series, for the monthly SST of the Gulf of California

As mentioned above, one of the goals to subdivide the series in two subperiods (1998–2006 y 2007–2015), was to ascertain if the general trend 1998–2015 is owed to El Niño events 2014–2015 which gave rise to SST increments greater than 1.5 °C. ENOS events of different duration and intensity were observed on both subperiods.

SST's spatial distribution mean overall conditions are shown in Fig. 7 and monthly climatology and its associated trend are shown on Fig. 8. In order to spatially compare both subperiods, SST temperature ranges were set at: <24 °C, >24 °C, ≤ 26 °C, and >26 °C. Spatial distribution for SST temperatures > 26 °C increased by 10% in the second subperiod, recording warmer water masses propagating inward. Along the mid-part of the Gulf, the area with SST in the range between 24 to 26 °C decreased by 8.5% during the second subperiod. The head of the Gulf and the great islands registered the least variability with barely a 1.5% less area covered by SST temperatures < 24 °C (see Fig. 7).

SST temporal distribution for the second subperiod (Fig. 8b) shows greater vari-ability with respect to the first subperiod (Fig. 8a), which might be correlated to longer and more intense ENSO events. Despite the methodological difference in trend oper-ators, linear trend and Theil-Sen analyses show a gradual SST temperature increase during both subperiods (Fig. 8a–b).

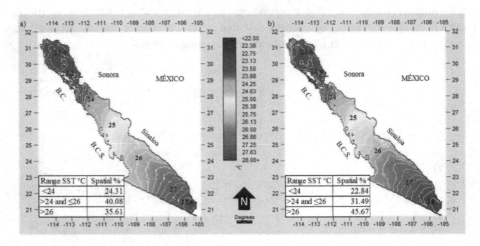

Fig. 7. Averages for the monthly SST of the Gulf of California, with isotherms at 0.2 °C of equidistance: 1998–2006(a) and 2007–2015(b)

Owing to seasonal SST variation, further analysis of spatial distribution for each winter and summer was carried out (Fig. 9), where surface circulation patterns are discernible: during winter months, SST gradient increases in a SE direction (likely the result of wind-driven anticyclonic gyres), and during summer SST gradient increase in a NW direction (most likely due to a reversal in wind direction).

Winter months, which usually display mean temperatures in the 18 to 25 °C range, show during years 2006, 2008, 2011, and 2012 the likely effect of wind-driven cir-culation: SST along the coastline of southern Sonora and parts of Sinaloa up to Mazatlán (latitude 23–24 N) is under 20 °C, while on average, those temperatures are recorded no further south than Yavaros (latitude 26–28 N) on Sonora's coast. Throughout summer, the winds from SE are not strong enough as to break the thermal stratification, therefore SST along most of the Gulf range in the upper bracket 28 to 31 °C, only the region around the great islands registered lower SST. Years 2004, 2006, 2009, 2011, and 2012 are noteworthy because surface waters with SST > 30 °C occupy over 50% of the Gulf's area. Particularly, in parts of 2014 and 2015 surface waters with SST > 30 °C spread over 65% and 90% of the Gulf's surface respectively.

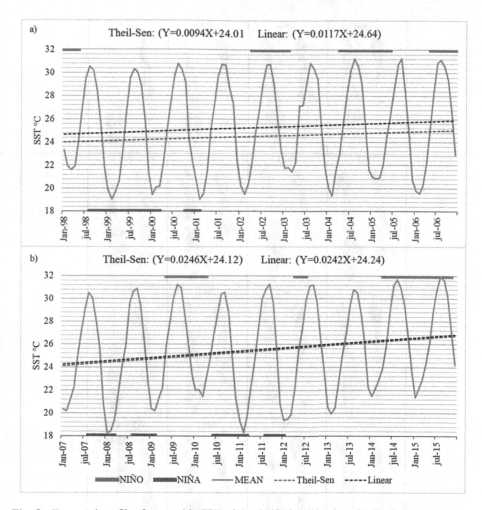

Fig. 8. Temporal profiles for monthly SST of the Gulf of California, with Theil-Sen and Linear trends: 1998–2006(a) and 2007–2015(b)

While for 2015, surface waters with SST above 31 °C scattered approximately over 30% of the Gulf surface. It is worth noting that for the months of May and November, a clear transition without definite circulation patterns takes place and SST range around the annual mean: 22 to 27 °C during May, and 23 to 28 °C during November (Fig. 6), with no particular spatial distribution.

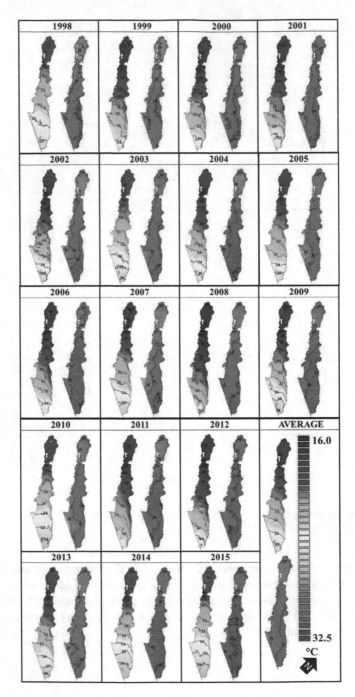

Fig. 9. Gulf of California, SST seasonal trend analysis, 1998–2015, spatial distribution of SST for annual winter and summer

4 Discussion

Notwithstanding minor irregularities, it has been concluded that SST temperatures in the Gulf of California show a rising tendency. The increase in the Gulf's sea surface temperature for the 1998–2015 period based on the Theil-Sen operator estimation is 0.72 °C, at an annual rate of 0.04 °C, 0.0033 °C monthly. Mean SST for the series is 25.42 °C. Long-term trend analysis by means of linear least square estimation revealed an estimated temperature rise of approximately 1.38 °C for the study period, at an annual rate of 0.08 °C, 0.0064 °C monthly. We believe our findings compare well with those obtained by Lavín et al. (2003) who using a similar methodology found a 1.16 °C temperature rising trend in a 17-year series of satellite images (1984 to 2000), 0.07 °C annually, 0.0057 °C monthly.

Spatiotemporal SST variability is largely due to the annual component (Soto-Mardones et al. 1999; Lavín et al. 2003), with the stretch from July to September exhibiting the least temporal variability and the highest SST (Soto-Mardones et al. 1999; Bernal et al. 2001). Spatial distribution-wise, the regions around the large islands and the head of the Gulf, while also displaying slight temporal variability, they register the lowest temperatures during any given year (Soto-Mardones et al. 1999).

Interannual variability is influenced by ENSO events (Herrera et al. 2007; Kessler 2006). We estimated a one to two-month delay for the ENSO signal to propagate from the Gulf's southern edge up to the great islands, where SSTA anomalies correlate with respect to the MEI index with r = 0.64. La Niña events are more evident during the summer months, while El Niño events are less frequent yet more intense. Marinone (1988), estimated that over 50% of interannual variability is owed to external forcing mechanisms linked to the Pacific Ocean. We found that 64% of the time SST temperatures are forced by ENSO events, 30% by Niño events, and 34% of the by Niña events, with fluctuating spatial distribution inside the Gulf.

We found that the SST's seasonal nature involve important spatial fluctuations related to the surface circulation system, which according to Lavín et al. (1997), and Bernal et al. (2001), is itself driven by the North American Monsoon system as stated by Englehart and Douglas (2006). We observed seasonal temperature distribution apparently owed to such wind influence: several winter seasons with SST temperatures below 20 °C were recorded along the southern Sonora and Sinaloa coastline up to Mazatlán, whereas those temperatures were previously recorded no further south than Yavaros on Sonora's coast. Moreover, in 2014 and 2015 particularly, surface waters with SST > 30 °C spread over 65% and 90% of the Gulf's space respectively. While in 2015, surface water with SST > 31 °C scattered approximately over 30% of the Gulf area.

Summarizing, there are three important remarks from seasonal trend analysis between the first and the second subperiod: 1. An apparent extension of summer suggested by SST temperatures reaching the 25 °C threshold 15.5 days sooner in May, coupled with a delayed drop from that same threshold 3.9 days later in November; 2. A −0.3 °C mean difference during the month of January seem to suggest winter season intensification; 3. During March, April, and December, mean SST temperatures have a 0.4 °C difference that could likely cause the early onset of summer and the winter delay.

Such seasonal differences might impact the development, distribution and abundance of several species that inhabit the Gulf (Lluch-Cota *et al.* 2007; Anda-Montañez *et al.* 2010; Brander 2010; Leitão *et al.* 2014).

The Gulf displays a strong seasonal SST signal (Soto-Mardones *et al.* 1999), therefore, any seasonal climatology change would imply alterations to the Gulf's general thermodynamic (Ripa 1997).

Acknowledgments. We would like to thank Consejo Nacional de Ciencia y Tecnología (CONACYT). Also, to Departamento de Investigaciones Científicas y Tecnológicas, Departamento de Investigación en Física, Departamento de Matemáticas, and particularly at Área de Cómputo de Alto Rendimiento at Universidad de Sonora for their valuable material and technical assistance, and for allowing us the use of their HPC computing facilities.

References

Anda-Montañez, J.A., Ramos-Rodríguez, A., Martínez-Aguilar, S.: Effects of environmental variability on recruitment and bioeconomic modelling in the Pacific sardine (Sardinops sagax caerulea) fishery from Magdalena Bay, Baja California Sur, Mexico. Scientia Marina, vol. 74, no 1 (2010). https://doi.org/10.3989/scimar.2010.74n1025

Baumgartner, T.R., Christensen Jr., N.: Coupling of the Gulf of California to large-scale interannual climatic variability. J. Marine Res. **43**(4), 825–848 (1985). (ID: 12174)

Beier, E.: A numerical investigation of the annual variability in the Gulf of California. J. Phys. Oceanogr. **27**, 615–632 (1997)

Bernal, G., Ripa, P., Herguera, J.C.: Variabilidad oceanográfica y climática en el bajo Golfo de California: influencias del trópico y pacífico norte. Ciencias Marinas, vol. 27, no. 4, pp. 595–617, December 2001

Brander, K.: Impacts of climate change on fisheries. J. Mar. Syst. **79**(3–4), 389–402 (2010)

Castro, R., Lavin, M., Ripa, P.: Seasonal heat balance in the Gulf of California. J. Geophys. Res. **99**, 3249–3326 (1994)

Douglas, M., Maddox, R.A., Howard, K., Reyes, S.: The Mexican monsoon. J. Clim. **6**, 1665–1677 (1993)

Eastman, J.R., et al.: Seasonal trend analysis of image time series. Int. J. Remote Sens. **30**(10), 2721–2726 (2009)

Englehart, P.J., Douglas, A.V.: Defining intraseasonal variability within the North American monsoon. J. Clim. **19**(17), 4243–4253 (2006)

Fernandes, R., Leblanc, S.G.: Parametric (modified least squares) and non-parametric (Theil-Sen) linear regressions for predicting biophysical parameters in the presence of measurements error. Remote Sens. Environ. **95**, 303–316 (2005)

Gutiérrez, O.Q., Marinone, S.G., Parés-Sierra, A.: Lagrangian surface circulation in the Gulf of California from a 3D numerical model. Deep-Sea Res. II **51**, 659–672 (2004)

Gutiérrez, M.O., López, M., Candela, J., Castro, R., Mascarenhas, A., Collins, C.A.: Effect of coastal-trapped waves and wind on currents and transport in the Gulf of California. J. Geophys. Res. Oceans **119**, 5123–5139 (2014). https://doi.org/10.1002/2013JC009538

Herrera-Cervantes, H., Lluch-Cota, D., Lluch-Cota, S., Gutiérrez-de-Velasco, S.: The ENSO signature in sea-surface temperature in the Gulf of California. J. Mar. Res. **65**, 589–605 (2007)

Idrisi-TerrSet, 18.09: Idrisi-TerrSet User Manual. Clark Labs, Clark University (2015). www.clarklabs.org

Kessler, W.S.: The circulation of the eastern tropical Pacific: a review. Prog. Oceanogr. **69**, 181–217 (2006)

Lavín, M.F., Beier, E., Badan, A.: Estructura hidrográfica y circulación del Golfo de California: escalas global, estacional e interanual. In: Lavín, M.F. (ed.) Contribuciones a la Oceanografía Física en México. Serie Monografías Geofísicas, Unión Geofísica Mexicana, vol. 3, pp. 139–169 (1997)

Lavín, M.F., Palacios-Hernandez, E., Cabrera, C.: Sea surface temperature anomalies in the Gulf of California. Geofísica Internacional **42**, 363–375 (2003)

Lavín, M.F., Castro, E., Beier, E., Cabrera, C., Godínez, V.M., Amador-Buenrostro, A.: Surface circulation in the Gulf of California in summer from surface drifters and satellite images (2004–2006). J. Geophys. Res. **119**, 4278–4290 (2014)

Leitão, F., Alms, V., Erzini, K.: A multi-model approach to evaluate the role of environmental variability and fishing pressure in sardine fisheries. J. Mar. Syst. **139**, 128–138 (2014). https://doi.org/10.1016/j.jmarsys.2014.05.013

Lluch-Cota, S.E., et al.: The Gulf of California: review of ecosystem status and sustainability challenges. Prog. Oceanogr. **73**, 1–26 (2007). https://doi.org/10.1016/j.pocean.2007.01.013

Marinone, S.G.: Una nota sobre la variabilidad no estacional de la región central del Golfo de California. Ciencias Marinas **14**(4), 117–134 (1988). https://doi.org/10.7773/cm.v14i4.611

Marinone, S.G., Lavín, M.F.: Mareas y Corrientes residuales en el Golfo de California. In: Lavín, M.F. (ed.) Contribuciones a la Oceanografía Física en México, Monografía no. 3, pp 113–139. Unión Geofísica Mexicana (1997)

Mascarenhas Jr., A.S., Castro, R., Collins, C., Durazo, R.: Seasonal variation of geostrophic velocity and heat flux at the entrance to the Gulf of California. Mexico. J. Geophys. Res. **109**, C07008 (2004)

NASA-OCW (National Aeronautics and Space Administration - Ocean Color Web, Aqua Modis Sensor) (2016). http://oceancolor.gsfc.nasa.gov/cgi/l3

NOAA-ESRL (National Oceanic and Atmospheric Administration - Earth System Research Laboratory) (2016). https://www.esrl.noaa.gov/psd/enso/mei/table.html

NOAA-ERDAPP (National Oceanic and Atmospheric Administration - ERDAPP Data Server, AVHRR Sensor) (2015). https://coastwatch.pfeg.noaa.gov/erddap/griddap/index.html

Ripa, P.: Toward a physical explanation of the seasonal dynamics and thermodynamics of the Gulf of California. J. Phys. Oceanogr. **27**, 597–614 (1997)

Roden, G.I.: Oceanographic aspects of the Gulf of California. In: van Andel, T.H., Shor Jr., G.G. (eds.) Marine Geology of the Gulf of California: A Symposium. Memoir American Association of Petroleum Geologists, vol. 3, pp. 30–58 (1964)

Soto-Mardones, L., Marinone, S.G., Parés-Sierra, A.: Variabilidad espaciotemporal de la temperatura superficial del mar en el Golfo de California. Ciencias Marinas **25**(1), 1–30 (1999)

Use of High Performance Computing to Simulate Cosmic-Ray Showers Initiated by High-Energy Gamma Rays

Cederik de León, Humberto Salazar, and Luis Villaseñor[✉]

Laboratorio Nacional de Supercómputo del Sureste de México,
Benemérita Universidad Autónoma de Puebla, 72570 Puebla, Mexico
cederik@gmail.com, lvillasen@gmail.com

Abstract. We use the supercomputer from the Laboratorio Nacional de Supercómputo del Sureste de México (LNS) to simulate secondary cosmic-ray showers initiated by gamma rays with energies between 100 GeV and 100 TeV. These simulations play an important role in the search for gamma ray bursts (GRB) in ground observatories, such as the High Altitude Water Cherenkov (HAWC) observatory located in Sierra Negra, Mexico. GRB are the most energetic explosions observed so far in our Universe and they have been observed only in satellite detectors such as Fermi/GBM, Swift/BAT and INTEGRAL. Their observation in ground observatories will constitute an important scientific breakthrough in the field of astroparticle physics. We use MPI to run simulation code in parallel on hundreds of CPU cores from the LNS. In particular we use the CORSIKA Monte Carlo shower generator with zenith angles of the primary gamma rays between 0 and 45° and azimuth angles between 0 and 360° with an spectral index of -2. We report on benchmark results on the speed and scalability of our code as a function of the number of CPU cores. The authors are members of the HAWC Collaboration, they use high performance computing to analyze the data collected with the HAWC Observatory.

Keywords: Gamma ray bursts · Extensive air showers
High performance computing · Simulations · Gamma rays

1 Introduction

The study of gamma ray bursts (GRB) requires the use of high performance computing (HPC) to simulate and reconstruct a large number of extensive air showers (EAS) initiated by gamma rays with different arrival directions and energies to fully comprehend the eventual observation of GRB in ground-based observatories, such as the High Altitude Cherenkov Observatory (HAWC) [1] and the Latin American Giant Observatory (LAGO) [2], in the near future.

The required computer resources for Monte Carlo simulation of EAS and their event reconstructions in our study of GRB exceed by far the capabilities of single desktop or workstation computers. Fortunately, we were able to use the HPC resources of the Laboratorio Nacional de Supercómputo del Sureste de México (LNS) [3] to simulate thousands of millions of EAS initiated by gamma ray primaries.

© Springer Nature Switzerland AG 2019
M. Torres et al. (Eds.): ISUM 2018, CCIS 948, pp. 182–187, 2019.
https://doi.org/10.1007/978-3-030-10448-1_17

1.1   The Cuetlaxcoapan Supercomputer at the LNS

One of the supercomputers located at the LNS is called **Cuetlaxcoapan**. This was the name of the place where the city of Puebla is located today; it means "place where snakes change skin" in Nahuatl language. This supercomputer consists of a cluster of the following nodes of Intel CPUs:

- 228 calculation nodes with two processors Intel Xeon E5-2680 v3 @ 2.50 GHz of 12 CPU cores each for a total of 5472 CPU cores and a RAM memory per node of 128 GB.
- 20 calculation nodes with two processors Intel Xeon E5-2680 v3 @ 2.50 GHz of 12 CPU cores each for a total of 480 CPU cores and a RAM memory per node of 256 GB.
- 20 calculation nodes with two processors Intel Xeon E5-2680 v3 @ 2.50 GHz of 12 CPU cores each for a total of 480 CPU cores and a RAM memory per node of 512 GB.
- 2 calculation nodes, each with 2 K40 Nvidia GPUs and 2 processors Intel Xeon E5-2680 v3 @ 2.50 GHz of 12 CPU cores for a total of 48 CPU cores and 11520 CUDA cores. Each node has 128 GB of RAM memory.
- 2 calculation nodes with two MIC (Many Integrated Core) Intel Xeon Phi Coprocessor 7250 with 61 active processing cores per processor for a total of 244 cores MIC. In addition, each node has two processors Intel Xeon E5-2680 v3 @ 2.50 GHz of 12 CPU cores each for a total of 48 CPU cores and a RAM memory per node of 128 GB.
- 6 managing nodes (login, queues and provisioning).
- 1.2 PB of storage capacity.

2   Monte Carlo Simulation and Reconstruction

2.1   Overview of Monte Carlo Simulations and Reconstructions of Extensive Air Showers

The main stages that require HPC to produce simulation data for further analyses of GRB are:

- Simulations of EAS induced by high energy gamma rays
- Scaler and event reconstruction produced by the EAS simulations
- Scaler and event data analysis.

The main process consists in the simulation of EAS initiated by gamma rays with energies in the 50 GeV to 100 TeV range for fixed spectral index and primary incident angles (theta for zenith, phi for azimuth). In addition, it is necessary to simulate background EAS consisting of gamma rays with uniform incident angular distributions, for theta values between 0 and 60° and for phi values between −180 and 180°. Since this procedure requires the simulation of GRB for different incident angles and incident energy, the complete study is highly demanding in HPC resources.

Figure 1 shows a simplified diagram that describes the entire simulation and reconstruction process. The process starts from the user input steer simulation file, this file contains all the information related to the EAS simulation characteristics, different stages are then needed in order to get, at the end, information that can be used in the analysis stage.

Simulation | Reconstruction Chain

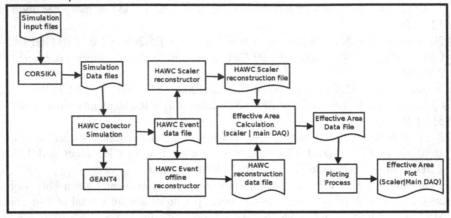

Fig. 1. Simplified diagram of the different stages required for the complete EAS simulation and event reconstruction process in the case of the GRB study for the HAWC Observatory.

2.2   EAS Simulation and Reconstruction Process at the LNS

Our GRB study was based on around 200 computer simulations that included all the stages shown in Fig. 1, each with 1 million EAS simulated with the MC EAS simulator called CORSIKA [4] and reconstructed with the HAWC custom made detector simulation and reconstruction software [5].

We generated collections consisting of 100 million and 700 million of EAS simulations, each collection with their own parameter configuration. Table 1 shows the configurations for different EAS simulation and reconstruction collections. Table 2 shows a graphical representation for the EAS development. These EAS are initiated by primary photon with energies of 50 GeV, 100 GeV, 1 TeV and 10 TeV (left to right, respectively). EAS profile changes with the primary energy.

Custom made scripts were made in order to generate and delivered the data ingest to the process described in Fig. 1; these scripts use the following input parameters:

- Simulation Name
- Primary zenith angles [From, To] [deg]
- Primary azimuth angles [From, To] [deg]
- Energy range [From, To] [GeV]
- Energy Spectral index
- Number of EAS to simulate by job
- Number of Jobs to be send

Table 1. Configuration used for the different EAS simulation and reconstruction collections, it includes the incident angles, zenith and azimuth, energy range and spectral index for each incident gamma ray.

Collection name	Primary zenith angle [deg]	Primary azimuth angle [deg]	Energy range [GeV]	Spectral index	Number of EAS per job	Number of jobs per collection
All sky	[0, 60] uniformly distributed	[−180, 180] uniformly distributed	[0.5, 1e4]	−2.0	1e6	100
Angular bin 0	[0, 20] uniformly distributed	Fixed value	[0.5, 1e3]	−2.0	1e6	200
Angular bin 1	[20, 40] uniformly distributed	Fixed value	[0.5, 1e3]	−2.0	1e6	200
Angular bin 2	[40, 60] uniformly distributed	Fixed value	[0.5, 1e3]	−2.0	1e6	200
GRB <YYMMDD>	Fixed value	Fixed value	[0.5, 1e3]	−2.0	1e6	700

This approach could help to enhance the full production of EAS simulated libraries and implement processes using HPC efficiently, depending on user requirements.

Table 2. Graphic representation of a vertical EAS initiated by a gamma ray with energies in the range between 50 GeV and 10 TeV [4]; note the change in the EAS profile as function of the primary energy.

50 GeV gamma ray	100 GeV gamma ray	1 TeV gamma ray	10 TeV gamma ray

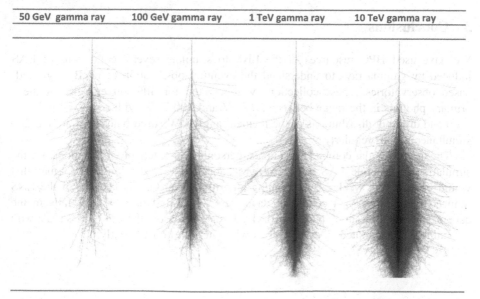

2.3 Computing Times

The computing times for EAS simulations can be reduced drastically using thinning [6] implemented in the EAS simulation software like CORSIKA and AIRES [7], this is helpful for searching the parameters values in pre-production EAS simulations with common computer hardware [8]; nevertheless in a full-production environment the use of these techniques could not be used due the statistical fluctuations and thinning, in large amount of trials, have to be treated in special ways [9–12].

The use of parallelization implemented in CORSIKA allows the calculation of a shower on many cores in parallel with MPI (message Passing Interface). The first interactions and secondary particles are handled with MPI and *subshowers* will run in parallel [4]; this will reduce the CPU time required to produce an EAS.

The CPU time for each computer job of one million EAS, using a vertical primary incident photon with energy range between 50 GeV and 1 TeV, spectral index of −2.0 and fixed incident angles, theta and phi, were around 1.5 hours per job.

The CPU time for each computer job of one 1 million EAS simulated using a vertical primary incident photon with energy range between 50 GeV and 10 TeV, spectral index of −2.0, the fixed incident angles, theta and phi were around 7 hours per job. In both cases we sent 200 simultaneous jobs to the LNS Cuetlaxcoapan supercomputer.

For the all-sky gamma ray background collections the configuration used consisted in a primary incident photon with energy range between 50 GeV and 10 TeV, spectral index of −2.0 and uniform distribution for incident angles theta and phi in the [0, 60] and [−180, 180] ranges, respectively. The CPU times were around 7 hours per job. In this case we sent 800 jobs to the LNS Cluster. The typical CPU time for a reconstruction of each EAS is around 0.5 h.

3 Conclusions

We have used HPC resources of the LNS to simulate several collections of EAS induced by gamma rays to understand the eventual observation of GRB in ground-based observatories. These collections were created for different energies of the a primary photons in the range between 50 GeV and 100 TeV, with a spectral index of −2.0 and different distributions of the incident angles. We used batches of around 200 simultaneous jobs regularly.

The use of regular computer resources, personal computers or workstations, for the simulation of a single EAS collection was banned due to the long CPU times that would be required: weeks if no thinning algorithms were used. The use of the LNS reduced these times to a couple of days. The MC simulation of EAS falls in the category of embarrassingly parallel workload, for this reason, the CPU times scale with the number of simulated EAS as well as with energy almost linearly.

References

1. Abeysekara, A.U., et al.: Daily monitoring of TeV gamma-ray emission from Mrk 421 Mrk 501 and the Crab Nebula with HAWC. Astrophys. J. **841**(2)
2. Bertou, X., LAGO Collaboration: The large aperture GRB observatory. In: AIP Conference Proceedings, vol. 1123, p. 197 (2009). https://doi.org/10.1063/1.3141355
3. Laboratorio Nacional de Super Cómputo del Sureste. http://www.lns.org.mx/infraestructura
4. Heck, D., Knapp, J., Capdevielle, J.N., Schatz, G., Thouw, T.: CORSIKA: a Monte Carlo Code to Simulate Extensive Air Showers Institute for Nuclear Physics. Forschungszentrum und Universität Karlsruhe, Karlsruhe College de France, Paris
5. Abeysekara, A.U., et al.: Data acquisition architecture and online processing system for the HAWC gamma-ray observatory. Nucl. Instrum. Methods Phys. Res. Sect. A Accel. Spectrom. Detect. Assoc. Equip. **888**, 138–146 (2018). https://doi.org/10.1016/j.nima.2018. 01.051
6. Kobal, M.: A thinning method using weight limitation for air-shower simulations. Astropart. Phys. **15**, 259 (2001)
7. Sciutto, S.J.: AIRES, a system for air shower simulation and analysis. In: Proceeding of 27th ICRC, vol. 1, p. 237 (2001)
8. de Dios Álvarez, J., Cotti, U., de León, C.: Computer time optimization in extensive air showers simulations. PoS (ICRC 2017), p. 292 (2017)
9. Billoir, P.: A sampling procedure to regenerate particles in a ground detector from a "thinned" air shower simulation output. Astropart. Phys. **30**, 270 (2008)
10. Stokes, B.T., Cady, R., Ivanov, D., Matthews, J.N., Thomson, G.B.: Dethinning extensive air shower simulations. Astropart. Phys. **35**, 759 (2012). arXiv:1104.3182
11. Kuzmin, V.A., Rubtsov, G.I.: No-thinning simulations of extensive air showers and small–scale fluctuations at the ground level. JETP Lett. **85**, 535 (2007)
12. Pierog, T., Engela, R., Hecka, D., Poghosyanb, G., Oehlschlägera, J., Veberic, D.: Ultra-high energy air shower simulation without thinning in CORSIKA. ICRC (2015)

Data Augmentation for Deep Learning of Non-mydriatic Screening Retinal Fundus Images

E. Ulises Moya-Sánchez[1,2(✉)], Abraham Sánchez[2], Miguel Zapata[3],
Jonathan Moreno[1], D. Garcia-Gasulla[1], Ferran Parrés[1], Eduard Ayguadé[1,4],
Jesús Labarta[1,4], and Ulises Cortés[1,4]

[1] Barcelona Supercomputing Center, Barcelona, Spain
eduardo.moyasanchez@bsc.es
[2] Posgrado en Ciencias Computacionales, Universidad Autónoma de Guadalajara,
Guadalajara, Mexico
[3] Ophthalmology, Hospital Vall d'Hebron, Barcelona, Barcelona, Spain
[4] Universitat Politècnica de Catalunya, Barcelona Tech, Barcelona, Spain

Abstract. Fundus image is an effective and low-cost tool to screen for common retinal diseases. At the same time, Deep Learning (DL) algorithms have been shown capable of achieving similar or even better performance accuracies than physicians in certain image classification tasks. One of the key aspects to improve the performance of DL models is to use data augmentation techniques. Data augmentation reduces the impact of overfitting and improves the generalization capacity of the models. However, the most appropriate data augmentation methodology is highly dependant on the nature of the problem. In this work, we propose a data augmentation and image enhancement algorithm for the task of classifying non-mydriatic fundus images of pigmented abnormalities in the macula. For training, fine tuning and data augmentation, we used the Barcelona Supercomputing Centre cluster CTE IBM Power8+ and Marenostrum IV. The parallelization and optimization of the algorithms were performed using Numba, and Python-Multiprocessing, made compatible with the underlying DL framework used for training the model. We propose and trained a specific DL model from scratch. Our main results are an increase in the number of input images up to a factor of, and report the information of quality images for. As a result, our data augmentation approach results in an increase of up to 9% in classification accuracy.

Keywords: Deep learning · Data augmentation
Retinal fundus images

1 Introduction

Fundus image is an effective and low-cost tool to screen for common retinal diseases [1]. In many countries a screening program for early detection of Diabetic

M. Torres et al. (Eds.): ISUM 2018, CCIS 948, pp. 188–199, 2019.
https://doi.org/10.1007/978-3-030-10448-1_18

Retinopathy (RD) has been implemented, however, it is possible to detect other retinal diseases using the same images [2]. There are two main retina images: ophthalmoscopy (with pupil dilation) and non-mydriatic (non-pupillary dilation) fundus images. One hand, ophthalmoscopy provide higher quality images [3]. On the other, some studies have found that non-mydriatic fundus images have a higher sensitivity and specificity [3], although non-mydriatic image quality is more vulnerable to distortions, artefacts, noise, colour distortions, blur, and low contrast [4].

The combination of non-mydriatic fundus photography with telemedicine has been shown great results for early detection and diagnosis [3], particularly in combination with automatic screening algorithms. Deep Learning (DL) algorithms have been shown able to achieve similar and even better-classifying performance than physicians in certain image screening classification tasks [5]. Within DL, the actual architecture of the model may have a limited effect on accuracy results [5]. Other aspects of DL training have been shown to have a great impact on accuracy, such as novel data preprocessing, data augmentation techniques, multi-scale network, and model hyper-parameter optimization [5, 6].

Data augmentation has a large impact on the improvement of the DL accuracy, particularly by reducing the impact of overfitting and increasing the generalization capacity of the network [7]. However, data augmentation is highly problem-specific and is typically guided by expert knowledge [7]. In this work, we propose a data augmentation and image enhancement algorithm for DL training, for the specific problem of automatic screening of non-mydriatic fundus images.

The dataset we work with, which we are currently unable to release, is composed of non-mydriatic colour fundus images. Each image is labelled by an expert ophthalmologist with the appearance of one or none of five possible pathologies. The number of labelled images per pathology is shown in Table 1. For training, fine tuning and data augmentation, we used the Barcelona Supercomputing Centre (BSC) cluster CTE IBM *Power*8+, while some Multiprocessing algorithms were executed in the Marenostrum IV supercomputer. The optimization and parallelization of the algorithms were performed using Numba, python multiprocessing. This allows us to produce code which is easily integrable with the same deep learning framework used for training the model (Keras [8] on top of TensorFlow).

Our data augmentation approach results in an increase in the number of training images of up to a factor of 1.58, while also enhancing the information quality of non-mydriatic fundus images. As a result, we obtain an improvement of up to 9% in image classification accuracy, while using the same convolutional neural network architecture and same hyperparameters.

2   Literature Review

The applications of DL algorithms to medical image analysis presents several unique challenges such as the lack of large training datasets, class imbalance and memory constraints [5]. DL methods have often been known as *black-boxes*.

In this context, and particularly in medicine, where accountability is important and can have serious legal consequences, it is often not enough to have a good prediction system.

According, to [5], the architecture of the DL network is not the most determinant factor when it comes to analysing its performance. For instance, in the Kaggle challenge for Diabetic-Retinopathy [9], many participants used the same DL architecture and yet had widely varying accuracy results [5]. Among the other factors that may significantly affect the performance of DL models is expert knowledge [5]. Understanding the particularities of the problem, and its most essential properties, allows machine learning experts to properly tune DL models for that particular problem. This tuning is of special relevance for data preprocessing, data augmentation, and model hyperparameter optimization [5].

DL models typically include millions of parameters (i.e., neuron weights) which are optimized during the network training phase to model a particularly complex function (e.g., that transforming a set of input pixels into a categorical label). Such a large search space requires many training instances to find a global minimum. However, when training instances are limited, one is forced to use the same instances many times for training the model. Eventually, this leads to overfitting, as the network is capable of memorizing the input, which leads to a bad generalization capacity. A bad generalization makes the model work very well for the training instances, but perform poorly for any other data. To delay and mitigate the impact of overfitting, it is common to use data augmentation methods [7]. Data augmentation is the process of generating variants of the available data instances, such that these variants can be used as new and different examples in the training of the network. The challenge in data augmentation relies on the generation of as many new training samples as possible, while adding the minimum amount of noise. Clearly, this a problem specific tasks, since certain approaches may be appropriate for certain problems only. For example, mirroring an image through the vertical axis is fine for images of dogs, but is not for classifying text.

Due to non-mydriatic images are more vulnerable to artefacts, noise, colour distortions, blur, and low contrast [4] the mydriatic images, then, we believe that is possible to use the image enhancing in order to do data augmentation of the dataset.

3   Dataset

The dataset we use contains screenings of non-mydriatic retinal fundus images, labelled for Pigmented abnormalities in the macula. The data was anonymized, labelled and shared by the staff of *Optretina* (which includes expert ophthalmologists) under a non-disclosure agreement. Image resolution range between 300 and 4000 pi, while colour depth is RGB 8-bit for all images. Table 1 shows the train, test and validation sets elements.

Table 1. Dataset without of data augmentation.

Sets	Train	Test	Validation	Total images
Pigmented abnormalities in macula	1033	256	323	1633
Not pathology images	1033	256	323	1633

4   Methods

We will present, our preprocessing method, image quality measurement, data augmentation based on image quality and DL architectures.

4.1   Preprocessing Cropping

Crop all the images, in order to remove the background of the retinal fundus image. To begin, a full resolution colour image $I(x,y)_{RGB}$ was converted to grayscale $I(x,y)$. Following, a Gaussian filter was used in order to reduce the noise using the Eq. 1 and convolution operation Eq. 2

$$g(x,y) = \frac{1}{2\pi\sigma^2} e^{-\frac{x^2+y^2}{2\sigma^2}}, \tag{1}$$

$$B(x,y) = I(x,y) * g(x,y) = \sum_{k_1=1}^{m} \sum_{k_2=1}^{n} I(x,y)g(x-k_1, y-k_2) \tag{2}$$

then a threshold was computed using the max arg of the histogram of the image, as you can see, the most frequently colour is the 0.

$$f(x) = \begin{cases} 1, & \text{if } I(x,y) \geq \arg\max(hist) \\ 0, & \text{otherwise} \end{cases} \tag{3}$$

and after that erosion $\ominus$ and dilation $\oplus$ of $I(x,y)$ by structure element $B = ones(5,5)$ is given by the expressions:

$$I(x,y) \ominus B = \bigcap_{b \in B} I(x,y)_{-b}, \tag{4}$$

$$I(x,y) \oplus B = \bigcup_{b \in B} I(x,y)_b \tag{5}$$

where $I(x,y)_b$ denotes the translation of $I(x,y)$ by b. These morphological operations were used to clean all the salt paper points inside of the circle. Finally, we use the binary images in order to compute the chord of the circle of radius r and perpendicular distance (height) form the centre of the circle as follows. In this case, our optimization technique was separate the open CV libraries (which are faster than numpy) and generate a multiprocessing pool process in python.

$$chord = 2r\sqrt{1 - (d/r)^2} \tag{6}$$

and we measure the length chord of the circle in horizontal and vertical in order to crop the image. The process is presented in Fig. 1.

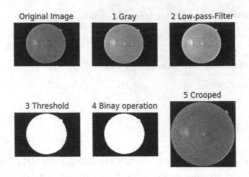

Fig. 1. Cropping process to the image

4.2   Image Quality

The image quality was measurement using 3 magnitudes: Signal to Noise Ratio, Contrast and a Blur index. These parameters are correlated, for instance, one image with high noise usually has, low contrast and high blur. According to several authors [10] the increase of noise can change the meaning in the DL classification. One of the main characteristics of non-dilate retina image is the lack of brightness due to the small amount of light. The small amount of light generates more noise than the signal. We use a crop and resize the image as input. We use the mean value of the pixel values of the grey image $Mean(I(x,y)$ and the variance $Var(I(x,y)$ to compute the Signal to Noise Ratio SNR as follows:

$$SNR = \frac{Mean(I(x,y))}{Var(I(x,y))} \tag{7}$$

In the Fig. 2 is possible to see the measure the effect of the noise in the mean value and variance in the same region. The signal to noise ratio is better if the number is greater than 1 this means that we have more signal than noise.

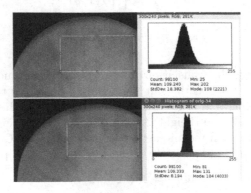

Fig. 2. Signal to noise ratio of the same region and its histogram

The blur was measure using the variance of the Laplacian convolution with the image. Although the Laplacian operator is well defined for any dimension $\Delta f = \sum_{i=1}^{n} \frac{\partial^2 f}{\partial x_i^2}$ we prefer using use their matrix representation to do a 2D convolution operator $(*)$ as follows with the image $I(x, y)$ in their matrix representation $I_{m,n}$:

$$\Delta_{i,j} = \begin{bmatrix} 1 & 1 & 1 \\ 1 & -8 & 1 \\ 1 & 1 & 1 \end{bmatrix} \tag{8}$$

$$Blur\_index = Var(I_{m,n} * \Delta_{ij}) \tag{9}$$

In Fig. 3 is possible to see effect of the noise in one image. The blur index can be change form 0 to a positive number.

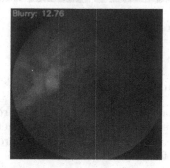

Fig. 3. Blur measurement using the variance of Laplacian of the image

The contrast was measured using a variation of the Michelson contrast definition. We divide the image histogram into two regions using the minimum luminance value of the $I(x, y)_{\min} = L_{min}$ and the maximum value $I(x, y)_{\max} = L_{max}$, after that, we sum all values. The contrast equation is

$$Contrast = \frac{I_{\max} - I_{\min}}{I_{\max} + I_{\min}} \tag{10}$$

Where $I_{\min}$ and $I_{\min}$ are defined by the following equations

$$I_{\min} = \sum_{i=0}^{L_{min}} L_i \tag{11}$$

$$I_{\max} = \sum_{i=L_{min}+1}^{255} L_i \tag{12}$$

Is possible to see that the contrast values are between $[-1, 1]$. In Fig. 4 is possible to see the contrast and the blur index values of two different images. One image with low contrast –0.81, with respect to the background and blur index 12.76 and the other with more contrast 0.8 and blur index of 133.57.

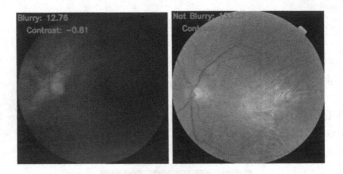

Fig. 4. Contrast and blur index measurement of two images.

4.3   Deep Learning and Data Augmentation

We propose a Convolutional Neural Network (CNN) architecture which exploits different small features specific for this illness. The network was training from scratch, selecting the hyperparameters using the supercomputing facilities. The architecture is detailed as follows:

```
Layer (type)                    Output Shape              Param #
=================================================================
conv2d_1 (Conv2D)               (None, 255, 255, 64)      832
_____
activation_1 (Activation)       (None, 255, 255, 64)      0
_____
max_pooling2d_1 (MaxPooling2    (None, 127, 127, 64)      0
_____
conv2d_2 (Conv2D)               (None, 125, 125, 64)      36928
_____
activation_2 (Activation)       (None, 125, 125, 64)      0
_____
conv2d_3 (Conv2D)               (None, 123, 123, 32)      18464
_____
activation_3 (Activation)       (None, 123, 123, 32)      0
_____
max_pooling2d_2 (MaxPooling2    (None, 61, 61, 32)        0
_____
flatten_1 (Flatten)             (None, 119072)            0
_____
dense_1 (Dense)                 (None, 64)                7620672
_____
```

activation_4 (Activation)	(None, 64)	0
dropout_1 (Dropout)	(None, 64)	0
dense_2 (Dense)	(None, 2)	130
activation_5 (Activation)	(None, 2)	0

Total params: 7,677,026

In all cases we use, *softmax* in the last dense and *ReLu* activation functions. Training from scratch is very computational exhausted and we use multi-GPU algorithm in the Minotauro (up to 4 K80) and CTE-Power 8 (up-to 2 P-100). Our main strategy to reduce the time per epoch was one hand make the preprocessing *off-line* and on the other do fine tuning to the learning rate.

Our main contribution in this paper proposed a data augmentation based on the quality of the image. For this paper we only present the case of noise reduction by low pass see Eq. 1 and contrast-enhanced using CLAHE (Contrast Limited Adaptive Histogram Equalization) [11] an example of the data augmentation is presented in Fig. 5.

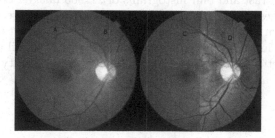

Fig. 5. A. Half of the original image, B. Half of the image with Gaussian blur as data augmentation, C. Half of original image and D. Half contrast enhanced CLAHE as data augmentation.

5   Results

5.1   Preprocessing: Cropping

Although the DL training was for small dataset we use our preprocessing cropping was applied to 227 905 images. Optimization idea of the algorithm first was, change some numpy functions for openCV functions, with this, we could reduce the time up to a factor of 7.12 for instance in chord computation (Eq. 6).

```
from numba import jit
@jit('f8(f8,f8)')
def f1(d, r):
    return  2*r*np.sqrt(1-d/r)
```

using the @*jit* decorator in a very simple way, we reduced the time of computation from $1\,\mu s$ using only numpy to $0.173\,\mu s$ using Numba, we believe that Numba offers the possibility to increase performance with almost the same syntactic sugar offered by python. Finally, we decide to use *multiprocessing* package with 5 pool process. The main result of the pool, was a reduction of the time was a reduction from $15.85\,ms$ to $9.67\,ms$ per image.

5.2   Image Quality

The image quality metrics was applied to 227905 images. The SNR, contrast, and blur index. Its possible to see that SNR and blur index have a mirror response. In a future work, we will analyse in detail this values. Our strategy in this for reducing the time case was using *multiprocesing* modules, in this case, we use 4 cores and get a reduction about the half of time by using one core. Figure 6 shows the snr contrast and blur histograms of 227905 images. Some bad quality and artefact images where our crop algorithm fails are presented in the Fig. 7 is possible to see that, even for a human can be difficult to extract the background. From the 227209 images our crop algorithm we detect 1540 fail images closer to 0.67%. The detection of this fails where computed using quality measurements, image histogram, and the central plot profile of the image.

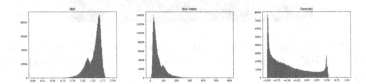

Fig. 6. Histograms of SNR, Contrast and Blur index measurement of the total dataset.

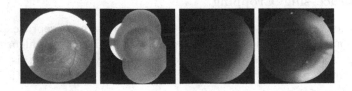

Fig. 7. Fail examples of cropping image.

5.3   Deep Learning and Data Augmentation

The baseline experiment is presented in Fig. 8 the accuracy (and the loss function) of the training and test sets. Is possible to see that the training curves have an important overfitting behavior due to the separation of the training and testing curves. One solution for this is a regularization process, such as data augmentation. Our data augmentation candidates was obtained using the mean value of SNR 1.542 ± 0.032, contrast -0.455 ± 0.2140, using the Eqs. 13 and 14. Our data augmentation was made correcting the bad quality images using clahe method for low contrast images and Gaussian filter for low *snr* images. Table 2 the test accuracy and the amount of data used in each training. Figure 9 shows the best case of training is possible to see how the overfitting is less than the baseline case. Our best result was showed how is possible to reduce the training overfitting increasing the accuracy in up to 9.08%.

$$Blur\_candidate = \begin{cases} 1, & \text{if } snr < mean(snr) - var(snr) \\ 0, & \text{otherwise} \end{cases} \quad (13)$$

$$Clahe\_candidate = \begin{cases} 1, & \text{if } contrast < mean(contrast) - var(contrast) \\ 0, & \text{otherwise} \end{cases} \quad (14)$$

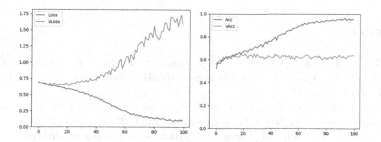

Fig. 8. Base Line training and test with out data augmentation. The accuracy (left) curves and the Loss (right) curves train and test. Is possible to see a overfitting behaviour between the train and test curves.

Table 2. Results of accuracy and the number of pathology images.

Case	Acc	Data
Base line	65.38%	1633
Cropping	67.11%	1633
Blur	69.60%	2041
Blur+CLAHE	71.32%	2591

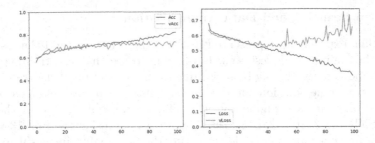

Fig. 9. Best train and test accuracy (left), train and test Loss (right) using Blur correction and CLAHE.

6   Conclusions

In this work we have presented, data augmentation method based on the quality of the images for CNN DL training using non-mydriatic retina fundus images. Due to their acquisition in poor illumination conditions, the images have low signal to noise ratio, low-contrast, and several artefacts, and thus, represent a real challenge to do a robust preprocessing process. All our algorithms were optimized with high-performance functions of python such as Numba or using multiprocessing. Our main result was showed how is possible to reduce the training overfitting increasing the accuracy in up to 9.08% in deep learning training using a target data augmentation taking into account the quality of the image.

References

1. Jin, K., Lu, H., Su, Z., Cheng, C., Ye, J., Qian, D.: Telemedicine screening of retinal diseases with a handheld portable non-mydriatic fundus camera. BMC Ophthalmol. **17**(1), 89 (2017)
2. Bennett, T.J., Barry, C.J.: Ophthalmic imaging today: an ophthalmic photographer's viewpoint-a review. Clin. Exp. Ophthalmol. **37**(1), 2–13 (2009)
3. Bruce, B.B., Newman, N.J., Pérez, M.A., Biousse, V.: Non-mydriatic ocular fundus photography and telemedicine: past, present, and future. Neuro-Ophthalmology **37**(2), 51–57 (2013)
4. Wang, S., Jin, K., Lu, H., Cheng, C., Ye, J., Qian, D.: Human visual system-based fundus image quality assessment of portable fundus camera photographs. IEEE Trans. Med. Imaging **35**(4), 1046–1055 (2016)
5. Litjens, G., et al.: A survey on deep learning in medical image analysis. Med. Image Anal. **42**, 60–88 (2017)
6. Lemley, J., Bazrafkan, S., Corcoran, P.: Smart augmentation learning an optimal data augmentation strategy. IEEE Access **5**, 5858–5869 (2017)
7. Perez, L., Wang, J.: The effectiveness of data augmentation in image classification using deep learning. arXiv preprint arXiv:1712.04621 (2017)
8. Chollet, F., et al.: Keras (2015). https://github.com/keras-team/keras
9. February 2018

10. Dodge, S., Karam, L.: Understanding how image quality affects deep neural networks. In: 2016 Eighth International Conference on Quality of Multimedia Experience (QoMEX), pp. 1–6. IEEE (2016)
11. Pizer, S.M., et al.: Adaptive histogram equalization and its variations. Comput. Vis. Graph. Image Process. **39**(3), 355–368 (1987)

Decision Support System for Urban Flood Management in the Cazones River Basin

A. Cristóbal Salas[1(✉)], J. M. Cuenca Lerma[1], B. Santiago Vicente[1], and H. L. Monroy Carranza[2]

[1] School of Engineering in Electronics and Communications, Universidad Veracruzana, 93390 Poza Rica, Mexico
acristobal@uv.mx, josecuencalerma@gmail.com, bardosantiago.v@gmail.com
[2] School of Architecture, Universidad Veracruzana, 93295 Poza Rica, Mexico
hmonroy@uv.mx

Abstract. Every year, the state of Veracruz suffers from constant torrential rains that produce overflows in rivers and streams as well as floods in urban areas. Due to the orography of the state, there are few hours for the evacuation of people from risk areas. That is why, this paper presents a software that helps the civil protection authorities to take preventive actions in cases of emergency due to extreme weather events. This software considers information such as: current amount of water in the region, rain forecast, soil porosity and orography of the region. With this information, the system generates a simulation of floods in that area. The system is implemented using parallelization of the problem domain and using multi-threaded techniques and distributed computation to reduce the execution time of the simulation.

The case of the region near the Cazones River basin is presented as an example of the utility of the system. It could simulate 72 h of rain falling in the area of 50 km × 20 km and showing the areas that could be affected during the flood.

Keywords: Flood simulation · Distributed · Multi-thread
Geographical information system · Decision making

1 Introduction

Floods are considered as natural disasters phenomenon that affect more people every year, mainly, in their finances [1]. There are several examples of these affectations like the Hurricane Gilbert which in 1988 impacted the city of Monterrey. Gilbert affected hundreds of people and it erased entire neighborhoods in the city due to its torrential rains [2]. Another example is the city of Acapulco which was affected by Hurricane Pauline in 1997 [3]. This Hurricane caused more than 400 deaths.

There are more examples of intense hurricanes that affected Mexican territory, like the hurricanes "Stan" and "Wilma" in 2005, affected the Mexican territory. The first landfall in San Andres Tuxtla, Veracruz causing more than 82 deaths. Other, Hurricane "Wilma" affected the entire Riviera Maya causing more than 8 deaths [4].

© Springer Nature Switzerland AG 2019
M. Torres et al. (Eds.): ISUM 2018, CCIS 948, pp. 200–207, 2019.
https://doi.org/10.1007/978-3-030-10448-1_19

According to the National Meteorological Service [5] belonging to the National Water Commission, Mexican federal government agencies report that by 2018, 14 hurricanes are expected to affect the Gulf of Mexico: seven tropical storms, four hurricanes of categories 1 and 2 and three hurricanes between Categories 3, 4 and 5. In Table 1 you can see a list of the last hurricanes (H), tropical storms (TS) and tropical depressions (TD) that have affected the state of Veracruz [6, 7].

Table 1. Recent meteorological phenomena in the state of Veracruz.

Year	Phenomenon	Category
2017	Katia, Franklin	H2, H1
2016	Danielle	TS
2014	Dolly	TS
2013	Barry, Fernand	TS, TS
2012	Ernesto	H2
2011	Arlene, Harvey, Nate	TS, TS, H1
2010	DT11, Karl, Matthew	TD, H3, TD

2   Related Works

Flood simulation using computer technology is quite common software in civil protection departments. For example, the city of Bangkok, Thailand developed a two-dimension simulation to analyze tsunami effects in the area [8]. Another simulation is presented in [9] where it was studied the effects of flooding in Japan; with this software, it was possible to replicate the tsunami occurred in 2011 in that city. Flood simulations have been also tested in New York city according to [10]. The information generated by the simulator is compared with the effects of Hurricane Sandy in 2012 in that city. Taiwan is another city that has run simulations to understand how the city can be affected by floods. This particular simulation operates with a real time data coming from weather forecast [11].

There are other computational systems that consider flooding, but they try to help the decision-making process. For instance, the software developed by the University of Twente [12], this university proposed a decision support system for flood control. This software considers hydrological, hydraulic and socio-economic models to evaluate a number of measures in Red River basin of Vietnam and China. In the same year, a similar software was presented in Italy and Greece [13]. This software uses meteorological forecast and data from sensors network to improve the decision-making process. Two years later, [14] published a multi-criteria decision support system for flood hazard mitigation and emergency. This platform combines value judgments and technical information to improve emergency management resource allocation. Some discussion about this type of software is presented in [15].

In [16], a Big Data based urban flood defense decision support system is presented. This system focusses on monitoring, analysis and mining of water levels and rainfall sensor data. As a consequence, software can predict the water level in the next six hours. Moreover, [17] analyze the importance of specialized decision-support systems and propose a framework to develop that kind of software.

3 System Design

The system has a client-server architecture (see Fig. 1) where the server module is responsible for computing the simulation and the client module is responsible for data visualization. Figure 2 shows the use cases for this distributed system. As can be seen, the entire system can be organized in three steps: defining a region, compute the simulation and data visualization. In the next section each step is described in detail.

3.1 Defining a Region

To define a region, user provides the four geo-positions representing the region to be analyzed. Each geo-position is acquired from the Google Maps API and they are defined by a triplet (latitude, longitude, altitude). Once defined, the entire region is divided in equilateral triangles. Each rectangle is represented as a 3D plane and it is described by an equation. Each plane computes the angle with respect to the three adjacent planes.

This angle represents the plane slope and it is used to compute the amount of water that the triangles should send to the adjacent rectangles according to the following rules: if the angle formed between the two adjacent planes is major or equal to zero then the triangle should receive water from the adjacent one. If angle is less than zero, then the triangle should send water to the adjacent one.

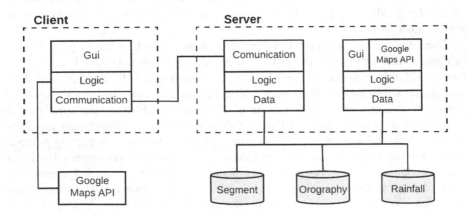

Fig. 1. Distributed system architecture

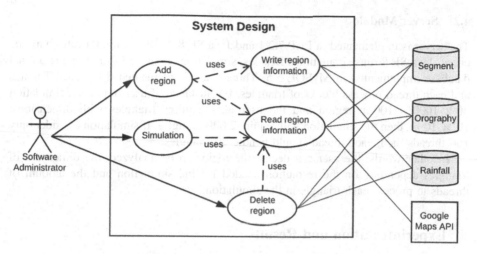

Fig. 2. Distributed system use cases.

The amount of water to be transmitted follows the next rule:

$$amount\ of\ water\ to\ be\ sent = \left\{ \frac{angle * 10}{9} \right\} \tag{1}$$

This simulation considers that the maximum angle between two planes is ±90° and according to this angle is the amount of water to be transmitted.

3.2   Compute Simulation

The server module computes the simulation in three stages: (1) compute the contributions of water based on the amount of water already contained in the triangle, the amount of rain falling, and the amount of water being absorbed by soil or going into the drain. (2) distribute the amount of water resulting from the previous computation between the adjacent triangles. (3) Compute the final amount of water in the triangle.

3.3   Data Visualization

During the data visualization step, the system shows the amount of water that finally remains in each rectangle. This data is displayed on Google Maps and the system creating a set of pictures in motion where the flood can be monitored.

4   Implementation

4.1   Client Module

This module is implemented using HTML5, CSS3, Javascript, jQuery and Google Maps API. jQuery is used to request data the server. Google Maps API also allows display the data in the digital Google's map.

4.2   Server Module

The server is implemented in PHP 7.2.1 and Java SE 8. PHP 7 communicates with the client. Java SE 8 runs simulations. Besides, simulation results are stored in a relational database implemented in MySQL 5.5. Threads are implemented using Java-Threads and each thread process blocks of triangles. For instance, if user requires a simulation of a 1000 × 100 m region and the user also requires triangles with dimensions: 10 × 10 m, then the simulation will require 2,000 triangles. If simulation consider only 100 threads then, each thread should handle 20 triangles.

In other words, the user can decide the region to be analyzed, the dimension of triangles depending on the resolution needed for the simulation and the amount of threads to process each triangle in the simulation.

5   Experimentation and Results

This research is being tested around the city of Poza Rica, Veracruz. This city has an area of 63.95 km^2 which represents 0.09% of the entire state. The city's weather is warm with an average temperature of 24.4 °C and an annual average rainfall of 1,010 mm [18]. The city is established along the Cazones river and it has several streams flowing inside the city [19] which are potential threat for population because of floods.

The city of Poza Rica has a register of a big catastrophe in 1999 where a tropical depression devastated the city. When this devastation occur, more than thirty neighborhoods were flooded, and thousands of inhabitants were affected [20, 21]. In addition, the city has suffered the passage of hurricanes and heavy rains in recent years as can be noticed in [22, 23]. The latest flooding occurred in September 2017 where more than 30 homes were flooded [24]. Due to the severities of this flood, Civil Protection authorities in the state of Veracruz proposed the following preventive measures such as: identify rivers and streams with rapid response, promote the development and implementation of a family civil protection plan, reinforce communication channels between authorities to improve the response in case of emergencies.

This area was selected for experimentation and more details can be seen in Fig. 3. In this experimentation, the region has defined as an area of 50 km × 20 km. This region was divided in 10 × 10 m equilateral triangles which means a total of 20 millions of them.

The simulation was tested in a computer with the following features 4 GB RAM, 500 GB hard disk and 2 GHz Intel Core i7. Test were made in two directions: (a) increasing the number of threads in a single Java application. (b) dividing the region to be analyzing in two and four pieces and run each sub-region in a Java application. In other words, the problem size was divided.

Fig. 3. Simulated of the region around the Cazones River.

Results of this experiments are presented in Table 2 where the time was measured in milliseconds.

Table 2. Processing time simulator.

Runs	Applications per run	Threads per application	Triangles per thread	Time (milliseconds)
4	1	1	5,000,000	1,570,175
4	1	2	2,500,000	1,105,344
4	1	4	1,250,000	700,704
4	1	8	625,000	626,384
4	2	1	2,500,000	1,104,192
4	2	2	1,250,000	700,128
4	2	4	625,000	696,672
4	2	8	312,500	247,968

From Table 2, it is possible to observe the impact of improving the entire system speedup when dividing the exploration area in smaller areas and assigning these new ones to different processes. Another optimization to the system speedup is when dividing the amount of work between several threads. Increasing the number of threads reduces the execution time until the computer's memory is exhausted.

6 Results Discussion

An important software requirement for the simulator, here presented, is to be useful in the decision-making process. The software itself would not be useful if it does not fulfill its mission of supporting decision making at the time of a flood. Among the advantages of this type of simulators are: (1) Identify the potentially vulnerable zones. (2) Estimate the economic losses caused by meteorological phenomena. (3) Locate the safe areas to establish shelters. (4) Train civil protection personnel to care for the population. (5) Provide evacuation routes for the population. (6) Establish times and strategies for the evacuation of the population considering the different means of transportation available in the city.

Although this software requires going through various verification processes and data validation processes to ensure the accuracy of the information provided; The software presented here is a first approach to the simulation of a meteorological phenomenon and it is very useful to start new planning processes. Among the planning processes are the following: generating environmental contingency scenarios useful for training civil protection personnel. These scenarios allow the design and adjustment of strategies to not only save lives but also to support other sectors such as the mobility of citizens in times of emergency, the planning of the distribution of survival packages or estimate the economic damage that can occur to local businesses.

Acknowledgement. This project is partially sponsored by the Ministry of Public Education through its Program for the Professional Development Program - PRODEP with registration key # UV-PTC-861 and the title: "Social strategies based on flood simulation for the houses located on the banks of the Cazones River in Poza Rica, Ver".

References

1. Forbes: Mexico are lost every year 230 billion dollar by floods. https://www.forbes.com.mx/mexico-pierden-230-mdd-cada-ano-by-flood/. Accessed 25 Jan 2018
2. Villasana, M.: 28 years hurricane Gilbert are met. http://www.milenio.com/policia/huracan_gilberto-28_anos_huracan_gilbertomilenio_noticias_0_812918815.html. Accessed 25 Jan 2018
3. Castro, C.: 20 years after Hurricane Pauline. https://www.elsoldeacapulco.com.mx/local/huracan-pauline-paulina-20-anos-aniversario-mexico-State-local-tragedy-pain-death-destruction-national-equals-warrior-local-acapulco-chilpancingo. Accessed 25 Jan 2018
4. Estrada, R.: The 7 most devastating hurricanes that have hit Mexico. http://www.elfinanciero.com.mx/nacional/los-huracanes-mas-devastadores-que-Han-beaten-a-mexico.html. Accessed 25 Jan 2018
5. Web page of Servicio Metereologico Nacional. https://smn.cna.gob.mx/es/ciclones-tropicales/temporada-de-ciclones-2018. Accessed 31 July 2018
6. Ochoa-Martínez, C.A., Welsh-Rodríguez, C.M., Bonilla-Jiménez, E., Morales-Martínez, M.A.: Fuentes de información sobre eventos hidrometeorológicos extremos en Veracruz de Ignacio de la Llave. Reality Data Space Int. J. Stat. Geogr. **4**(3), 66–73 (2013)
7. Luna-Lagunes, J.I.: Danielle 2016. Mexican Government (2016). https://www.gob.mx/cms/uploads/attachment/file/123932/resumenes.pdf
8. Ohira, W., Honda, K., Nagai, M.: Tsunami inundation damping performance of based on mangrove two-dimensional numerical simulation. In: 2015 IEEE International Geoscience and Remote Sensing Symposium (IGARSS), Milan, pp. 2727–2730 (2015). https://doi.org/10.1109/igarss.2015.7326377

9. Koshimura, S., Hino, R., Ohta, Y., Kobayashi, H., Murashima, Y., Musa, A.: Advances of tsunami inundation forecasting and Its future perspectives. In: OCEANS 2017 - Aberdeen, Aberdeen, pp. 1–4 (2017). https://doi.org/10.1109/oceanse.2017.8084753
10. Wang, H.V., Loftis, J.D., Liu, Z., Forrest, D., Zhang, J: The advancement on the storm surge and street-level inundation modeling - a case study in New York during Hurricane Sandy City. In: OCEANS 2014-TAIPEI, Taipei, pp. 1–8 (2014). https://doi.org/10.1109/OCEANS-TAIPEI.2014.6964508
11. Huang, C.-J., Hsu, M.-H., Yeh, S.-H.: Distributed computation of 2D modeling inundation. In: 2015 6th International Conference on Computing, Communication and Networking Technologies (ICCCNT), Denton, TX, pp. 1–6 (2015). https://doi.org/10.1109/icccnt.2015.7395222
12. Booij, M.J.: Decision support system for flood control and ecosystem upgrading in the Red River basin. In: Water Resources Systems—Hydrological Risk, Management and Development, pp. 115–122. International Union of Geodesy and Geophysics (2003). Publ. no. 281
13. Abebe, A.J., Price, R.K.: Decision support system for urban flood management. J. Hydroinform. **7**(1), 3–15 (2005)
14. Levy, J.K., Hartmann, J., Li, K.W., An, Y., Asgary, A.: Multi-criteria decision support systems for flood hazard mitigation and emergency response in urban watersheds1. J. Am. Water Resour. Assoc. **43**(2), 346–358 (2007)
15. Levy, J.K., Gopalakrishnan, C., Lin, Z.: Advances in decision support systems for flood disaster management: challenges and opportunities. Int. J. Water Resour. Dev. **21**(4), 593–612 (2005)
16. Yang, T., Chen, G., Sun, X.: A big-data-based urban flood defense decision support system. Int. J. Smart Home **9**(12), 81–90 (2015)
17. Muste, M.V., Firoozfar, A.R.: Toward generalized decision support systems for flood risk management. In: 3rd European Conference on Flood Risk Management, E3S Web of Conferences, pp. 1–12 (2016). https://doi.org/10.1051/e3sconf/20160720017
18. Encyclopedia of Municipalities and delegations, Poza Rica. http://siglo.inafed.gob.mx/enciclopedia/EMM30veracruz/municipios/30131a.html. Accessed 25 Jan 2018
19. Pereyra-Díaz, D., Pérez-Sesma, J.A., Salas-Ortega, M.D.: Hydrology. http://cdigital.uv.mx/handle/123456789/9650. Accessed 25 Jan 2018
20. Gaona Moon, F.: Remember Poza Rica in the tragedy of floods in 1999. http://imagendelgolfo.mx/resumen.php?id=204083. Accessed 25 Jan 2018
21. Escamilla, E.: 17 years of severe flooding are met in Poza Delicious; SPC conduct mock. http://www.jornadaveracruz.com.mx/Post.aspx?id=161005_092150_499. Accessed 25 Jan 2018
22. E-Consultation in Poza Rica Families fear losing everything by Hurricane Franklin. http://www.e-veracruz.mx/nota/2017-08-09/municipios/familias-en-poza-rica-temen-perderlo-todo-por-el-step-de-franklin. Accessed 25 Jan 2018
23. E-Consultation continue rains in the state of Veracruz. http://www.e-veracruz.mx/nota/2017-09-30/state/continue-rains-in-the-state-of-VERACRUZ. Accessed 25 Jan 2018
24. Olmedo, M.: Affected more than 30 homes by the overflowing of the river Cazones. http://formato7.com/2017/09/25/affected-more-than-30-housing-for-the-overflow-del-rio-cazones/. Accessed 25 Jan 2018

Author Index

Printed in the United States
By Bookmasters